# THEMES IN DRAMA

*An annual publication*
*Edited by James Redmond*

9

*Editorial Advisory Board*

# THE THEATRICAL
# SPACE

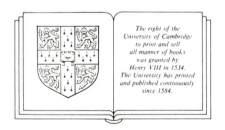

The right of the
University of Cambridge
to print and sell
all manner of books
was granted by
Henry VIII in 1534.
The University has printed
and published continuously
since 1584.

CAMBRIDGE UNIVERSITY PRESS

CAMBRIDGE

LONDON   NEW YORK   NEW ROCHELLE
MELBOURNE   SYDNEY

PN
2122
T54
1987

Published by the Press Syndicate of the University of Cambridge
The Pitt Building, Trumpington Street, Cambridge CB2 1RP
32 East 57th Street, New York, NY 10022, USA
10 Stamford Road, Oakleigh, Melbourne 3166, Australia

First published 1987

Printed in Great Britain at The Bath Press, Avon

*British Library cataloguing in publication data*
Themes in Drama,  9
1.  Drama – History and criticism – Periodicals
809.2'005 PN1601

Library of Congress catalogue card number 82–4491

ISSN  0263–676x
ISBN  0  521  33471  3

1-12-87

# Contents

# *Themes in Drama* volumes and conferences

The first eleven volumes in the series *Themes in Drama* are

1    *Drama and Society*
2    *Drama and Mimesis*
3    *Drama, Dance and Music*
4    *Drama and Symbolism*
5    *Drama and Religion*
6    *Drama and the Actor*
7    *Drama, Sex and Politics*
8    *Historical Drama*
9    *The Theatrical Space*
10   *Farce* (1988)
11   *Women in Theatre* (1989)

Papers are invited for the following volumes, and should be submitted in final form to the Editor before 1 February in the year indicated (potential contributors are asked to correspond with the Editor well in advance of these dates):

12   *Drama and Philosophy* (1988)
13   *Violence in Drama* (1989)
14   *Melodrama* (1990)
15   *Madness in Drama* (1991)

*Themes in Drama* conferences, 1988

Annual conferences are held at the University of London and at the University of California. The subject each year is that of the volume in preparation. The 1988 conferences will be on 'Drama and Philosophy'. Details of the conference in California may be obtained from *Themes in Drama* Conference, University of California, Riverside, Ca. 92521. Details of the conference in London may be obtained from the Editor.

James Redmond, Editor, *Themes in Drama*, Westfield College, University of London, London NW3 7ST

# Contributors

Stephanie K. Arnold, *Department of Theatre, University of California, Riverside*

Christopher Baugh, *Drama Department, University of London Goldsmiths' College*

Barbara T. Cooper, *Department of French and Italian, University of New Hampshire*

Halina Filipowicz, *Department of Slavic Languages, University of Wisconsin, Madison*

William W. French, *Department of English, West Virginia University*

John Spalding Gatton, *Honors Program, University of Kentucky*

Jonathan Haynes, *Literature and Languages Division, Bennington College*

Michael Issacharov, *Department of French, University of Western Ontario*

Vera Jiji, *Department of English, Brooklyn College, City University of New York*

Pamela M. King, *Department of English, Westfield College, University of London*

Stanley V. Longman, *Department of Drama, University of Georgia*

Charles R. Lyons, *Department of Drama, Stanford University*

Mary Kay Martin, *Department of Dramatic Art, University of California, Berkeley*

James S. Moy, *Department of Theatre and Drama, University of Wisconsin, Madison*

James E. Robinson, *Department of English, University of Notre Dame*

Hanna Scolnicov, *Department of Theatre Studies, The Hebrew University of Jerusalem*

Niall W. Slater, *Department of Classics, University of Southern California*

Sharon Tyler, *Department of English, University of California, Riverside*

Adrian Weiss, *Department of English, University of South Dakota*

Albert Wertheim, *Department of English, Indiana University*

# Illustrations

# Editor's preface

This is the ninth volume of *Themes in Drama*, which is published annually. Each volume brings together reviews and articles on the theatrical activity of a wide range of cultures and periods. The papers offer original contributions to their own specialized fields, but they are presented in such a way that their significance may be appreciated readily by non-specialists.

Each volume indicates connections between the various national traditions of theatre by bringing together studies of a theme of central and continuing importance. The annual international conferences (see p. vii) provide an opportunity for scholars, critics and theatrical practitioners to exchange views, and many of the papers in the volumes are revised versions of papers read and discussed at the conferences. The present volume reflects the range and quality of the 1985 conferences on 'The Theatrical Space'. Contributions are invited for volumes 12, 13, 14 and 15; they should follow the style of presentation used in this volume, and be sent to

James Redmond
Editor *Themes in Drama*
Westfield College
University of London
London NW3 7ST

# Transformations of space in New Comedy*

## NIALL W. SLATER

The birth of New Comedy is accompanied by a simultaneous transformation of both physical and imaginative space in the Greek theatre. This transformation ratifies and gives presence to a number of internal transformations of comedy in the century between Aristophanes and Menander. The New Comedy which emerges is both physically and imaginatively detached from the city which gave it birth. This detachment in turn is the source of New Comedy's remarkable endurance as a form: it becomes mobile, even universal, as it is carried throughout the Mediterranean world by the great Hellenistic acting companies, the Artists of Dionysos. In this form New Comedy impinges upon the Roman mind and theatrical tradition. Plays of the New Comedy repertoire are transformed by Plautus and others into Latin versions conceived for a new physical space. In the hands of Plautus a new dimension of imaginative space comes to the fore as well, but Terence and other Roman writers return to Greek conceptions of space.

I shall look chiefly at the beginning and end of New Comedy in the ancient world, that is, the transition from Aristophanes to Menander and from Greek to Roman comedy. I will deal more briefly with the conventions of space in New Comedy proper, which are for us more familiar. We begin then in the fifth century BC.

Comedy for us begins with Aristophanes and the Theatre of Dionysos on the south slope of the Acropolis in Athens.[1] This theatre, a model for many others built after the fifth century throughout the Greek world, may be divided into three major components: the *skene* (a low stage with backdrop building), the orchestra (or dancing place), and the *cavea* (or seating area – originally just a grassy slope, later provided with permanent marble seats). Thus it appears on our archaeological reconstructions of the fifth-century theatre, a tripartite division of form and function, but in fact this is a single, unified, hieratic space, a place where the entire city of Athens comes together to worship the god of theatre, Dionysos.

The center of this space is the chorus in its dancing place. Admittedly we

* A draft of this paper was read at the *Themes in Drama* International Conference held at the University of California, Riverside in February 1985.

are heavily influenced in this judgement by Aristotle's account of the
development of tragedy, which asserts that drama began in choral performance: only gradually did the poets add first one, then two, and finally three
actors to respond to, and interact with, the chorus.[2] For our purposes it does
not matter whether Aristotle had sound historical evidence for this tidy
evolutionary scheme. The main point is that Aristotle, like the contemporary Greek audience, saw the centrality of the twenty-four singers and
dancers who composed the chorus.

This centrality had an obvious physical dimension we can best appreciate by considering the scale of Greek theatres. In its later development the
Theatre of Dionysos in Athens seated as many as 17,000 spectators, the
fourth-century BC theatre at Epidauros over 20,000. Even under optimal
acoustic conditions, one wonders if the choral part of the performance
might not have been the bulk of what a spectator seated above the *diazoma*
(about halfway back) would have heard.[3] The chorus in the orchestra
dominated the visual aspect of performance as well, especially in comedy
where their costumes might be the most striking part of the production:
consider the plays with animal choruses such as *Wasps* or *Birds*. Visually
and aurally then, the performance for a significant portion of the audience
would have been the chorus. This is far from asserting that the actors, and
the story they enact, were unimportant. I suggest only that virtually any
modern performance of Aristophanes (except those done in Greece in the
ancient theatres) fundamentally distorts our spatial experience of the plays.
In an indoor theatre the action and the actors dominate the space, and the
chorus is somehow squeezed into a part of the stage. This is a radical
reversal of the great open orchestra and small stage of the fifth century. The
world of Old Comedy was fundamentally a choral space, in which the
twenty-four amateurs of the chorus, trained in song and dance by the poet,
functioned as both center and bridge, the heart of the performance and a
mediation between the whole city, present as audience, and the by now
professionalized actors on the stage.

The free interaction in Old Comedy between chorus and audience,
chorus and stage, and even stage and audience demonstrates the essential
unity of this space. One of the most distinctive features of Old Comedy
makes this clear: the direct address of chorus to audience in the form known
as the *parabasis*.[4] With the stage temporarily cleared of actors the chorus
turns to the audience and, at first dropping their characters, speaks directly
to them. The *parabasis* may contain comments of the poet on his own work,
as in the *Knights* (lines 507–19), where the chorus explains why
Aristophanes has hitherto had his plays produced in the name of Kal-
listratos rather than his own, or the revised *parabasis* to the *Clouds* (lines 518–
62), in which the chorus upbraids the audience for failing to appreciate the
first version of the play. The *parabasis* also contains address to the gods and

comments on matters of current political interest in Athens, which, though now given in character, have little to do with the action of the play proper; for example, the chorus of *Clouds* complain that, though they produced thunder and lightning, even accompanied by a lunar eclipse, the audience has ignored these omens and elected Kleon (one of Aristophanes' favorite targets) to public office (lines 575–94).

The free interaction of chorus and stage is equally clear, though we can already see a move away from such freedom in the course of Aristophanes' career. In both the early plays *Acharnians* and *Wasps*, the chorus is hostile to one of the leading characters. Dicaeopolis, having made a separate peace with Sparta, is pursued by the chorus of old Acharnians who want the war to continue and threaten to kill Dicaeopolis by stoning for his treason (line 295). The chorus of old jurymen in *Wasps* threaten to assault Bdelycleon with their stingers (lines 403 ff.) when he attempts to keep his father Philocleon from joining them. The comedy of these scenes will not work unless the potential of the chorus storming the stage is real. Members of the chorus do go on stage in a co-operative effort in the *Peace* (lines 425–519). The god of War has buried the goddess of Peace in a cave and sealed her in with stones. The chorus assist in removing the stones and hauling Peace (a statue of the goddess) out of the cave with ropes. This was probably done using the *ekkyklema*, or rolling stage wagon with ropes, for the chorus run out into the orchestra.[5]

The interaction of stage and audience includes both direct address to the audience and comments by one character to another on the audience. In the *Knights* Demosthenes asks the Sausage-seller if he can see the audience (line 163, literally 'the rows of people') as a prelude to asking if he wants to rule all Athens (embodied in that audience) and her empire. In the *Frogs* Dionysos and his slave Xanthias incorporate the audience into the story by referring to them as the parricides and oath-breakers who populate Hades, in which they have just arrived (lines 274–6). Just a few lines later, Dionysos, terrified by the underworld monster Empusa, appeals for protection to his own priest sitting in the front row of the theatre. We have no ancient evidence for how this scene was played, but the suggestion of some modern translators that Dionysos should cross the orchestra to his priest's throne in the front row only enacts the fusion of imaginative space implicit in the line.

I have undertaken this perhaps too lengthy review of interaction between performers and audience to remind us of one very important but sometimes neglected fact: there is no dramatic illusion as we would conceive it today in Old Comedy.[6] To speak of the *parabasis* or direct audience address as 'breaking the illusion' implies what is not really there to begin with, a consistent attempt at an illusionistic representation of reality. This is a theatre in which the imaginative space embraces both performers and

audience without creating an illusion. In the *Peace* Trygaeus flies up to
heaven on the back of an enormous dung beetle, which was actually flown
through the air by the *mechane* or crane. The chorus, however, present when
we meet Trygaeus on earth, is still there in the orchestra when the scene
switches to Mt Olympus. The poet does not worry about their transport –
the imaginative (but non-illusory) space has carried them along. In the
same way Dionysos incorporates the audience in his theatrical world by
making them the dead who populate Hades.

This unified imaginative space is beginning to break up toward the end of
Aristophanes' career, even as the divisions of physical space in the theatre
deepen. It is at the end of the fifth century that we first find stone bases for
the *proedria*, the front-row seats of honor, thus marking a permanent
division between audience and performers.[7] At the same time the chorus
becomes less and less involved in the action, and by the time of
Aristophanes' last play, *Wealth*, is so inorganic to the action that the choric
odes are not recorded in our manuscripts, only the notation 'Chorus'
separating scenes. Aristotle says the choruses became simply musical
interludes, divorced from the action.[8]

Between the last play of Aristophanes and the substantial remains we
have now recovered of Menander, we have numerous fragments of Greek
comedy but none extensive enough to allow us to assess the use of
imaginative space. By the time we reach Menander, the unified space of
Old Comedy has broken apart and illusion, borrowed from tragedy along
with the romantic recognition plots of late Euripides, has triumphed. At the
same time the reconstruction of the Theatre of Dionysos by the Athenian
statesman Lycurgus has physically divided the space as well. To this period
date the permanent stone seats we now see in the theatre and the raised
stage.[9]

The clearest indication of this break-up of the theatrical space is the new
role of what was once the central element of the comic performance: the
chorus. In Menander the chorus has become a conventionalized band of
(often drunken) revellers who break up the action of the play but in no way
interact with the story. We see this in the *Dyskolos* where, at the end of what
we can now call a first act, the slave Daos says he sees a crowd of Pan-
worshippers coming and withdraws (lines 230–2).[10] Each of Menander's
plays for which we possess the end of the first act has some such reference
there to the approach of the chorus. Although the chorus clearly performed
in subsequent act-divisions, no one on stage makes further reference to it.
The role of the chorus is thus a complete reversal from our experience of Old
Comedy. Far from being a bridge between audience and stage as it once
was, tying the theatrical space together, it now functions as a framing
device, cutting off the world of illusion from that of the spectators.

The world of the stage has shrunk in both temporal and spatial dimensions in the process. Time is eminently flexible in Old Comedy. Dicaeopolis sends Amphitheos off to Sparta to negotiate a private peace in the *Acharnians*, and Amphitheos returns in less than forty-five lines. Later in the same play Dicaeopolis celebrates the Rural Dionysia, which fell sometime in December. Move on a few lines, and the celebration of the Anthesteria, a late-February festival, is in progress. By contrast Menander carefully places any large time gaps in the action during the choral entr'acte, that is, hidden behind the frame around the action. In the first act of the *Dyskolos* Sostratos sees and addresses the young girl with whom he has fallen in love. The chorus of Pan-worshippers then covers a sufficient gap in time for Sostratos to go into Athens from the country setting of the play and come back, while at the same time the slave Daos fetches the young girl's brother from a nearby farm.

The imaginative space has sharply contracted. In the *Birds* Aristophanes' characters found a new city in the sky, halfway between earth and heaven. By the end of the play they have starved Olympus into submission by a blockade, and Peithetairus has seized Zeus' power and become the new king of the universe. The world of New Comedy is purely domestic, most often a quiet residential street in Athens where private comedies of marriage or reconciliation are played out with no effect on anyone beyond the participants.

The Theatre of Dionysos as rebuilt by Lycurgus gives architectural embodiment to the newly divided and framed imaginative space. The most important element here is the raised stage. The fifth-century theatre had certainly had some form of low platform stage, if only for acoustical reasons, but as we have seen in Aristophanes' *Peace*, physical interaction between stage and chorus remained possible. No question, perhaps, among many tangled problems in interpreting the remains of the Theatre of Dionysos has been more hotly disputed than that of when the raised stage was introduced. By 'raised' we mean here one of at least six to eight feet which completely cuts off access between stage and orchestra. Pickard-Cambridge argues vigorously against the raised stage both from the plays of Menander and the scanty and difficult remains of the theatre itself, but he admits that the contemporary theatre of Epidauros had a raised stage.[11] I believe that the most economical hypothesis ascribes the raised stage, which all agree the Theatre of Dionysos in Athens acquired at some point, to the Lycurgan rebuilding, but for our purposes that is not necessary. Menander's plays were performed throughout the Greek world. That the late fourth-century theatre of Epidauros performed his and other plays of New Comedy with a raised stage and no stage/chorus interaction is proof that the imaginative space of stage and chorus had been divided – architecture merely ratified this.

The transformation of space which brings New Comedy into being is now complete. The unified, non-illusory, and hieratic space of Old Comedy has divided into three parts: a world of illusion on the stage, an extraneous chorus, and the now secularized audience. The subject matter of comedy becomes domestic and thereby broadens its appeal greatly. The political comedy of Aristophanes had no appeal outside Athens; we have no records of any performances after his lifetime outside the city. Menander's young lovers, though, appealed to Greek-speaking audiences from Athens to Alexandria to Syracuse. Wherever conquest and trade carried the Hellenistic Greeks, the touring Artists of Dionysos followed.

It is in this form, as touring performance, that Greek drama reaches south Italy and from there touches the Romans. Of the first generation of Roman dramatists we have too little to judge their use of space, but from the second generation, active from at least the last decade of the third century BC down to the 180s, comes Titus Maccius Plautus, in whose hands New Comedy and its concepts of space undergo some surprising transformations.

Our evidence for the physical state of the early Roman theatre is even more exiguous than that for fifth-century Greece. From south Italian vase paintings of theatre scenes and internal evidence we conjecture the stage to be a low wooden platform with a backdrop of three housefronts.[12] These theatres were temporary structures, erected only for the festivals; Roman moral conservatism prevented the erection of a stone theatre in Rome until that of Pompey in 55 BC. Of chorus and orchestra in this theatre there is no trace. We are much nearer the world of travelling players setting up their stage in tavern yards and markets than the great stone theatres of the Greek world.

This transformation of physical space becomes in the hands of Plautus a transformation of theatrical space as well. The chorus had become in New Comedy a barrier between stage and audience, a frame around the world of illusion. Once the chorus is banished, the way lies open again for direct appeals from stage to audience in the form of monologue, aside, role-playing, and comments on the play as play.[13]

Many, if not all, of Plautus' plays are based on the New Comedy repertoire of the touring Artists of Dionysos.[14] Plautus does much more than translate these plays into Latin: he reconceptualizes them theatrically. The result is a combination of Greek New Comedy with native Italian dramatic forms, especially the Atellan farce, an improvisational form with stock characters often compared to *commedia dell' arte*. Plautus' literary drama displays many features of improvisation which draw the audience into the process of play-making and thereby moves towards re-unifying the theatrical space that Menandrean illusionism and fourth-century theatre architecture had divided.

The new dimensions of theatrical space in Plautus are apparent the moment the prologue speaks. Menander uses divine prologues like Pan in the *Dyskolos* or Fortune (*Tyche*) in the *Aspis* to convey background information on the story and characters we are about to see. Plautine prologues, by contrast, invite the audience to participate in the creation of the theatrical world. The prologue to the *Truculentus* comes forward to ask the audience in Plautus' name for use of a small part of their city in which to erect Athens for the duration of the play – and waits for a nod of approval from the crowd.[15] Mercury, speaking the prologue of *Amphitruo*, even plays with the notion that he can change the genre of the play in response to audience reaction. First he announces a tragedy, then pretends to be startled by a negative reaction from the crowd. After all, they had come to hear a comedy. Mercury promises to change the play to a comedy – but jokes that all the verses will stay the same anyway (lines 50–5).

Plautus' extensive use of eavesdropping scenes also serves to unite theatrical space. In Menander the eavesdropping scene functions primarily as a means of gaining information – with occasional comic twists when information is misunderstood or wrong. Smikrines in the *Aspis* learns of the supposed death of his nephew Sostratos by eavesdropping on the boy's slave, Daos. Most of the plot complications in the *Samia* depend on old Demeas' false belief, acquired through eavesdropping, that his son has fathered a child by his (Demeas') mistress. In Plautus eavesdroppers take on a function of the now-vanished chorus – to comment on, and guide the audience's response to, what they overhear. The eavesdroppers function in effect as an onstage audience. A good example of this is the scene in the *Pseudolus* where Pseudolus and his master Calidorus eavesdrop on the great entrance *canticum* of the slave-dealer Ballio (lines 133ff.). The eavesdroppers acquire no new information: their function is to remind the audience of its proper response to Ballio through their outraged asides against him in particular and slave-dealers in general.

From commentary and reaction it is but a step to manipulation. From those eavesdropping scenes Plautus develops his later plays in which the clever slaves in effect improvise the plot of the play. The situations are standard New Comedy dilemmas: a young lover needs money to buy his girlfriend from the slave-dealer. He lacks the wit to do this himself but relies on the wiles of his slave to raise the money, usually by cheating the young man's father. In Plautus' hands this situation becomes the occasion for improvisational plotting, as in the *Persa* where Toxilus (atypically here a slave) devises a scheme to sell a freeborn girl (disguised as a Persian captive) to the slave-dealer. He can then use the money to buy his own love from the slave-dealer, then reclaim the phony 'Persian girl' as freeborn. We can already see in this play a joy in improvisation for its own sake: Toxilus coaches his fellow conspirators in their parts and insists on seeing his plot played out to the end – even some parts which prove unnecessary.

This improvisational reworking of New Comedy reaches its climax in what is perhaps Plautus' finest play, the *Pseudolus*, and in the process creates a new kind of imaginative theatrical space. Pseudolus, the clever slave of the title, becomes in effect playwright of his own play, explicitly acknowledged in a monologue in which he becomes a poet, who can, as he says, 'make a lie seem like truth' (lines 401–3). He creates the plot, finds an actor to play his script, coaches that actor through his performance, and celebrates a dramatic victory at the end.

This creation of a play-within-the-play is a remarkable metaphorical transformation of space. Aristophanes had played with elements of dramatic self-consciousness – for example in the *Frogs* where the slave Xanthias comments on the usual jokes Aristophanes' rivals would give slave characters in his situation. Such self-consciousness in Aristophanes is sporadic, not programatic, and Menander in New Comedy suppresses any such self-consciousness in favor of illusionism, architecturally and theatrically framed. Plautus, transposing these stock comedies of love, separation, and reconciliation to the stage of his simple street theatre, sees the possibility of fusing native Italian improvisational theatre with the Greek New Comedy tradition. The result is a radically new form we may legitimately call metatheatre.

Plautine metatheatre differs from the theatrically self-conscious drama of the Renaissance and after, which Lionel Abel has dubbed metatheatre, primarily in its focus on the figure of an on-stage playwright, one character who through control of the other characters, whom he manipulates like actors, brings the plot of the play into being. Heroism in Plautus is the ability to create and control theatrical space.

In this Plautus had no successors. Terence returns to the conventions of Greek illusionism. Once the Romans begin to build large stone theatres, drama is already a frozen form at Rome, trapped in an equivalent of the nineteenth-century proscenium picture frame. New Comedy comes into being through a simultaneous restriction of physical and imaginative space: the raised stage and the restriction of comedy to domestic subject matter. Plautus shows that New Comedy was capable of further transformation, but his lead was not followed.

The basic form of New Comedy is still alive, of course, but it has by and large remained faithful to its original restrictions of space. Some very interesting experiments with comic metatheatre, such as Molnar's *The Guardsman*, have been made in this century – but that is a subject for another day.

## NOTES

1 All Aristophanes' plays for the City Dionysia were produced here. There was also a Lenaean festival, for which there may have been a separate theatre, but the fundamental conception and physical realization of space would have been essentially the same as in the Theatre of Dionysos; see C. W. Dearden, *The Stage of Aristophanes* (London: Athlone Press, 1976), pp. 1–8, and R. E. Wycherley, 'Lenaion', *Hesperia*, 34 (1965), 72ff. There are no remains of the fifth-century theatre *in situ*. A. W. Pickard-Cambridge, *The Theatre of Dionysos at Athens* (Oxford: Clarendon Press, 1946), hereafter cited as *TDA*, remains the fundamental account. Though *TDA*, Dearden, and many other secondary works still attribute the conglomerate walls in the shrine and the theatre to the fifth century, excavation in 1963 showed them to be fourth century: see P. Kalligas, *Archaiologikon Deltion*, 18 (1963), *Chronica*, 12–18. An excellent recent discussion taking into account the evidence of Kalligas is F. E. Winter, 'The Stage of New Comedy', *Phoenix*, 37 (1983), 38–47.

2 Aristotle, *Poetics* 1449a.

3 Acoustical tests carried out in the 1950s showed that, even with a low wooden stage and backdrop to focus the sound, it would be very difficult to hear the actors beyond the first *diazoma*. The much steeper angle of the theatre at Epidauros accounts for the far better acoustics of that theatre.

4 See K. Dover, *Aristophanic Comedy* (Berkeley and Los Angeles: University of California Press, 1972), pp. 49–53, for a sensible brief discussion. There is a thorough study in G. M. Sifakis, *Parabasis and Animal Choruses* (London: Athlone Press, 1971). More recently see also A. M. Bowie, 'The Parabasis in Aristophanes: Prolegomena, *Acharnians*,' *Classical Quarterly*, 32 (1982), 27–40.

5 Dearden (above, note 1), pp. 62–4.

6 Sifakis (above, note 4), pp. 7–14.

7 Bases for such *proedria* were found re-used in a drain: see *TDA* (above, note 1), pp. 19–21, and O. A. W. Dilke, 'The Greek Theatre Cavea', *Annual of the British School at Athens*, 43 (1948), 165–6. The dating of these blocks by letter forms has been hotly debated; I believe them to come from near the end of the century, but a new study of these is in order.

8 Aristotle, *Poetics* 1456a.

9 On the Lycurgan theatre, see *TDA* (above, note 1), pp. 134–68. Pickard-Cambridge does not believe in the raised stage for this period, but see below, note 11.

10 The same thing occurs at *Aspis* 246–9, *Epitrepontes* 169–71, and *Perikeiromene* 261–6.

11 *TDA* (above, note 1), pp. 148–56, on archaeological remains in Athens. The question is bound up with that of the *proskenion*, a structure in front of the stage building (*skene*), whose existence in the Lycurgan theatre is well attested: see *TDA*, p. 157. I believe the only reason for creating this new structure is to support the raised stage. I am happy to find that Winter (above, note 1), whose study only came to my attention while revising this article for publication, takes a similar position. Pickard-Cambridge's attempts to prove that there was stage/

chorus interaction in the fourth century BC (*TDA*, pp. 160–6) through internal evidence of the plays remain doubtful, and his one proof from a Menander play is rejected in the latest commentary: Gomme and Sandbach, *Menander: A Commentary* (Oxford: Oxford University Press, 1973) on *Theophoroumene* 30. On Epidauros and the performance advantages of the raised stage, see *TDA*, pp. 209–15.

12  M. Bieber, *History of the Greek and Roman Theatre* (Princeton: Princeton University Press, 1961), pp. 129–46; W. Beare, *The Roman Stage*, 3rd edn (London: Methuen, 1964), pp. 176–83.

13  On all these techniques and Plautine metatheatre in general, see my *Plautus in Performance: The Theatre of the Mind* (Princeton: Princeton University Press, 1985). For a brief account of the disappearance of metatheatrical references in the transition from Old to New Comedy, see my 'Play and Playwright References in Middle and New Comedy', *Liverpool Classical Monthly*, 10 (July 1985), 103–5.

14  A. S. Gratwick in *Cambridge History of Classical Literature*, vol. II, ed. E. J. Kenney and W. V. Clausen (Cambridge: Cambridge University Press, 1982), pp. 77–84, 96–103.

15  *Truculentus* 1–4:

> Perparvam partem postulat Plautus loci
> de vestris magnis atque amoenis moenibus,
> Athenas quo sine architectis conferat.
> quid nunc? daturin estis an non? adnuont.

# Theatre space, theatrical space, and the theatrical space without*

## HANNA SCOLNICOV

At Whitsuntide of the year 1547, the leading citizens of the town [of Valenciennes] presented the life, death, and Passion of Our Lord on the stage of the mansion of the Duke of Arschot. The spectacle lasted twenty-five days, and on each day we saw strange and wonderful things. The machines [*secrets*] of the Paradise and of Hell were absolutely prodigious and could be taken by the populace for magic . . . We saw water change into wine so mysteriously that we could not believe it, and more than a hundred persons wanted to taste this wine. The five bread and two fish seemed to be multiplied and were distributed to more than a thousand spectators, and yet there were more than twelve baskets left.[1]

In the Valenciennes Passion Play, the miracles of the multiplication of the loaves and of the transformation of water into wine were materially demonstrated. This illusion could be created within the scope of the performance because the acting space is an autonomous space which does not have to submit to natural laws. Within it, the theatre is liberated from the universal co-ordinates of time and space, to roam freely between Paradise and Hell, Mount Tabor and Jerusalem.

Every performance defines its own boundaries in relation to its own space–time structure. It is only within these circumscribed limits that its inner logic can function. These boundaries are set up by each production within a given space. This may be a building especially designed for theatrical performances, or it may have been intended by the architect for some other purpose, or it may be a natural open-air setting, etc. The physical space in which a performance takes place is its *theatre space*. Within a given theatre space, the production will create its own *theatrical space*, which, in a theatre, might be confined to the stage alone or appropriate the aisles and balconies or even extend to encompass the audience sitting in the auditorium.

Unlike 'theatrical space', 'theatre space' is an architectural term. From the point of view of the production, the theatre space is a given space, full of

---

* A draft of this paper was read at the *Themes in Drama* International Conference held at the University of London, Westfield College in March 1985.

potential, but also beset with limitations. As an architectural space, the theatre space is part of everyday space and exists independently of, and prior to, any performance. When we come to Vicenza to see Palladio's Olympic Theatre, it is its theatre space that we admire.

Although the theatrical space is created by the performance within the theatre space, that is, within everyday space, it stands apart from it. In every performance, the actors define their particular space through word, movement and gesture, and with the aid of props, scenery, lighting and acoustic effects. In that space alone their play has physical extension.

II

The theatrical space has two main characteristics: it is cut off from the everyday, and within its boundaries it achieves freedom from the everyday. As Ionesco has shown us, the clock on stage can chime any arbitrary number of times and in any random order, and the ringing of the doorbell may signify that there is either somebody or nobody behind the door.[2] Just as Dr Faustus in Marlowe's play can summon the spirits only after he has circumscribed himself in a magic circle, so the performance can achieve freedom from everyday limitations only within the boundaries of its own theatrical space.

The severing of the theatrical from the everyday space has structural parallels and historical connections with the separation between sacred and profane space as described by Ernst Cassirer, Mircea Eliade, Susanne Langer and others. In his discussion of the mythical forms of thinking, Cassirer shows how the sacred space is conceived as set apart from everyday space and as qualitatively differentiated from it. He points out that the very word 'temple' is indicative of the separation between sacred and profane spaces, being derived from the Greek root *tem-*, which means to cut or delimit.[3] Hence, the temple is the place cut off for consecration. From the same root are derived in Latin both *templum* and *tempus*.[4] Both time and place as symbolic forms of thinking thus grow from the same basic act of distinguishing by cutting.

Eliade takes up Cassirer's concept of the sacred place and enriches it. For the archaic source of the Western idea of the temple, he goes to Ovid's *Fasti*, from which he quotes the story of the foundation of Rome. As Ovid tells the story, Romulus chose the day of the festival of Pales to mark the line of the city walls, following a hieratic series of steps:

> A trench was dug down to the solid rock, fruits of the earth were thrown in the bottom of it, and with them earth fetched from the neighbouring soil. The trench was filled up with mould, and on top was set an altar and a fire was duly lit on a new hearth. Then pressing on the plough-handle he drew a furrow to mark out the line of the walls.[5]

The founding of Rome is described as a cutting-off and consecrating of a particular space. According to Eliade, city walls were originally erected not for military protection but as a magical defence,

> for they marked out from the midst of a 'chaotic' space, peopled with demons and phantoms, an enclosure, a place that was organised . . . provided with a 'centre'.[6]

The sacred circle, cut off and delimited, consecrated and imbued with strength and significance, is highly suggestive in relation to the theatrical space.

As Greek theatre developed from religious ritual, it inherited from the latter its spatial organization. The *orchestra* in which the chorus danced, with the altar at its centre, is a reminder of the sacred nature of the theatrical performance: it is a sacred circle transformed into a theatrical space.

Although the theatre detached itself from religious ritual, people remained attached to it much in the same way. The theatrical experience remained close to the religious experience. The catharsis experienced in tragedy, according to Aristotle, is not far from the religious experience of purification and rebirth. Like ritual, a performance brought the community together on religious festivals, and was an occasion for the reaffirmation of shared values and beliefs. The lasting attachment of the people to their theatre is evidenced even today by theatres being constructed and reconstructed one upon another just as temples are. They too become venerated places to which people will readily come back for more of the same kind of experience.

### III

Despite the structural similarities between them, the theatrical space differs from the sacred space in one important aspect. While ritual is strictly enclosed within the sacred space, the theatrical space allows the actors to 'have their exits and their entrances'. But, at the same time, the theatrical space remains cut off from everyday space. In other words, the theatrical space extends beyond the limits of the visible acting area, but without blurring the distinction between itself and everyday space. The character who leaves the visible theatrical space may be going to another room, invisible to the audience, to meet some other characters, or he may return to the stage after having completed a long journey. The characters on stage can discuss what is happening in some other place, or wish to leave their present surroundings for some distant land. Whether far off or close by, all these other places serve as important extensions of the theatrical space and, in the terms of the play, are very real spaces, despite the fact that they remain unseen.

The unseen theatrical space is no less real and dramatically important than the visible theatrical space. Actions of great moment like Macbeth's murder of Duncan, may take place off stage, in what I propose to call *the theatrical space without* as opposed to *the theatrical space within*. The difference between them is the difference between perceived space and conceived space.[7]

In the novel all space is conceived, because its apprehension is always mediated by words, so that there can be no real perception of space. But, in the theatre, the theatrical space within is perceived directly and sensuously, and the theatrical spaces outside can be conceived as extrapolations of the concrete visible space on stage.

The theatrical space without adds an extra dimension to the performance. For, whereas the visible theatrical space is wholly within the given theatre space, the theatrical space without extends as far as the playwright wills it to, thus demanding an imaginative response on the part of the spectators.

The theatrical space without should not be confused with the everyday world outside the theatre. A character who exits the stage does not walk off into the dressing room. And when the performance is over, the characters do not go out and mingle with the audience wrapped up in their overcoats and trying to reach various means of transportation. While the *actor* may do all these things, the character has no existence outside the theatrical space.

The transcendence of the theatrical space without also underlines the separateness of its perceived counterpart. Even when it engulfs the spectators, the theatrical space is not part of everyday space, but a delimited space, a magic circle marked off from the mundane and ordinary. The audience then feels the heightened theatrical effect of being drawn into the theatrical space, leaving their everyday existence behind.

The separateness of the theatrical space is a necessary condition of any performance. Even forms of theatre which seem to abolish the distinction between the two spaces, for example, street theatre, in fact intrude into everyday space, and their whole effect depends on the spectators' awareness that this is play, not reality. In order to enjoy street theatre, one must eventually realize that these are actors who are pretending to fight rather than people engaged in a real street brawl. Their 'as if' activity cuts them off from everyday space and sets them apart in a theatrical space. Although street theatre repudiates conventional theatre space by avoiding the theatre building, it cannot escape carrying around itself its own theatrical space.

In the same spirit of knocking down the barriers that divide art from reality, theatre from everyday life, Kruse and Graumann, in a recent paper, pose a rhetorical question:

> Should the theatre be a place of festive atmosphere, detached from everyday life, so that a visit to the theatre becomes a special undertaking for which one

has to prepare and dress up; or should the theatre belong to the profane sphere, and be approached in an everyday attitude and in everyday clothing, just like other everyday business?[8]

But, surely, whether or not one chooses to 'dress up' for the theatre, one cannot approach the theatre 'just like other everyday business' because it is not an everyday business. However revolutionary the performance, it does not, in itself, effect a political revolution in our everyday world. As I understand it, the theatre does not belong to the 'profane sphere', but is a special secular development of the sacred space, and dressing up for it is part of our modern-day ritual preparation for attending this special communal event.

The theatrical space has a double nature: as it has visible extension in the theatre, and by extrapolation also beyond it, it is created by the performance; but to the extent that it is predetermined by the text, both in dialogue and stage directions, it is an inbuilt structural dimension of the play itself. The twin concepts of the theatrical space within and without provide a very handy set of critical terms for dramatic analysis, though from an unusual angle. Any play, genre, or dramatic style, may be characterized by the particular balance it strikes between the theatrical space within and without and the relative meaning it attaches to them. In other words, far from being accidental or arbitrary, the articulation of the theatrical space is, at its best, an expression of the playwright's philosophical stance. As such, it becomes of thematic and structural importance to the play. An analysis of the spatial conception of a play, especially of the theatrical space without, can thus lead us directly to a consideration of its innermost problems.

IV

When turning to the plays, it is always best to start with Greek tragedy, where dramatic form appears in its purest and simplest lines. In the absence of stage directions, the discussion of the theatrical space in Greek tragedy must rely on historical and archeological research on the one hand, and on the written dialogue on the other.

The relationship between the theatrical space within and without is dependent to a large extent on the use of doors or passageways which communicate between the two. According to accepted opinion, the Greek actors entered the theatre space either through the wing entrances or through up to three doors in the background *skene*. These two kinds of entrances connect the scene with two different kinds of spaces without, the one far off, the other close by.

The two wing entrances were used for characters arriving from afar. Harold Baldry explains the evolution of these conventionalized entrances:

In later years a general theatre convention arose corresponding to what the Athenian audience could see: as the Piraeus lay to their right, entrance from harbour or market place in the play must be on that side; entrance from open country, on the spectator's left.[9]

Thus, the historical development is from the actual sensuous perception of the everyday space surrounding the open-air theatre to a conventional attribution of meaning to the two entrances, irrespective of the actual whereabouts of the audience. Roman drama further systematized this convention, assigning the right-hand side entrance to those arriving from the forum, and the left-hand side one to those arriving from the harbour and from foreign parts.[10] The process described by Baldry is a movement from the perception of actual space to its conventionalization in theatrical terms, so that it no longer depends on any one particular theatre space. Any playwright writing within this tradition would shape his theatrical space without in accordance with the convention. This convention transforms what was originally, in Athens, a perceived space into a conceptualized or conceived space.

Also conventionalized is the use of the doors in the *skene*. The *skene* served as a neutral architectural façade, which could represent, according to need, a palace, temple, tent or cave.[11] The action always unfolds in front of this façade, but the characters can exit into the 'house' or come out of it on to the stage. Thus what by convention lies behind the visible façade is a very near theatrical space without, continuous with the theatrical space within, an interior from which the characters issue.

In *King Oedipus*, the *skene* represents the palace into which Oedipus rushes when he discovers the incriminating truth of his identity. Jocasta's suicide and Oedipus' self-blinding both occur off stage,[12] inside the palace, that is, in the near-by theatrical space without. What has taken place off stage is narrated by an eye-witness, an attendant who comes out of the palace.

The attendant concludes his recitation by pointing out that 'the doors are opening'.[13] Usually this would be the sign for the opening of the central doors and the wheeling out of the *ekkyklema* with its burden of horror. Here it is difficult to tell whether the blind Oedipus stumbles out or whether he is revealed on the *ekkyklema*. Like the attendant, this piece of machinery, this 'thing wheeled out', is a conventionalized mechanism for revealing what has gone on in the near-by theatrical space without, by physically pushing the without into the within.[14]

But the theatrical space without of the play is not confined to that which lies behind the doors of the *skene*. Characters arrive from far off, from Delphi or Corinth, through the wing entrances. As in some perspective paintings, the action that unfolds in the foreground is given depth by two differently distanced planes which form its background. The best indication of these two planes in the play is provided by the two messengers, indifferently called in some translations 'messenger' and 'attendant'. But the Greeks called the one *angelos*, the other *exangelos*, or the messenger who told news from a distance as opposed to the messenger who told what was doing in the house or behind the scenes.[15] Both are dramatic functions rather than characters in their own right, each bringing news from his part of the space without.

While the action of the play is limited to one place, there are many references to other places. Taken together, these places form a virtual geography around Thebes. The action depends, to a large extent, on reports of characters who have travelled to Thebes from one of these peripheral places. Creon comes back from Delphi with an oracle, the *angelos* arrives from Corinth with his news of the death of Polybus, and the Shepherd is summoned from Mount Cithaeron, where he is grazing his flocks. Oedipus' own voyage from Corinth to Thebes antedates the events of the play, but is also recounted. This wider geographical area accommodates the various events that are excluded from the concentrated plot which unfolds in the visible theatrical space. Seen from this angle, it is the theatrical space without that guarantees the unity of place in the theatrical space within and, along with it, also the two other unities.

The theatrical space without provides all the necessary points of reference: Mount Cithaeron, the crossroads, and Corinth, which together define the world of the characters. As a baby, Oedipus was transported from Thebes, via the mountain, to Corinth; as an adult, he traced his way back. The *angelos* too has travelled between these two cities. It is almost natural that the fatal meeting should have taken place at the crossroads, between Thebes and Corinth. Another important point of reference is the Oracle at Delphi: Laius, Oedipus, Creon, all have consulted it. The theatrical space without is thus in constant interaction with the theatrical space within, intruding upon its sense of security, preserving the memory of things past, de-stabilizing the tenuous equilibrium of the space within.

v

The manipulation of the theatrical space without enables Sophocles to extend the scope of the action while, at the same time, preserving the dramatic unities. Nineteenth-century realistic theatre, standing firmly in the classical tradition, puts the theatrical space without to similar use. But the perceived perspective has been turned round 180 degrees. In the Greek theatre, the action developed outdoors, in front of the *skene*, so that the inside of the house was relegated to the theatrical space without and the backdrop was an architectural façade pierced with doors. Ibsen's middle-period realistic plays call for a drawing-room setting, and the doors lead to other, unseen rooms in the house, as well as outdoors. It is now the interior of the house which constitutes the theatrical space within, providing the necessary environment for intimate, private conversation.

In the elegant and slightly pretentious formality of the drawing room, Ibsen places his middle-class characters. His detailed stage directions as well as many textual references make it almost possible to draw a mental plan of the whole house which lies beyond this one room and with which it is connected through the stage doors. And beyond the house are the streets and other houses of Christiania. The playwright would like the good citizens of that city who watch his play to believe that what they see on stage is what is happening in a particular sitting room similar to their own and in the same city. He would like them to identify the theatrical space without with their own everyday space.

In *Hedda Gabler*, the heroine complains of her boredom and explains its cause: 'It's this middle-class world that I've got into.'[16] When asked by Ejlert Lövborg what was it that had made her cross-question him in the old days about his debaucheries, she answers hesitatingly and only after repeated promptings:

> Do you find it impossible to understand that a young girl, when there's an opportunity . . . in secret . . . That one should want to have a glimpse of the world that . . . that one isn't allowed to know about?[17]

When the men prepare to go to Judge Brack's all-male party, Hedda expresses her fantasy-wish to be present there, invisible, 'so as to hear a little of your gaiety – uncensored'.[18] Afraid as she is of scandal, Hedda adheres to the strict moral codes of her society, class and era, but by nature she is intrigued by what is considered in her *milieu* immoral conduct. She lacks the courage to follow her own desires and remains imprisoned within her elegant parlour.

It is only Hedda's imagination that dares be unconventional, and it is only through vicarious experiences that it can be both provoked and satisfied. Lövborg's exploits provide her with this necessary stimulation. Her peculiar fantasy is for Ejlert to come back 'with vine leaves in his hair, flushed and confident'. This unrealistic Dionysiac figure crystallizes Hedda's passionate and frenzied nature. It is a figure liberated from the encumbering bourgeois house in which she finds herself entrapped in the role of a young married wife, facing the prospect of motherhood. The Dionysiac figure represents the liberation of all the sexual fantasies which Hedda cannot but repress. It is her wild animal in a cage.

The spatial relations between the drawing room and the space without are transformed by Ibsen into a theatrical expression of the central theme of *Hedda Gabler*. The theatrical space within, the drawing room with its dried lavender smell, becomes the symbol of the powerful repression that the heroine suffers. In the theatrical space without there are the houses of Judge

Brack and Mademoiselle Diana and Ejlert Lövborg's rooms, all of which represent, for Hedda, that freedom from middle-class propriety she secretly yearns for. Further off, in a provincial town, there is also the house of the District Magistrate, the house Thea has dared leave, spurning bourgeois morality in a way Hedda would never dare to do. The aunts' house too forms part of this space without, although it represents an antipode to the other houses. The spinster aunts are models of resignation and acceptance, parsimony and self-abnegation. They have internalized bourgeois morality and for them there is no contradiction between their personal aspirations and the social norms.

Looking at *Hedda Gabler* from the angle of the theatrical space without and its relation to the theatrical space within takes us straight into the heart of the play. The spatial articulation is not an extraneous aspect of the drama, but a basic dramatic category. *Hedda Gabler* is a play that stands firmly in the tradition of the classical theatre, placing the individual in the centre and investigating his relationship with the surrounding world. The make-up of Hedda's personality is reflected by the spatial relations between the drawing room with its attached inner room and the space outside. While the other characters come and go, Hedda never leaves the stage until the very end, when she shuts herself off in the inner room and commits suicide.

## VI

In both *Oedipus* and *Hedda Gabler*, the configuration of the theatrical space expresses the central concerns of the two playwrights. For Sophocles, the movement between the theatrical spaces within and without demonstrates the ironic and inscrutable workings of fate or the intrusion of the metaphysical into everyday life. For Ibsen, the interplay between inside and outside spaces represents the destructive effect of the conventions and norms of society on a particular nature. In both cases, the spatial conception is intimately related to the basic philosophical and religious positions dramatized by the action of the two plays.

The conception of the stage as a room has come to dominate a large section of modern drama as a result of its focusing on the individual and on his intimate relationships. But this outward structural uniformity should not efface the different meanings attached to these different rooms.

Harold Pinter chose to call his dramatic *début* simply *The Room*. He sees in the room a basic unit of space, within which skeletal situations can be developed. In his programme notes to the Royal Court Theatre production of *The Room*, Pinter outlines the various possible permutations of the interaction between a man, a room and a visitor:

> Given a man in a room and he will sooner or later receive a visitor. A visitor

entering the room will enter with intent . . . The man may leave with the visitor or he may leave alone. The visitor may leave alone or stay in the room alone when the man is gone. Or they may both stay together in the room.[19]

Pinter toys with these elements much as Kandinsky plays with the confrontations between straight and curved lines or between different colours.

Pinter's articulation of the theatrical space is minimalistic and conceptual. He strips off characterization, plot, and cultural and historical setting, in order to reveal the impassionate outline, the basic structure of the theatrical event. This is similar to reducing a holy icon to a set of geometrical shapes. But certain meanings attach to the very structure itself, for Pinter thinks of his characters as

> . . . scared of what is outside the room . . . we are all in this, all in a room, and outside is a world . . . which is most inexplicable and frightening, curious and alarming.[20]

Pinter describes the outside in terms reminiscent of Eliade's 'chaotic space, peopled with demons and phantoms'. Pinter formulates here what for him is the central theatrical opposition between the within and the without. The without is a potential menace, an unknown threatening to intrude upon the relative and fragile security of the within. Separating the two – or connecting them, as the case may be – is the door. As Pinter puts it:

> The world is full of surprises. A door can open at any moment and someone will come in.[21]

This conceptual scaffolding forms the core of the play *The Room*. It is tricked up to look like a naturalistic play, but derives its powerful meaning from its deep structure. The room rented by Rose is described as warm and cosy. It forms part of a large house belonging to Mr Kidd. His tenant, Rose, speculates about who lives in the damp basement. Besides a door which leads onto the landing, the room has a window which looks onto the street. Outdoors it is freezing cold and getting dark, inside there are a gas fire and the homely pleasures of bacon and eggs and 'nice weak tea'.

The hyper-realistic style of the play is shaken by occasional intrusions of improbabilities, as when the landlord is unable to answer the simple question, 'How many floors you got in this house?' He says he used to count them in the old days, but can no longer keep track of them.[22] The dialogue half-suggests that Mr Kidd's bizarre answers are due to age and deafness, but also that they should not be taken at face value, on a merely naturalistic level. There are other upsetting details: Rose does not seem to know which room in the house is occupied by the landlord himself. Rose's visitors, the young couple Sands, have come in search of a room; they too are trying to establish their own little space, warm and secure. Their search turns out to be threatening to Rose's peace of mind, as 'the man in the basement' has indicated room number seven, Rose's own room, as a vacancy.

Most disturbing of all is the dark and damp basement, a theatrical space without which menaces the small warm room Rose struggles so hard to maintain. Her room forms a small habitable and hospitable haven within the large boarding house. Underneath is the basement, in which a black blind man is lurking, waiting for his chance to enter the room. His enigmatic figure is ominous and unsettling, threatening to destroy the temporary refuge Rose has succeeded in building herself.

Once he gains access into her room, the man gets a strong grip on Rose with his puzzling message: 'Your father wants you to come back home.' It is this word 'home', repeated, questioned and asserted, that makes Rose capitulate and revert to some old layer in her biography, in which she was called Sal. Her resistance crumbles down, she becomes tender to the point of physically touching the man,[23] at which moment her husband Bert re-enters the room and brutally reasserts his dominance over her in a violent *coup de théâtre*.

Pinter manipulates the theatrical spaces within and without to represent the psychoanalytic layers of the human soul. At first sight, his room might seem another variation on Ibsen's drawing room leading off to other spaces both inside and outside the house. But Pinter's house has been stripped bare before being redecorated with naturalistic detail. This stripping has transformed the house from an imitation house, similar to 'real' houses, into a basic structure which organizes space in a particular manner, attaching relative meanings to the different spatial units. Although it is redecorated to look like a real room, the room no longer represents an ordinary room. Its meaning depends on its position within the other spaces defined, but not depicted, in the play.

VII

Despite the differences between them, the three examples analysed so far, the classical tragedy, the realistic tragedy, and the hyper-realistic play, share the same basic structural principle: a theatrical space within, clearly distinguished from the theatre space on the one hand, and from the theatrical space without on the other.

Some twentieth-century playwrights have tried to shade off these clear-cut boundaries for special effects. The opening scene of Pirandello's *Six Characters in Search of an Author* pretends to be a rehearsal of another play called *Mixing It Up*. In other words, we are asked to believe that no theatrical space is being conjured up, that all we are seeing is part of the theatre space. This only accentuates the theatricality of the six characters who walk into the rehearsal. They introduce themselves as theatrical characters who carry in themselves a drama which they are compelled to play out. This drama is inseparable from its particular theatrical space. As the daughter puts it:

> I am dying to live that scene . . . The room . . . I see it . . . Here is the window . . . in front of the window the little mahogany table with the blue envelope containing one hundred *lire* . . .[24]

Another playwright who manipulates the classical spatial conception for the sake of heightened theatricality is Michel de Ghelderode. In his *Three Actors and their Drama*, the central characters are three actors who perform a short melodrama. As actors in the play, their theatrical space is the theatre space. As characters in the play-within-the-play, their theatrical space is defined by an incongruous *mélange* of Gothic, Empire and Louis XVI elements.[25] The subject matter of the play is the actors' inability to keep apart the two planes of existence: they act out their theatrical personas in everyday life, and they let their own 'persons' slip into the performance. But, as in Pirandello, the actors too are no more than dramatic characters themselves, so that the blending of real with theatrical space is merely illusory.

One could go on and on analysing intresting uses and manipulations of the theatrical space and the relation between the within and the without. I should like to conclude by examining two plays which provide extreme examples of the treatment of space in the theatre. These plays do not conform to the classical spatial pattern, but offer radical alternatives to it. My first example is medieval, the second contemporary.

VIII

Unlike the plays treated so far, the *Corpus Christi Play* has no theatrical space without. This is only to be expected of a cycle of plays that encompasses the history of the world from the Fall of the Angels to the Last Judgment. It is an all-inclusive play, that embraces all time and all space, excluding nothing. Its inner logic demands that everything take place within the theatrical space. The short plays which make up the cycle do not necessarily establish a consecutive story-line but present an *ensemble*, like the countless picture-Bibles to be found in medieval churches, executed in relief, painting or mosaic.

The two known methods of performance of the great cycles, the processional pageant and the theatre-in-the-round, create this all-inclusive theatrical space by different means. The York Cycle can be taken as representative of the first method, that of *décor successif*. The play is closely related to the town of York itself. The production was a local affair, that employed all the talent and means at the disposal of the wealthy guilds, and was regulated by the governing body of the town. The procession wound its way around the town, stopping at appointed stations, and performing the whole cycle at each station,[26] thus literally permeating the whole town. One finds here that the theatrical space and the theatre space become coextensive, spreading out to the very walls of the town. These walls become the crucial delimiting line between the sacred and the profane spaces. Through its processionary movement, the religious performance reaffirms the sacred nature of the space within the town walls, which comes to represent, for the duration of the play, the whole universe.

This brings us back to Ovid's story of the foundation of Rome by building an altar over the fruit-filled trench and then raising a rampart around it. Plutarch said that 'they gave the name of world [*mundus*] to that trench as to the universe itself'.[27] The festive procession of pageants, following in the steps of the Corpus Christi procession itself, thus re-establishes the town's sacred precincts. The processional religious performance sanctifies the town of York in the sense outlined by Eliade:

> In fact the idea of a sacred place involves the notion of repeating the primeval hierophany which consecrates the place by marking it out, by cutting it off from the profane space around it.[28]

In Eliade's analysis, the sacred place, be it temple or city, 'is always a meeting place for the three cosmic regions',[29] hell, heaven, and earth. Thus, what seems to be most daring in the medieval theatre, the representation of God and His act of creation, is in no way a desecration when presented in the newly re-established sacred space, in the town which forms the theatrical space of the *Corpus Christi Play*. Within it, the separate pageants might represent partial theatrical spaces, but they should be regarded as parts of the play as a whole, which, as it represents the history of the world, encompasses the whole *mundus* enclosed within the town walls. The spectators as well as the actors are engulfed within this re-enactment of the Christian story of the world; nobody is excluded and there can be no theatrical space outside.

The all-inclusiveness of the cycle-play is even more prominent when performed in the round, as in the Cornish Cycle. Here spectators as well as actors are enclosed within the same round earth rampart, which marks the boundaries of the sacred space. The various 'places' and 'houses' are all simultaneously visible, and Jesus' journey from the Lake of Galilee to Jerusalem is performed literally by the actor crossing the *platea* from a particular 'place' to a designated 'house'. Jerusalem does not constitute a theatrical space outside because it is part of the within, as are all other places. The theatre-in-the-round is a self-contained microcosm, for which there can be no theatrical space without. As Elie Konigson puts it in his *L'Espace théâtral médiéval*,

There is no exiting from the acting space because there is no exiting from the
world. Between Paradise and Hell there is no place for an unhallowed outside,
where the actor could take off his character.[30]

Both methods of representing the *Corpus Christi Play*, the procession of
pageants as well as the theatre-in-the-round, reinforce the scope and
meaning of the play by widening the theatrical space within, until nothing
is excluded. The theatrical space engulfs the whole of the theatre space, so
that they become indistinguishable. The very nature of this play negates the
possibility of any theatrical space without.

IX

My last example differs from all my previous ones in that it deliberately and
explicitly addresses itself to the problem of the theatrical space. In his play
*Offending the Audience*, Peter Handke sets out to demolish the conventional
mimetic views of the theatre and consequently the very idea of theatre. In
his introductory note, Handke supplies the term *Sprechstück* by way of genre-
definition. The words of the *Sprechstück* 'don't point at the world as
something lying outside the words but to the world in the words themselves', and these words 'give no picture of the world but a concept of it'.[31]

The four speakers in *Offending the Audience* speak directly to the audience
and point out that they share the same time–space continuum. In the
process of tearing up the theatrical conventions, the speakers carefully
phrase them:

> There is no invisible circle here. There is no magic circle. There is no room for
> play here. We are not playing. We are all in the same room. The demarcation
> line has not been penetrated, it is not pervious, it doesn't even exist.[32]

By insisting that the demarcation line does not exist, the speakers force on
us the awareness that in the theatre, as a rule, there is just such a
demarcation line, just such a separation between the space inside the magic
circle and the space outside it.

When performed, this piece is often taken to be merely offensive, a
hurling of abuse at the conventional theatre audience, *pour épater les
bourgeois*. But the play is in fact an important conceptual and theoretical
piece. The abuse is the emotional outlet for the theoretical attack which has
been launched at the audience. This attack is tantamount to a profanation
of the sacred theatrical space. Handke insists on the audience regarding the
theatre space as part of their everyday space. He refuses to admit the
possibility of demarcating part of the theatre space so that it will represent
another, theatrical space. He desecrates the theatrical space, throwing out
all its idols: the scenery, the actors impersonating characters, the special
lighting, the plot – all are cleared out leaving a bare stage from which

speakers – not actors – address the audience sitting in a fully lit auditorium on an equal footing with them.

This bold and outrageous procedure pulls the carpet from under its own feet: where can the theatre go from here? But Handke himself would have us regard his *Sprechstücke* merely as 'autonomous prologues to old plays', which 'do not want to revolutionize but to make aware'.[33] In other words, after *Offending the Audience* we should become aware of the problematic status of the theatrical space in which alone the theatrical illusion can be maintained.

In modern drama, the theatrical space, instead of remaining implicit in the formal setting of the play, has been brought into the foreground and made into a theoretical and philosophical issue. Space is no longer a mere environment in which the protagonists move. It has become a theatrical object in its own right, often replacing the traditional subject matters of drama. The concepts of theatre space, theatrical space and theatrical space without offer useful critical tools for a synchronic analysis of spatial configurations and their meanings in totally different types of theatre.

## NOTES

1  H. d'Outreman, *Histoire de la ville et comté de Valenciennes* (1639), in A. M. Nagler, *A Source Book in Theatrical History* (New York: Dover Publications, 1952), p. 47.

2  Eugène Ionesco, *The Bald Soprano*.

3  Ernst Cassirer, *The Philosophy of Symbolic Forms* (New Haven: Yale University Press, 1955), p. 99.

4  *Ibid.*, p. 107.

5  *Ovid's Fasti*, IV, 821–5, with trans. by J. G. Frazer (London: Heinemann, Loeb Classical Library, 1951).

6  Mircea Eliade, *Patterns in Comparative Religion* (London: Sheed & Ward, 1958), p. 371.

7  I have analysed Shakespeare's use of the theatrical space without in my paper 'The Undiscover'd Country: The Theatrical Space Without in *Hamlet*', to be published in the Proceedings of the 1984 Conference of the Association Shakespeare Française.

8  Lenelis Kruse and Carl F. Graumann, 'The Theatre as Interaction and as Interaction Space', in James F. Arnott, Joëlle Charian, Heinrich Huesmann, Tom Lawrenson and Rainer Theobald (eds.), *Theatre Space: An Examination of the Interaction between Space, Technology, Performance and Society* (Munich: Prestel Verlag, 1977), p. 157.

9  Harold C. Baldry, 'The Theatre and Society in Antiquity', in J. F. Arnott *et al.* (eds.), *Theatre Space*, p. 9. See also in James Redmond (ed.), *Drama and Society*, Themes in Drama 1 (Cambridge: Cambridge University Press, 1979).

10  For a detailed discussion of the Roman convention and its Greek origins, cf. George E. Duckworth, *The Nature of Roman Comedy* (Princeton, NJ: Princeton University Press, 1971), pp. 85–7.

11 Cf. Harold C. Baldry, *The Greek Tragic Theatre* (London: Chatto & Windus, 1971), pp. 49–50.

12 Cf. *ibid.*, p. 51.

13 Sophocles, *The Theban Plays*, trans. E. F. Watling (Harmondsworth: Penguin, 1947), p. 61.

14 Cf. Baldry, *The Greek Tragic Theatre*, pp. 51–3.

15 The term *exangelos* appears to have been first used by Aeschylus, as reported by Philostratus (ii/iii ct. A.D.). See H. G. Liddel, R. Scott and H. S. Jones, *Greek–English Lexicon*, 9th edn, 1940.

16 Henrik Ibsen, *Hedda Gabler and Other Plays*, trans. Una Ellis-Fermor (Harmondsworth: Penguin, 1950), p. 306.

17 *Ibid.*, pp. 316–17.

18 *Ibid.*, p. 323.

19 Quoted by Martin Esslin, *Pinter: A Study of his Plays* (London: Eyre Methuen, 1973), p. 40.

20 Interview with Kenneth Tynan, in Esslin, *Pinter*, p. 35.

21 Interview with John Sherwood, in Esslin, *Pinter*, p. 38.

22 Harold Pinter, *Complete Works: One* (New York: Grove Press, 1976), p. 108.

23 *Ibid.*, p. 125.

24 Luigi Pirandello, *Naked Masks*, ed. E. Bentley (New York: E. P. Dutton & Co., 1952), p. 223.

25 Michel de Ghelderode, *Seven Plays*, trans. George Hauger (New York: Hill & Wang, 1960), vol. I, p. 133.

26 Richard Beadle and Pamela M. King (eds.), *York Mystery Plays*, 'General Introduction', p. xvii. Other scholars, such as E. K. Chambers and G. Wickham, take different views of the method of presenting the pageants. But their interpretations do not affect my main point.

27 Quoted by Eliade, *Patterns in Comparative Religion*, p. 373.

28 *Ibid.*, p. 368.

29 *Ibid.*, p. 377.

30 E. Konigson, *L'Espace théâtral médiéval* (Paris: Centre National de la Recherche Scientifique, 1975), p. 278.

31 Peter Handke, *Kaspar and Other Plays*, trans. M. Roloff (New York: Farrar, Straus and Giroux, 1969), n.p.

32 *Ibid.*, p. 10.

33 Note on *Offending the Audience* and *Self-Accusation*, *ibid.*

# Character and theatrical space

CHARLES R. LYONS

In one of Samuel Beckett's recent plays, a middle-aged woman rocks in a chair.[1] Our physical vision of the space she inhabits is limited to the small area of light into which she moves as she rocks forward. She listens, as we spectators do, to a voice that tells a strange story of a woman who gradually abandons her search for 'another creature like herself' and retreats to a rocking chair to wait for her death. The figure we see appears to invoke that voice by speaking the single command 'More.' The voice falters three times, and the woman provokes it to resume by repeating the command. Each response, however, assumes a weaker tone; and, eventually, the voice fails and she issues no more commands. The woman stops her rocking, and we suspect that she has either died or has approached death. Beckett's brief, unelaborated drama features only one character, uses no physical space other than that occupied by a rocking chair, and performs within twenty minutes.

Beckett's later plays, which have become progressively simpler in terms of their theatrical demands, have taught us the communicative potential of the single figure speaking and listening in an unelaborated scene.[2] Their dependence upon a minimal use of scenic devices and physical action does not suggest a retreat from theatricality but, rather, proves Beckett's faith in the communicative power of simple dramatic images. *Rockaby* demonstrates clearly that a playwright's essential resource is the image of a human character who exists in dimension and duration. No theatrical representation of human experience can be performed that does not exhibit a human figure in space and reveal itself in time. Whatever scenic conventions operate, the spectator will perceive the actor in some visual field and the play will unfold during the time required for the performance. In reducing the components of performance to minimal realizations of images of character, space, and duration, Beckett has shown us that these elements are not only fundamental but sufficient. The simple representation of the woman rocking in a chair listening to her own voice develops an image of experience that encompasses an indefinite but extended period of time and the character's movement through a public space to an increasingly restricted private world. The bare but rhythmic text details a story of her withdrawal from the search for another and her retreat into the rocking chair in which her mother died. That equivocal narrative, which holds only speculative authority, provides the only means of investing significance in the radically limited image of theatrical space the performance exploits. Beckett's exercises in theatrical simplicity clarify the operation of the basic conventions of dramatic form and illuminate the principles of their use. Understanding the processes by which a play such as *Rockaby* establishes suggestive images of character, space, and time helps to illuminate the means by which dramatic texts hold meaning for us. The performance of this provocatively simple work demonstrates the fact that the dramatic image of character within space and time is irreducible and that it is impossible to separate the image of theatrical space from the image of character.

In the past fifty years, with some exceptions, the principal movements in criticism have been markedly non-mimetic.[3] As the emphasis in Shakespearean criticism shifted from the analysis of character to the function of language, the term *character* seemed to disappear from the critical lexicon. When Maude Bodkin implemented Freudian and Jungian constructs to analyze the totality of *King Lear* as the representation of the consciousness of its hero, Goneril and Regan became functions of the father's unconscious, and in her terms they operate not as discrete dramatic characters but as figures that embody the father's fear of children.[4] In phenomenologically oriented criticism, most brilliantly exercised in the study of seventeenth-century French drama,[5] the idea of individual character is subsumed by a notion of the *consciousness* of the text, a kind of persona that substitutes for the self of the writer; and the critical act produces a vision of that consciousness, built up of the various metaphoric alignments, paradigms, or conceptual structures sustained throughout the writer's work. In Marxian criticism, *character* may read as *character*, but the notion of human identity itself shifts to become a screen upon which the attitudes and perceptions of a class display themselves. In the exercises of structuralist and post-structuralist criticism, the idea of *character* as the representation of human consciousness does not obtain. Characters exist in relationship to other characters, differentiated according to the categories by which the text organizes itself, an organization that reflects certain systems of cultural value unself-consciously.

Each of these non-mimetic critical strategies demands that we perceive the language of the text as a partially transparent epithelial surface that, paradoxically, both masks and discloses the structure underneath. That is, at a literal level the text operates as an aesthetic displacement of an inner dynamic. In that sense, the critical act does not study the text as the reflection of an objective reality but, rather, translates the explicit text into a language that discloses the latent content. The nature of the substructure perceived, of course, depends upon the assumptions of the critical strategy. The organization of the latent content may be seen as a manifestation of socio-economic forces, as the representation of a psychic transaction that reveals the functioning of the unconscious, as a reflection of the organizational patterns of the writer's consciousness, as a variation of a culturally determined myth, or as a transitive *space* that displays the disjunctively accumulated cultural residue of a series of temporal moments.[6]

In non-mimetic critical analyses, the individual dramatic figure functions merely as a unit of the surface or literal level of the text. That is, the *character*, per se, operates as a symbol, sign or trope among other symbols, signs, or tropes that must be translated within the terms of the perceived substructure. These critical strategies, of course, have released the dramatic text from a naive mimetic approach in which the value of the play was determined by its ability to mirror an objective reality truthfully. And yet, however liberating the non-mimetic critical strategies have been, they have not been able to deal with the phenomenon of the text in performance as effectively as with the phenomenon of reading. In fact, the typical practitioners of New Critical, phenomenological, structuralist, and post-structuralist perspectives have been acutely uncomfortable with theatrical performance as the vehicle for the transmission of the texts they favor. This discomfort is understandable because, in performance, the spectator receives the text only through the physical representation accomplished by human beings in an actual space. It is difficult to accomplish the New Critical processing of a text, realigning corresponding metaphors and perceiving implicit linguistic paradigms, when one's attention is focused on individual actors speaking the text in a direct, line-by-line sequence. Correspondingly, when the images of a text are distributed among a complex of personalities, it is difficult for the phenomenologist to hear the idiosyncratic voice of the single consciousness. Whereas the structuralist would deny the existence of that voice and focus on the text in performance as the compound of a series of semiological systems or codes, verbal and non-verbal, the spectators' engagement with the performance, as with the ritual, would preclude their consciousness of the hidden significance of the organizational principles enacted. In the structuralist's terms, the experience of performance is aesthetic, the discovery of the implicit structure is a scientific process. The text may be vulnerable to a structural analysis, but performance provides an inappropriate condition for that activity; and performance, as well, is subject to the operation of different systems of categorization. Of course, theatrical performance, in which the image of the playwright as an individual creative subject is destroyed by the extra-textual intervention of director, designers, and actors might seem the quintessential post-structuralist activity. Here, of course, the sense of the dramatic text as an arbitrary collection of the traces of disparate meanings should be evident. However, the unity provided by the continuity of the presence of the actor/character tends to obscure the collision of readings that precedes the performance.

We need to confront the fact that the image of character in space and time constitutes an irreducible aesthetic unit. No critical system can erase the presence of the human image that occupies the space of the stage. When we posit analogies among the arts, we often discuss language as the medium of the playwright, considering words to be equivalent to the painter's pigment. However, the ratio painter/pigment : playwright/language is not accurate. The playwright's medium is the representation of character. The playwright, unlike the writer of prose fiction or epic poetry, cannot communicate directly to the reader or spectator, but speaks through the individual character. Each textual segment is mediated through the voice of a dramatized *persona*, physically present before the spectator. Each statement is communicated as the assertion, perception, image of a *persona*. The representation of character – to use Dryden's felicitous phrase, 'the painting of the hero's mind' – is the representation of consciousness: the dramatization of a consciousness perceiving the scene, including other characters, perceiving or imagining itself within that scene, and formulating, processing, or responding to that perception. The perception and mediation of images, grounded in the *persona* assumed by the actor, constitutes the primary aesthetic instrument at the playwright's disposal. While it is possible to use critical systems to construe latent organizational principles, the data with which we work in that project comes to us through the agency of character.

I want to assert emphatically that I am not calling for a return to the methodologies of Edward Dowden or A. C. Bradley, who accepted the mimetic value of Shakespeare's plays so unequivocally that they believed certain dramatic characters to supersede the texts that house them.[7] The specific detail of Shakespeare's representation of behavior in combination with Bradley's own mimetic sensibility prompted him to build images of character that exemplified the received psychological theories with which the late nineteenth century evaluated human behavior. Rather than using *character* in Bradley's sense, I am attempting to exercise a functional concept that is more equivalent to the formal schemas that Gombrich identifies in his discussion of representation in Western painting.[8] The plays of Samuel Beckett expose the conventionality of the theatrical idea *character* by revealing that *character* is less the mirroring of an entity whose counterpart or type exists in 'reality' and is more a perceptual formula that playwright, *character*, and spectator apply to the voicing of a discourse that would, otherwise, be inexplicable in its present circumstance. In Beckett the sense of character as subject is hypothetical, speculative, transitive. The notion of self or subject constitutes a fragile tissue that connects character to narrative, character to scene, and character to immediate moment. That connection – made by the actor and the spectator – is self-consciously hypothetical; and the spectator's acceptance of the *character* as the nexus of images of space and time should be tentative.

We recognize the impossibility of creating images of consciousness that are independent of images of scene and duration since consciousness cannot perceive itself outside of a spatial and temporal situation. In turn, we cannot imagine a human figure fully removed from space and time. Language, of course, is the principal vehicle by which the playwright represents the mental processes that build images of individual dramatic character. Language is also the primary instrument in the dramatic representation of place. Even though the dramatic scene is physically depicted by the space of the stage itself, the playwright establishes the significance of the *mise en scène* through the language the characters speak as they voice their perception of the environment in which they exist.

When we read prose fiction, we may create an image of the *persona* of the storyteller whatever person the narrative employs. In dramatic performance, however, the presence of actors, representing characters, replaces the image of the single storyteller with the illusion that the behavior of the *dramatic personae*, which we observe directly, is self-interpreting. Dramatic performance eliminates the intervening presence of the storyteller and substitutes the theatrical enactment for the narration. Performance presents the illusion that the co-ordinates of the dramatized event are not enclosed within the narrative consciousness of a single storyteller. The playwright, thereby, creates the illusion that he is removed from the event of the performance. One of the formal consequences of the apparent absence of the playwright's voice is that the illusion of place, the fictional scene of the drama, must be created visually by elements of scenery and by the language spoken by the characters. The reader of a piece of fiction may, indeed, posit an image of a world that contains the narrative but that world is not present as a physical part of the aesthetic event of reading, whereas in dramatic performance an image of the scene is always present in the perceivable space that holds the actor. Therefore, the experience of observing a dramatic performance differs from the experience of receiving a narrative from reading or listening to a recitation. The performance takes place within some architectural container in an area marked off as the scene of the action performed.[9] That actual space may hold specific objects and qualities that make historical, sociological, or aesthetic references, but the stage becomes a fictional scene principally through the voiced perceptions of the characters who inhabit it.

It is rare when a dramatic work makes no visual or spoken reference to one or more of the perceptual schemes by which we conceptualize an idea of place. For example, the playwright may refer to an image of space by the use of direct visual quotation. The scenographic image may figure an actual site by representing sufficient unique details to stimulate the knowledge-able spectator to read the scene as a duplicate of an existing referent. The portico of Inigo Jones' St Paul's in the first scene of Shaw's *Pygmalion* and the interior of Sant' Andrea della Valle in Puccini's *La Tosca* function as aesthetic substitutes of actual buildings. The playwright may also make reference to an idea of space by the exercise of either iconographic or conventional signs. In *Richard II*, for example, Shakespeare undoubtedly used the actor's movement from the upper stage of the Globe to the platform at that moment when Richard cries 'Down, down I come like glist'ring Phaëton . . .' (III, iii, 178). Here the actual physical structure of the theater functions as a three-dimensional emblem of an architectural structure, a sign that is like its actual referent only in a limited sense. That is, the tiring house of the Globe provides an architectural configuration that allows movement from an upper story to a lower level without making specific visual reference to the exterior of a palace in general or to the actual site of Barkloughly Castle (Harlech) in Wales. The kind of site referred to – the elevated place at which the monarch can display himself to a public in contrast to the courtyard which is a place of assembly – is, in many actual buildings, a practical architectural icon of political hierarchy. Shakespeare uses the tiring house in *Richard II*, consequently, as the representation of a typical architectural structure that itself supports a ritualistic represen-tation of political authority. The tiring house itself is neither an icon nor an emblem; for that particular moment of the play it functions as an image of a structure that holds iconographic value as the character uses the physical space and his movement within it as a political and as a psychological gesture. In a few moments, the spectators release the value that Richard's language assigns to the relationship between tiring house and platform and perceive the space as another kind of site. Serlio's engraved representations of the three types of scene required in the sixteenth-century Italian theatre include a highly conventionalized abstraction of a city street with the mundane buildings required for urban comedy (plate 1), an equally condensed display of a street with the buildings that figure in tragedies – palaces, churches, and edifices of state (plate 2), and a highly decorative forest glade that provides the appropriate environment for pastoral drama (plate 3). Each of these scenes refers to highly generalized concepts of space, and audiences would expect a different kind of behaviour to take place in each of the environments displayed.

The playwright may also suggest through metaphor the relationship of the scene to an object, idea, concept, or value. In Ibsen's *Brand* a scenic location such as the Ice Church represents a natural phenomenon, a glacial crevice, that the community has named the Ice Church because its physical

1 This firſt ſhall be Comicall, whereas the houſes muſt be ſlight for Citizens, but ſpecially there muſt not want a brawthell or bawdyhouſe, and a great Inne, and a Church; ſuch things are of neceſſitie to be therein.

(Sebastiano Serlio, *Architettura*. Venice, Paris 1537–47. This text is from the first English edition, of 1611, as are the illustrations.)

characteristics resemble the architecture of a church. The Ice Church, however, functions in the play as a conceptual structure in which Brand explores the antithesis between his realization of an absolute commitment to God and the compromises demanded by his interaction with others. The site is not, of course, the visual representation of a metaphor but, rather, a visualization of the space that allows the character to use his perception of the scene metaphorically in order to conceptualize antithetical visions of experience.

The point that I make in this very brief analysis of the use of scene in dramatic performance is that the representation of place is made through processes of visual and verbal reference. The playwright uses reference according to a variety of systems by which space is conceptualized: as a

2 Houſes for Tragedies, muſt be made for great perſonages, for that actions of loue, ſtrange aduentures, and cruell murthers ( as you reade in ancient and moderne Tragedies ) happen always in the houſes of great Lords, Dukes, Princes, and Kings. Therefore in ſuch caſes you muſt make none but ſtately houſes, as you ſee it here in this figure . . .

physical artifact such as St Paul's in Covent Garden that itself holds varied aesthetic, political, social, economic significance; as an emblem of political hierarchy as in Shakespeare's use of the simple spatial analogy between the structure of a palace and the tiring house; as a physical image that can communicate social significance through vulnerability to categorization as in the Serlian scenes; or as a physical presence that can receive meaning from a dramatic character by being perceived in relationship to something else (glacial crevice as Ice Church). Ibsen's use of the fundamental spatial images of height and depth, both in the physical representation of place and in the character's reference to places apart from the represented scene, builds upon a cultural scheme that assigns values to the ideas 'high' and 'low': he represents those values, however, not as absolutes but as conceptual forms through which the characters think of themselves in the world.

The words of the text establish both the literal identification of a site – Thebes, Argos, the sacred Grove at Colonus, the cliffs at Dover, the Cachon

3 The Satiricall Scenes are to reprefent Satirs, wherein you muft place all thofe things that bee rude and rufticall, as in ancient Satirs they were made plaine without any refpect, whereby men might underftand, that fuch things were referred to Rufticall people, which fet all things out rudely and plainely: for which caufe Vitruuius fpeaking of Scenes, faith, they fhould be made with Trees, Rootes, Herbes, Hils, and Flowres, and withfome countrey houfes, as you fee them here fet downe. And for that in our dayes thefe things were made in Winter, when there were but fewe greene Trees, Herbs and Flowres to be found; then you muft make thefe things of Silke, which will be more commendable then the naturall things themfelves: and as in other Scenes for Comedies or Tragedies, the houfes or other artificiall things are painted, so you muft make Trees, Hearbs, and other things in thefe; the more such things coft, the more they are efteemed, for they are things which ftately and great perfons doe, which are enemies to nigardlineffe.

country – and also convey the character's subjective response to that space. The imagination of the audience transforms the actual physical dimensions of the stage into an assimilated image of scene derived from observing the behavior of characters within that space, behavior that is, predominately, verbal. In other words, the scene of a dramatic event is an image of place within the spectator's imagination, stimulated by the ways in which the

characters speak of the site and relate to it. In the process of accepting the
illusion of the event, the spectator imposes an extrapolated image of place
upon the physical space of the stage, expanding, contracting, qualifying,
and altering the physical dimensions of the stage to correspond to the image
of space and situation created by the representation.

The space that surrounds the character, the site itself and the objects and
other characters it contains, provide the fictional mind of that figure with
material that will generate substantive images that inform his consciousness. The character will perceive objects, spaces, and other characters and
will mediate these objectivities into the images that constitute his conscious
awareness of himself in the world. Scene in that sense is crucial to the
development of an image of character since the objectivities of the scene
provide the consciousness of the character with the immediate images with
which it constitutes itself. I use the term *objectivities* to refer to the character's
perception of the scene that surrounds him, the physical space and the
human and inanimate objects it contains. When I use the word *scene*, I refer
to the totality of these objectivities.

My use of the term *scene* derives from its inclusive significance in Kenneth
Burke's pentad of five dramatistic terms: Act, Scene, Agent, Purpose,
Agency.[10] Burke, of course, uses *scene* to refer not only to physical location
but to the political, ideological, and psychological 'situation' in which an
act takes place. While Burke does not define the term in the same language
that I use, his notion of *scene* includes the composite image of place and
situation created by the response of characters to their physical and social
environment. In drama, scene encompasses situation through the representation of the characters' perception. My analysis of the function of space in
tragedy considers the interaction of character and scene in which the mind
of the character invests the dramatized space with meaning and the objects
of the scene provide the consciousness of the character with the images with
which it conceptualizes itself. The playwright has the physical resources of
the space of the stage, the possibility of transforming that space by
scenographic illusion, and the subjective perceptions of the scene that are
spoken by the characters themselves. As I have emphasized in these
introductory pages, the sense of place that these mediations build provides
the most important means of building an image of scene. The history of
scenography and its relationship to dramatic texts is a fascinating study,
but my discussion in this essay confronts more fundamental conventions of
dramatic structure. My insistence upon the irreducibility of the image of
character in space in time is, I recognize, a clear departure from more
orthodox discussions in which scene is analyzed as an independent component of the dramatic event.

The spectator sees the character in the site and, as well, watches the
character himself respond to his self-conscious image of himself in the site.
In other words, the spectator sees the character in space and observes the

character perceiving the scene and conceptualizing his relationship to that site. The spectator sees the scene, in space and situation, as an objective presence and notes the difference between that presence and the character's mediated vision of it. When I use the pair of terms, *perception* and *mediation*, I do not limit perception to the process of receiving data from the senses but, rather, to the interaction of perception and cognition discussed by Piaget in psychological terms and by both Gombrich and Arnheim in visual terms.[11] *Mediation*, the process in which a character creates and exercises a subjective image of what he has perceived, is not – as my earlier discussion might suggest – the second phase of a two-part action: what happens after perception. The physical processes of seeing are themselves informed, if not directed, by the conceptual schemes that order that perception. In order to represent the individuality of a character, the playwright must reveal the subjective difference between his perception of the world and that of other characters. The playwright, therefore, creates the individuality of character by revealing, in his language, the conceptual schemes that inform his perception of the scene.

The character's perception of the world may be the most communicative instrument in qualifying the nature of the scene, but the sense of place established by the performance is not identical to that perceived by the hero, because this individual character and his or her perception remain objective entities within the field observed by the spectator. The uniqueness of the character's vision differentiates him in that field. Lear's perception and mediation of the storm in act III exemplifies this process. While Bodkin and others have discussed the storm as a metaphor that reproduces in nature Lear's tempestuous consciousness, the dramatized phenomenon of the storm is independent of him, an objective presence that Lear experiences.[12] The storm is not a mimetic reproduction of his mind; the storm is discrete. To see the relationship of Lear and the storm differently is to ignore the fundamental convention of character and scene in which the playwright represents the dramatic figure using the details of the scene to exercise the processes of consciousness that create his character. Shakespeare establishes Lear's subjectivity, the uniqueness of his consciousness, by dramatizing the highly individualized processes in which he perceives the physical phenomena of the storm and uses them to conceptualize his personal experience.

Initially Lear invokes the storm to take revenge on those who have betrayed him. In this sense, he perceives the storm as his own agent, the potential instrument of revenge against his daughters:

> And thou, all-shaking thunder,
> Smite flat the thick rotundity o' th' world.
> Crack nature's molds, all germains spill at once,
> That makes ingrateful man!

(III, ii, 6–9)

However, at that point, in a curious transition, he distances himself from
the storm, de-personalizing it. He declares that the storm cannot be unkind
to him because he did not give it a kingdom. He moves toward a different
perspective in which he associates the storm with Goneril and Regan, and
he claims that the storm is their agent. At this moment he sees himself not as
the source of the storm's energy or as its controller but, rather, as the
recipient of its hostility. Lear's first two perceptions of the storm – his sense
that the tempest could serve as the instrument of his revenge and his
interpretation of the natural phenomena as the agents of his daughters'
hostility towards him – are ego-centered visions. Later, however, Lear
moves from these highly subjective interpretations of the storm into a
recognition that the storm is a hostile natural force that inflicts suffering
upon those people in his kingdom who have neither shelter nor protective
clothing:

> Poor naked wretches, wheresoe'er you are,
> That bide the pelting of the pitiless storm,
> How shall your homeless heads and unfed sides,
> Your loop'd and window'd raggedness, defend you
> From seasons such as these? O, I have ta'en
> Too little care of this!
>
> (III, iii, 28–33)

Freed from the rational egocentricity that marked his sanity, he
encompasses compassion for others as he experiences his own suffering.
Moving into the hovel, Lear focuses upon Poor Tom, the disguised Edgar,
as the object of his sympathy, extending the perception he gained of the
suffering of the 'poor naked wretches' of whom he has taken too little care.
However, initially his concern for Poor Tom assumes that this man
reproduces his own suffering; and he uses the naked man as an image of his
own experience.

> Has his daughters brought him to this pass?
> Couldst thou save nothing? Wouldst thou give 'em all?
>
> (III, iv, 62–3)

In another transition, Lear reverses himself. Rather than seeing Poor Tom
as the image of himself, he attempts to identify himself with the naked
madman; and he strips off his clothes to demonstrate that identification:

> Thou wert better in a grave than to answer with
> thy uncover'd body this extremity of the skies. Is man
> no more than this? Consider him well. Thou ow'st the
> worm no silk, the beast no hide, the sheep no wool, the
> cat no perfume. Ha! Here's three on's are
> sophisticated. Thou are the thing itself;
> unaccommodated man is no more but such a poor, bare,
> forked animal as thou art. Off, off, you lendings!
> Come, unbutton here.
>
> (III, iv, 100–8)

First Lear imposes his own identity on the figure of Poor Tom, and then he reverses that process and perceives his fundamental human nature in the image of that creature. He attempts to enact that perception by making himself as naked as Poor Tom. This scene constitutes an important moment in Shakespeare's representation of Lear's consciousness. However, at the same moment at which they recognize this important stage in the development of Lear's perception of others, spectators may well be aware that the object that stimulates Lear's sharper vision is a false one. That is, Shakespeare establishes a painful paradox in stimulating Lear's authentically compassionate moment with an inauthentic image: the disguised courtier, Edgar, who performs the role of the naked madman. Lear, whose madness seems real, directs his sympathy towards Edgar whose actual identity is masked by the disguise of madness. Whereas the suffering that the disguised Edgar represents is an authentic problem – and Lear's perception of this reality is a valid realization of his personal and political failure to attend to it – Shakespeare does not present his hero in direct relationship to that public world – only the representation of it through Edgar's performance of Poor Tom.

The text establishes the storm as an independent presence in order for Lear to use its phenomena in a sequence of images in consciousness with which he confronts the extremity of his situation. His processes of self-conceptualization manifest both the irrationality of his increasing madness – seen in the ways in which he personifies the storm – and the insight his individual suffering stimulates – seen in his compassion for the victims of the storm in general and Poor Tom in particular. We cannot understand the processes in which Shakespeare builds the image of Lear's character unless we confront the fundamental relationship between character and scene in which the playwright reveals the dramatic figure's perception and mediation of the discrete fictional phenomena that constitute the space in which he exists.

At this point in my discussion, it would be useful to concentrate upon a text in which the principal character invests a major physical location with clearly subjective significance. *Brand* serves this purpose well because Ibsen's use of the antithesis of Ice Church and village church provides an easily recognized organizational scheme in which the hero is able to conceptualize his experience. Brand's vision of these two locations demonstrates the process in which a playwright uses the character's perception of scene to reveal the individuality of character, and my following discussion clarifies that Ibsen's topography in *Brand* is not an independent communicative instrument but is, on the contrary, indivisible from the representation of character.

In the opening moments of the drama, as Brand walks through a mountain storm, approaching his native village after an absence of many years, he first meets a peasant and his son. The peasant is traveling to visit his dying daughter who desperately wants his blessing before she dies. As the danger from the storm increases, the peasant refuses to continue the dangerous journey, and Brand despises his lack of commitment to this single act. Brand perceives the other man's choice in schematic terms: the difference between the implementation of an absolute ideal and the exercise of compromise. Brand continues through the storm, encounters Agnes and Einar, and then the demented adolescent girl, Gerd. Gerd makes the first reference to the Ice Church. His response to her evocation of this place reveals that it is a natural crevice in the mountain that the villagers identify as the Ice Church because the ice-paved floor and the curving arches of drifting snow form a structure that resembles a vaulted nave. Gerd adamantly clings to the notion that it is an actual church. For her, the site offers freedom or safety from the falcon that she imagines pursues her. Gerd perceives the Ice Church as a sanctuary from the threatening falcon and the taunts of the cruel villagers. She sees the village as the place of foulness in contrast to the pristine isolation of the Ice Church. Brand perceives the Ice Church as threatening and dangerous:

> Never go there; a sudden gust of wind
> Has often been enough to crack the glacier;
> A shriek, a rifle-shot, is enough –
>
> . . .
>
> Danger lies there; you must fear it!

Gerd replies, pointing down toward the village:

> Foulness lies there; you must fear it![13]

Brand perceives the difference between the Ice Church and the village church as an opposition between two forms of worship, a conflict that reflects his unequivocal interpretation of the peasant's choice between the absolute act and the compromising safer course. Brand uses the contrast between the Ice Church and the church in the village to define his own choice between an individualistic, absolutist worship of God and a more traditional life of serving a congregation. Initially he elects the choice marked by the village church, and he descends to the village to take up his life as a village priest.

   In the course of the drama, Ibsen's hero uses his vision of these physical locations to conceptualize antithetical modes of being: the absolute commitment to an ideal opposed to compromise; isolation opposed to relationship; a spiritual atemporality opposed to the experience of change and mutability; and asceticism opposed to sexuality. When we look closely at the processes of dramatic representation that Ibsen employs, we realize that the significance of these two scenic locations derives primarily from Brand's subjective interpretation of their personal significance. Neither place is a discrete or independent communicative unit in Ibsen's play. It would be foolish, of course, to assert that the opposition between the heights and the depths is independent of cultural or literary significance; however, Ibsen does not rely upon the typical cultural or psychological significance of that antithesis. He develops the spectator's sense of the significance that these two physical stations hold for the principal characters as they invest the Ice Church and the village church with meaning from their own experience. We witness them using the physical attributes of that location to comprehend and express the antitheses that they confront in their experience. The process is reflexive: the character endows a place with meaning drawn from his experience and then conceptualizes his experience using the attributes of that place in a form of metaphoric thinking.

The criticism of Ibsen's drama tends to identify the iconographic value of his typical landscape by assigning fixed values to the heights, the depths, the forests, and oceans that provide the larger geographic scene of the dramas.[14] These metaphoric readings interfere with our recognition of Ibsen's use of the fundamental dramatic conventions I have been discussing. For example, the characters' spoken perceptions of the site form a composite image of space that is not resolved into a single, unified perspective. Gerd sees the Ice Church as a sanctuary; Brand sees it as a precarious structure that could fall at the slightest sound. However, he also associates it with the type of absolute commitment to an ideal that he desires constantly. In the same sense, he perceives any relationship that compromises the discipline of his ideal as the antithesis of that which is represented by the Ice Church. In the course of his life, he rejects and renounces all that would bind him in relationship to others. He denies his son by refusing to take the sick child to a warmer climate, and the boy dies. He refuses to bless his mother because she is unwilling to give up her wealth. Eventually, he renounces Agnes, whose sexuality provides his greatest temptation. He uses the money left to him by his mother to build a new village church, and when even that action does not satisfy him, he retreats to the Ice Church, attempting to lead the villagers to this sanctuary that he prizes more than the new village church. There he encounters the phantom of Agnes and, once again, within the structure of the Ice Church, he must confront and renounce the temptation of sexuality. He identifies this spectre with the falcon that pursues Gerd. The demented young woman thinks he refers to the bird that preys on her; she shoots her rifle, and the Ice Church crashes down in an avalanche that kills Brand, Gerd, and – by implication – the entire village.

Because of its image in the minds of Brand and Gerd, the physical scene of the Ice Church assumes the significance of a sanctuary and retreat from the relationships marked by the imaginary presence of the falcon and the spectre of Agnes; and yet, the denial of relationship encompassed by that

image proves destructive. The idea or image 'Ice Church' accumulates a
compound number of associations and references in the course of the
drama. The paradigmatic antithesis of the Ice Church and the village
church is itself a simple structure but one that accommodates a wide range
of meanings. None of the individual characters, not even Brand, holds a
clear, comprehensive sense of that potential significance. The spectator
should not resolve the conflicting perceptions of the site into a single,
unequivocal dramatic symbol. On the contrary, members of Ibsen's
audience should recognize that the place, 'Ice Church', as scenic location
and idea, is part of an organizational scheme whose value derives from its
usefulness as a means of representing the processes of the character's
thought. The Ice Church has no absolute meaning; it forms a visual and
verbal image that completes the paradigm Ice Church and Village Church
and allows the characters, particularly Brand, to explore the differences
between the absolute and the relative, asceticism and sexuality,
atemporality and mutability, isolation and relationship, the metaphysical
and the physical. The actual physical structure, therefore, stimulates a
conceptual scheme that sustains the abstract series of antitheses in their
specific realizations at critical points in the progress of the drama. For
example, as a functional image, the Ice Church allows the spectator to
connect the falcon that pursues Gerd with the temptation that Agnes
presents to Brand and, therefore, to see the physical station of the Ice
Church as a manifestation of Brand's ascetic sexual denial and to realize
that the object that pursues him is as subjective and potentially illusory as
that which preys on Gerd. The uses to which both Brand and Gerd put the
idea 'Ice Church' should clarify that the site is not a discrete metaphor but,
rather, an 'objectivity' that reveals the metaphoric nature of their processes
of conceptualization. The communicative unit consists of the interaction
between the objective scene – in this case the Ice Church – and the
character's concept of it. The Ice Church has no fixed, independent
meaning in Ibsen's tragedy; it functions as a structure that receives
meaning rather than as a symbol that projects meaning. As a general rule,
the scene in drama operates as a matrix that accepts the values that are
assigned by the characters as they voice their perception of the site and its
significance. This point, of course, constitutes the principal assumption on
which my discussion of theatrical space builds: the physical representation
of scene, however specific the conventions of a moment demand that it be,
provides a form upon which the perceptions of the characters impose
significance. The spectator's idea of the meaning of that space is an image
that assimilates or accommodates those perceptions. The scene rarely has a
fixed significance, but, rather, almost always holds a functional, transitive
value.

Even though I use the compound model of spectator, performance, and reception, this discussion of drama is not a study of its reception, nor a phenomenology of performance. My model of spectator and performance does not, for example, take into consideration the subjectivity of the spectator and the uniqueness of his or her responses to the performance, nor the variations that would be informed by psychological difference and historical situation. This discussion of character and space is not concerned with the reception of specific dramatic texts but, rather, with certain fundamental theatrical conventions or structural paradigms. These conventional schemes operate as stimuli to the spectator during the performance. The hypothetical witness to whom I refer, therefore, is a potential spectator rather than an actual member of an audience situated historically within an identifiable place and time. This model does not refer to an actual performance or even a possible performance but, rather, refers to the potentiality for communication in performance that is implicit in the texts I discuss. The image of space created by an individual performance will, of course, be the product of the aesthetic processes I have discussed and those highly individualized circumstances that inform reception at a specific place and time.

## NOTES

1 Samuel Beckett, *Rockaby and Other Short Pieces* (New York: Grove Press, 1982).
2 Charles R. Lyons, *Beckett* (New York: Grove Press, 1984, and London: Macmillan, 1983), pp. 176–82.
3 The obvious exception, of course, is Erich Auerbach, *Mimesis: The Representation of Reality in Western Literature*, trans. Willard Trask (Princeton: Princeton University Press, 1953). However, with his historical framework and through detailed explication of representative segments of texts, Auerbach produces a formal examination of developing narrative conventions. Francis Fergusson's notion of 'histrionic sensibility' in *The Idea of a Theatre* (Princeton: Princeton University Press, 1949) exercises a neo-Aristotelian perspective in combination with his use of ritual theories from the Cambridge Anthropologists, through Kenneth Burke. However, this book, while very influential, implements older theories rather being itself an original critical document.
4 *Archetypal Patterns in Poetry* (London: Oxford University Press, 1934), pp. 13–25).
5 See Georges Poulet, *Etudes sur les temps humains* (Paris: Plon, 1956); Jean Starobinski, *L'Oeil vivant* (Paris: Gallimard, 1961).
6 Jacques Derrida, *Of Grammatology*, trans. Gayatri C. Spivak (Baltimore: Johns Hopkins University Press, 1976), pp. 99–102.
7 A. C. Bradley, 'The Rejection of Falstaff', *Oxford Lectures in Poetry* (London: Macmillan, 1909), pp. 247–73.
8 E. H. Gombrich, *Art and Illusion* (Princeton: Princeton University Press, 1960).
9 Even in performances which take place on a bare stage with no theatrical embellishment, the spectator views the actor in a defined field of vision.

Contemporary performance has frequently attempted to merge the area of viewing and the dramatic field, withdrawing the implicit barrier between observer and observed, but the explicit self-consciousness of these efforts documents the difficulty of violating the spectator's function of being a witness to an event rather than a participant in it.

10 Kenneth Burke, *A Grammar of Motives* (Berkeley and Los Angeles: University of California Press, rev. edn, 1961), pp. 3–15.

11 See for example, Jean Piaget, *La Psychologie de l'intelligence* (Paris: Armand Colin, 1947); E. H. Gombrich, *Art and Illusion* (Princeton: Princeton University Press, 1960); and Rudolf Arnheim, *Visual Thinking* (Berkeley: University of California Press, 1969).

12 See Walter Sokel, *The Writer in Extremis* (Stanford: Stanford University Press, 1959), p. 39 for the opposite point of view. Sokel sees the relationship between Lear and the storm as a precursor of the relationship between character and scene in Expressionism: '. . . the heath scenes in the third act of *King Lear*, in which nature becomes a dynamic projection of a raving mind, are very close to Expressionism.'

13 Trans. Charles R. Lyons. See Lyons, *Henrik Ibsen: The Divided Consciousness* (Carbondale: Southern Illinois University Press, 1972).

14 See, for example, Brian Johnston, 'The Metaphoric Structure of *The Wild Duck*', *Contemporary Approaches to Ibsen* (Oslo: 1979–80), p. 83.

# Spatial semantics and the medieval theatre*

## PAMELA M. KING

From the manner in which liturgical tropes apparently used the interior of the Romanesque church, comes an understanding of the nature of the playing space in outdoor vernacular religious drama which has proved both useful and tenacious. The *locus*, or *sedes*, is recognized as the unit of specified place, often sacral in significance, like the crib or Easter Sepulchre, the focus of performance analogous with the altar, the focus of worship. As simple tropes extend into narrative drama, a multiplication of *loci* occurs within one play, as in the Fleury *Play of Herod*, where both crib and Herod's court are thematically opposed foci of action. The area between and around the *loci*, where commuting and other non-specifically localized action takes place, is known as the *platea*. Glynne Wickham confidently asserts,

> These two concepts, *platea* or acting area, and *loca* or symbols for identification of place, are the basis of all medieval stagecraft and of the Public and Private Theatres of Elizabethan England.[1]

Certainly any cursory examination of text and stage directions in, for instance, *The Castle of Perseverance*, the *N-Town Plays* or *Ane Satire of the Three Estates*, shows that the fundamental concept of the use of the theatrical space involves a division between *locus*, or scaffold, and *platea*, or, confusingly, 'place'. What is more, the configuration of scaffolds within the playing space appears, in some places, to have maintained the traditional orientation of the church, with heaven in the East. In processional productions, such as the York Cycle, we could argue that the pageant waggon continues the function of *locus* – ark, crib, Eden – and the street around, the *platea*. There is scant evidence that all the waggons drew up together to form the traditional configuration at any one station, although the idea should not be dismissed as a possibility. Within the York Cycle there is one interesting parallel with the Fleury play in that *Herod and the Magi* was played with two waggons. The Goldsmiths supplied the Magi and the

* A draft of this paper was read at the *Themes in Drama* International Conference held at the University of London, Westfield College in March 1985.

Bethlehem *locus*, whereas the Masons were responsible for supplying Herod's court. It seems probable that there are other instances less clearly documented in which a similar arrangement may be envisaged. In the Coventry Pageant of the *Shearmen and Taylors*, a play which demands multiple locations of action, there is at least that famous stage direction,

Here Erode ragis in the pagond and in the strete also.[2]

More expansive raging takes Herod out of his *locus* into the *platea*. The discreet functions of *locus* and *platea* are, then, widely accepted, and visualizing the space in these terms seems more appropriate at least than the stage-on-wheels. The *locus* is a confined area, probably dependent to a large degree on static placing of scenic elements and actors to create visually intelligible context, even arrangement like a devotional picture. The *platea* is the location of movement and action, of transition between those pictures. In that it represents non-localized space, it tends to be thematically neutral except where the journey or procession is thematically important within the play. In a drama dedicated to the articulation of man's relationship with the Deity according to an almost feudal order, the movement or disorder of the *platea* alternating with the order presented by the *loci* presents constantly a spatial articulation of the central pre-occupations.

Recent years have seen many advances in particular reconstructions of staging. In the field of Corpus Christi drama in particular the labours of the Records of Early English Drama, uncovering large quantities of often inconclusive evidence, have led us to question the tidy picture of the development of medieval stagecraft depicted by earlier scholars. The popularity of descriptive reconstructions based on fragmentary record material has in its turn led to actual theatrical reproductions from which interesting empirical observations have been derived about how the space operates. From reports of reconstructed performance comes an increasing awareness of the diverse relationships that the complex theatrical space created between the world of the play and that of the audience. Previously it appears that most accounts assumed that the audience observed, interpreted, learned, but on a plain consistently distinct from the players. Reconstructions have led to observations on how the audience becomes 'involved' in the elements of the play which use the *platea*. Of course they do not really join in, but we are struggling now to articulate the nature of the observable changing relationship between play and audience within this complex space.

One very useful piece of recorded observation of the phenomena is to be found in Meg Twycross's account of 'Playing "The Resurrection"'.[3] She here confirms that the space divides clearly into the traditional functions of *locus* and *platea*, but also demonstrates that different spaces are intelligible in terms of the nature of the contract between the play and the audience at any individual point in the action:

> The extreme distancing comes when the 'framing effect' of the waggon posts and fascia is exploited so that the playwright, in the midst of events, suddenly resolves the action into a familiar picture.

By contrast, the physical closeness of action in the street,

> made audience very much an active factor in performance,

but,

> despite lack of physical separation, the actors are still inhabitants of the world of the play, the audience still onlookers. The illusion is not 'broken'.[4]

'Distancing', 'active factor' and 'broken' all suggest that we now need a vocabulary not for defining elements within the space itself, but to describe this sophisticated contract between play and audience which generates meaning; what is, effectively, the contribution of the use of space to the semantics of the play.

The figural approach has long been used by literary analysts, such as V. A. Kolve[5] and Erich Auerbach,[6] to demonstrate the manner in which script generates meaning. It has the advantage of being a habit of thought familiar to dramatist and audience, as well as being a system of analysis accessible to medievalists. Certainly the breaking down of the use of the space into figural elements can complement analysis of text. But *figura* are necessarily static. What the use of space in theatre depends upon and what the audience responds to is not a fixed arrangement, but a series of figurally inspired signals. What is here proposed, therefore, is that the figural approach can usefully import selected terms from semiotics[7] in this area where empirical observation seems to ask for a more articulate means of expression.

When we conventionally talk of 'playing space', we mean delimited space, with defined boundaries, chiefly that between the stage, or world of the play, and the 'real' world of the audience. One factor which all observations of *locus* and *platea* productions seem to have in common is that barriers between different spaces within the playing space are more carefully and consistently maintained than this assumed barrier between audience and play. David Parry, producer of the York Cycle in Toronto has observed the following:

> Here was a child who obviously wanted to sit down, but the conditions were extremely wet, and he didn't want to get his bottom wet, so he went and sat at the foot of Pilate's throne. It didn't obtrude at all . . .[8]

We also tend to make the assumption about theatre space that the audience, in the act of buying their tickets, separate themselves from the rest of the world. David Parry again observed,

... the general reaction, once people had realised how the thing operated, was that they could move in and out of what was going on ... These plays are obviously part of the whole continuum of life.[9]

These phenomena peculiar to fixed and processional *locus* and *platea* productions invite explanation.

Our most important piece of original evidence about the nature of space is the diagram (plate 4) which accompanies the text of *The Castle of Perseverance*.[10] Richard Southern's reconstruction of this space[11] was based on the assumption that it showed a theatre, a contained space, on the not unreasonable basis that some Cornish rounds survive, as do some manuscript illuminations which seem to show playing in rounds. Southern was succumbing to a need to define the whole area occupied by play and audience, cut off from the rest of the world. Since his work appeared, individual place and scaffold plays have been excepted from the pattern which he suggests. Paula Neuss's work on the staging of the Cornish *Creacion of the World*,[12] for example, suggests a semicircular arrangement. The Banns of *The Castle of Perseverance* suggest that it is to be played 'on the green',[13] and commentators have moved towards a consensus view that the plan is not a drawing of a theatre, but the design for a set which may or may not then be put into an existing round. The containing space, if any, is not shown. If we can look at the diagram freed from the idea that it represents an area marked out as a theatre, we can begin to look at how as a set design it delimits different types of space. Different types of space are more important than the contained nature of the space itself.

Figurally the plan is, in many respects, straightforward. The dominant feature is the castle itself with Mankind's bed beneath it. The action concerning the virtues is concentrated here. It is a castle fortified against vice. The other dominant feature of the plan is the circle:

> This is the water a bowte the place, if any ditch may be mad ther it schal be played or elles that it be strongly barred all abowt and lete nowth over many stytelerys be withinne the place.

The definition of this feature as the outer boundary of the theatre in Southern's account depends on 'a bowte the place'. As Natalie Crohn Schmitt has demonstrated, however,[14] 'a bowte' can be used in the sense of 'to go about', and 'place' could be the *locus* of the castle. It certainly seems ambiguous enough to allow flexible interpretation. Practical considerations, if the play is a touring production as the Banns suggest,[15] make it distinctly more likely that the ditch is a moat around the castle. Feudal allegories of the late medieval period in sermon and poetry frequently placed God as the lord of a moated castle. Outside the circle are the scaffolds, which do not assume prominence because they are not illustrated,

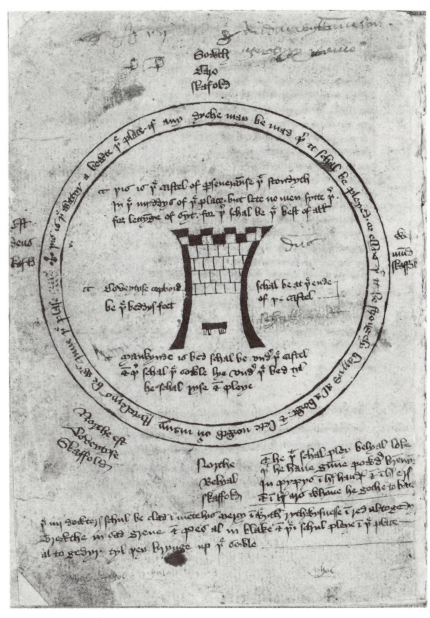

4 'The Castle of Perseverence'. (By permission of the Folger Shakespeare Library)

only labelled, probably because some standard construction type was envisaged by the artist.

The placing of the scaffold of God is very interesting. Conventionally God, heaven, is in the East, as is the case here; but in feudal allegory the castle is the seat of the Deity. The dual location of the *loci* of virtue on this plan takes us some way towards understanding the figural meaning of the space, and, by extension, the placing of the audience as is directed on the plan. Above the castle is written,

> This is the Castle of Perseverance that standyth in the myddyl of the place but
> lete no man syte ther for lettynge of syt for that schal be the best of al.

The action of the play, the battle of vice and virtue for the soul of man on his journey from cradle to grave, is conducted at a tropological level. The good and bad angels, the virtues and vices, the moated castle called Perseverance, all pertain to the spiritual progress of one man, like the pilgrimage of Will to Truth in *Piers Plowman*. The set in that respect represents the microcosm, the soul of man. The set also, however, is a figure of the macrocosm of the universe, since the scaffolds, Heaven, Hell, Flesh and World, represent properties of the entire universe, constant features against which the drama of Mankind is literally acted out.

The placing of the audience, or their exclusion from the castle area, seems to fit with this interpretation of the space. They are not apparently controlled outside the moat, amongst the scaffolds, an area which represents the universe as they understand it, and Mankind's life is spent largely in the same *platea*, Langland's 'field full of folk', peopled by the audience. As the chief thrust of the play is a warning against covetousness specifically, that is given prominence, a scaffold in the North East on the plan. The people's spiritual state during the course of the play is, however, constant, whereas Mankind's is dynamic. The area associated with spiritual growth is the area of the castle which is specific to him. The audience therefore are not allowed there – as well as 'for lettynge of syte' – but are themselves given figural meaning peopling the *platea* of the universe beneath the *loci* which are fixed topographical points, indices of mortal existence. The barrier of the moat is thus figurally the important division between the world at large and its temptations, and individual moral fortification. Heaven remains in the East as God, of course, presides over good and evil alike. As the world outside the moat is a mimetic presentation of everywhere at all times, it can have no containing boundaries.

Figural analysis thus attributes broad semantic values to elements of the plan and places the audience intelligibly within it. The members of the audience share a common figural identity. But we still have to articulate how the audience perceive that figural role, how they submit to delegating action to the performer playing Mankind. Meg Twycross's audience clearly acknowledged that,

> the actors are still inhabitants of the world of the play, the audience still onlookers. The illusion is not 'broken'.[16]

Individual audience members do not rush to enter the castle, do not attempt to join in and 'destroy the play'.[17] What is happening is that the audience, whilst aware of different levels of physical barrier within the play, also remain aware of the non-topographical barrier between real world and world of play. They recognize that the space in which they figure is not the real universe but a sign of it. Most theatrical spaces are icons of some real topography.[18] In this instance, the plan does not represent an image icon, which suggests identity of detail between set and world, but a metaphorical icon, having bare reference points. The audience communally understands the iconic nature of the space in the same way as one can look at a map, put a pin in it and say, 'We are here', without trying to get into the map. The pin is delegated to act as a metaphorical icon of the traveller – it can also be moved around iconically to represent where one has been and where one might go. Mankind in *The Castle of Perseverance* is the metaphoric icon of each member of the audience. In this manner 'illusion is not "broken"', but the audience is 'very much an active factor'.

But we have already seen that the figural meaning of this set and of all *locus* and *platea* spaces, depends on the 'active' role of the audience being engaged and disengaged at different points in the action, in different places within the space. In fact, of all the theatrical systems identified by Elam,[19] tone, mime, gesture, etc., the system governing the use of space is the first one to strike the spectator. He absorbs the syntax of spatial relationships on entering the space and prepares to apply the cultural codes available to him to elicit meaning from that space. In *The Castle of Perseverance*, interstitial placing clearly functions as a syntactic system which may be interpreted according to the theory of proxemics, 'the interrelated observations and theories of man's use of space as a specialized elaboration of culture'.[20] The proxemic system with which everyone is familiar involves the way in which we distinguish between personal space, social space and public space. The acceptable limits of these cannot be assumed to be the same for all cultures in all ages, but the response elicited from an audience by a performer at public distance on a scaffold is clearly different from that when the performer enters the social space on the *platea*. Violation of the personal space of an individual audience member is best observed when a masked vice-figure decides to move in close and pick on someone at random. Normal transcodification breaks down here, as the mask withholds normal facial expression which is important at this proximity. When the proxemic code fails to match the kinesic or gestural code the audience member responds by sensing an invasion of personal space. The importance of interstitial placing, and the possibilities afforded by its manipulation, are witnessed by Meg Twycross again[21] when she notes that to observe in a Resurrection play the laments of the three Maries at the tomb of Christ, 'at a distance, as private persons undergoing emotional crisis', becomes tedious; but,

> set them down in the audience, on their level . . . and their role suddenly becomes quite different. They are almost agitators, incitors to emotion.

In auditorium or fixed-form theatre, the interstitial relationship between audience member and play is constant. The individual is isolated in his own allocated space, his seat, where he privately decodes information from various systems, not necessarily replicating the information of the playwright, actor or director. *The Castle of Perseverance* and other plays like it depend on informal, or semi-fixed theatrical space. In this, and particularly because of constantly changing interstitial relationships between the audience and the play, the spectator is forced to respond as part of a unit. His response, then, is social rather than personal. The social response in which the audience as social unit affirms communally the meaning generated by the play, is entirely in keeping with the role of information systems in determinist drama. The meaning of the theatrical space in *The Castle of Perseverance* depends on the meaning of the everyday space consented to by the audience, and the articulation of that meaning rests to a great extent upon the use of the space.

Similar criteria may be applied to processional Corpus Christi drama. The figural reading of bible-history drama has already been supplied in part in the chapter on Adam and Eve in Erich Auerbach's *Mimesis*.[22] Auerbach supplies an excellent model for a figural reading of text which can be extended into space. His argument hinges upon the view that the momentous or mythic is merged with the topical or everyday by rhetorical means. The high style, *sermo gravis*, and low style, *sermo humilis*, are deliberately mixed in religious drama in order stylistically to embody the philosophical Bernardine mystery of the dual nature of Christ, who by humility is exalted:

> The medieval Christian drama falls perfectly within this tradition. Being a living representation of Biblical episodes as contained with their innately dramatic elements, in the liturgy, it opens its arms invitingly to receive the simple and untutored and to lead them from the concrete, the everyday, to the hidden and the true.[23]

The choice of metaphor here is interesting – 'opens its arms invitingly . . . to lead . . .'. Again the question of audience 'involvement' is being courted:

> And the spirit of the form which encompasses them is the spirit of the figural interpretation of history. This implies that every occurrence, in all its everyday

reality, is simultaneously a part in a world-historical context through which
each part is related to every other.[24]

By drawing analogies with the figural interpretation of history, in which
Old Testament events are types of New Testament events, Auerbach
demonstrates the manner in which the audience is engaged in biblical
drama, by, at its most banal, the way it impresses its relevance upon them.
His reading is, however, based solely on text, or rhetorical style of
discourse. The other theatrical systems at work in these plays support the
figural reading of the text.

As the best place to examine the way the systems are established in a play
is the beginning, it is proposed to consider the opening of the whole York
Cycle, God's first speech in the Barkers' *Creation and Fall of Lucifer*.
Elizabeth Burns has pointed to the manner in which certain induction
techniques operate in a play to define space and to establish rhetorical
boundaries.[25] The speech which opens the York Cycle represents a very
special type of induction:

> GOD:  *Ego sum Alpha et O: vita, via, veritas, primus et novissimus.*
> I am gracious and great, God without beginning,
> I am maker unmade, all might is in me;
> I am life, and way unto wealth-winning,
> I am foremost and first, as I bid shall it be.
> My blessing of blee shall be blending
> And hielding, from harm to be hiding,
> My body in bliss ay abiding,
> Unending, without any ending.[26]

The first stanza, spoken by a masked actor, an iconic symbol of the
Godhead, establishes by deixis the properties of the Godhead as first and
last, without beginning and ending. The cycle's function is to denote all
sacral history, but what God's first speech establishes, by reference to His
eternal present, is the connotative property inherent in patterned history; in
other words it proposes that the represented events are not simply part of
historical time, but of all time and time now as represented in the church
calendar with its recurrent Christmas and Easter. The properties of time in
the cycle are established rhetorically by the first and last lines, ending in
'without beginning' and 'without ending' respectively. Historical time is
thus adumbrated through the proposal of a direct relationship between the
fictional 'now' of the plays and actual time to which the audience belongs.

The space occupied by God is identified by deixis:

> Bainly in my blessing I bid at here be
> A bliss all-bielding about me,
> In the which bliss I bid at be here
> Nine orders of angels full clear,
> In lofing ay-lasting at lout me.

*Then the angels sing 'We praise thee O God, we acknowledge*
*thee to be the Lord.'*

Here underneath me now a nexile I neven
Which isle shall be earth. Now all be at once
Earth wholly, and hell, this highest be heaven.

(lines 20–7)

As God speaks, the space to which He refers must be realized as an iconic
diagram as the waggon opens out to reveal heaven, earth and hell-mouth.
The discourse uttered by God is, of course, itself iconically related to the
Christian concept of creation by word.

Induction techniques in the theatre more commonly serve to point the
illusion of space and time – the Prologue to Shakespeare's *Henry V* is a
classic example. Here, however, the technique is short-circuited in order to
propose that the space and time iconically represented are closer to the
everyday world, rather than more remote. All systems here conspire to
'open their arms invitingly' as Auerbach perceives.

As the space is rendered intelligible in terms of time and place in this
manner, the audience must be absorbing the interstitial relationships of the
parts of the diagram of heaven, earth and hell and interpreting them. Just as
the important is foregrounded, downstage, on the proscenium set, on the
multilevel pageant-waggon, high is important and admirable; low is less
important, evil. In this instance the *locus* itself is semantically subdivided.
The space they perceive does not in this instance contain the audience,
which is why it is a diagrammatic rather than a metaphorical icon. The
establishing of diagrammatic intelligibility of all that follows in the cycle
depends upon this first play and the way in which it displays the universe in
almost two-dimensional terms. The method is one fitting and familiar to a
society accustomed to emblematic modes of expression, such as the *arma
Christi* or heraldry.

The waggons, or *loci*, of the following plays, and their use of the *platea*, all
depend syntactically upon the first waggon for their meaning. Angels and
devils in the Virgin's house or Pilate's wife's bedchamber, are synecdochi-
cally dependent on the initial diagram of heaven and hell. More import-
antly, the action which moves into the *platea*, shepherds and soldiers, the
ordinary mortals of the cycles, fabled for their anachronistic discourse,
invade the social space of the audience whilst remaining tied by synecdoche
to the earth-space indicated on waggon one.

Concurrently with this dependency, the cycle of course extensively
employs conventional theatrical synecdoche, what Umberto Eco calls,
'member for its class'.[27] Herod's throne represents his court; three soldiers
and three women represent a massacre. Only the first and last plays do not
depend on synecdoche to establish place, since they are the framing icons
which render the world of the play intelligible. As the action on the *platea*

Scale: 1 ft.

5 A hypothetical reconstruction of the York Mercers' *Doomsday* Pageant Waggon. (By permission of Peter Meredith, University of Leeds)

throughout the cycle has explored the role of the audience within the world of the play, in the Last Judgement the souls of the damned and the saved rise up from the *locus* of earth as intelligible figures to whom action has been delegated in the same manner as with Mankind in *The Castle of Perseverance*.

In processional plays, therefore, the important boundaries are those between different loci, particularly heaven, earth and hell, rather than between play and audience. It is again important to the figural meaning of the cycle that, although the boundary of 'illusion' cannot be 'broken', it is desirable not to reinforce it physically, but rather to create a counter-illusion, that of the world of the play running over into the world of the audience at the edges. Various sign-systems can be shown to achieve this effect in the York *Crucifixion*. In this play, the soldiers come from the *platea* and use the language of everyday workmen, like Auerbach's Adam and Eve, whilst they attach Christ to the cross on the ground. As the cross is raised on the waggon, the interstitial relationship between Christ and the audience is radically altered and is immediately followed by direct address:

> All men that walk by way or street,
> Take tent ye shall no travail tine.
> Behold mine head, mine hands, and my feet,
> And fully feel now, ere ye fine,
> If any mourning may be meet,
> Or mischief measured unto mine.
> My father, that all bales may beet,
> Forgive these men that do me pine.
> What they work, wot they not;
> Therefore, my father, I crave,
> Let never their sins be sought,
> But see their souls to save.[28]

The deixis which refers in turn to Christ, to the audience and to God, combined with the complexities of interstitial placing, briefly proposes iconic identity between the audience and those who performed the Crucifixion.

Just as the boundaries between play world and audience world are manipulated, so too boundaries between audience and the rest of the world at any given moment are unclear in processional production, as David Parry confirmed.[29] Delimitation of playing space into *locus* and *platea* combines with a significant abstention from dividing playing space from audience, theatre from the world. This is the way in which space operates semantically in a theatre of which Auerbach says,

> ... there is but one place, the world, and but one action —man's fall and redemption ... the whole is always borne in mind and figurally represented.[30]

What is offered here is no more than an approach to a possible approach, born out of the belief that in medieval drama studies we need to explore methods of analysis which can be applied to all the systems at work, not only the verbal, and one which caters for the moving, changing combinations of signs where the figural describes only the static. Empirical observation of plays in reconstruction invites the formation of predictive models. Of course any such model is only as good as the data it can be formed on, and staging evidence is fragmentary, modern audiences decode and respond differently. A multi-systems approach to medieval drama still seems desirable and not at all incompatible with the traditional figural method.

## NOTES

1 Glynne Wickham, *Early English Stages 1300–1576* (London: Routledge & Kegan Paul, 1980), p. 160.
2 Hardin Craig (ed.), *Two Coventry Corpus Christi Plays*, EETS e.s., 87 (1957), 27.
3 Meg Twycross, 'Playing "The Resurrection"', *Medieval Studies for J.A.W. Bennett Aetatis Suae LXX*, ed. P. L. Heyworth (Oxford: Clarendon Press, 1981), pp. 273–96.
4 *Ibid.*, pp. 277, 274, 275.
5 V. A. Kolve, *The Play Called Corpus Christi* (London: Edward Arnold, 1966).
6 Erich Auerbach, *Mimesis: The Representation of Reality in Western Literature* (Princeton: Princeton University Press, 1953), especially chapter 7, 'Adam and Eve', pp. 143–73.
7 Keir Elam, *The Semiotics of Theatre and Drama* (London: Methuen, 1980) provides useful models. I should also like to acknowledge the valuable advice received from Jackie Johnston, doctoral candidate at the University of York, in this area.
8 David Parry, 'The York Mystery Cycle at Toronto, 1977', *METh*, 1:1 (1979), 19–31, 26.
9 *Ibid.*, 25.
10 Mark Eccles (ed.), *The Macro Plays*, EETS o.s., 262 (1969).
11 Richard Southern, *The Medieval Theatre in the Round: A Study of the Staging of The Castle of Perseverance and Related Matters* (London: Faber & Faber, 1957).
12 Paula Neuss, 'The Staging of *The Creacion of the World*', *Medieval English Drama: A Casebook*, ed. Peter Happe (London: MacMillan, 1984), pp. 189–200.
13 Eccles, *The Macro Plays*, p. 7.
14 Natalie Crohn Schmitt, 'Was there a Medieval Theatre in the Round? A Re-examination of the Evidence', *Medieval English Drama Essays Critical and Contextual*, ed. Jerome Taylor and Alan H. Nelson (Chicago: University of Chicago Press, 1972), pp. 292–315, 297.
15 Eccles, *The Macro Plays*, p. 7.
16 Twycross, 'Playing "The Resurrection"', p. 275.
17 One of the accusations levelled at character B by character A when both are masquerading as audience members in Henry Medwall's *Fulgens and Lucres*, ed. Peter Meredith (University of Leeds, School of English, 1981), p. 11.
18 Elam, *The Semiotics of Theatre and Drama*, pp. 21ff.

19  *Ibid.*, e.g. p. 37.
20  *Ibid.*, quoting Edward T. Hall (1966).
21  Twycross, 'Playing "The Resurrection" ', p. 283.
22  Auerbach, *Mimesis*, pp. 143–73.
23  *Ibid.*, p. 155.
24  *Ibid.*, p. 156.
25  Elizabeth Burns, *Theatricality: A Study of Convention in the Theatre and in Social Life* (London: Longman, 1972), pp. 23ff.
26  Richard Beadle and Pamela M. King, *York Mystery Plays: A Selection in Modern Spelling* (Oxford: Oxford University Press, 1984), pp. 2–3.
27  Elam, *The Semiotics of Theatre and Drama*, p. 29, quoting Umberto Eco (1976).
28  Beadle and King, *York Mystery Plays*, p. 220.
29  Parry, 'The York Mystery Cycle at Toronto, 1977', *passim*.
30  Auerbach, *Mimesis*, p. 158.

# The Elizabethan audience on stage*

## JONATHAN HAYNES

The 'extra-dramatic' moments of Elizabethan drama, when an actor steps out of the dramatic illusion and suddenly occupies the same space as the audience in the theater, have exercized a certain fascination over modern theoreticians of the theater, both critics and avant-garde directors and playwrights. As the theater of the twentieth century sought, for reasons of its own, to escape from the box formed by the proscenium into a more flexible theatrical space, the spatial conventions and the related conventions governing the dramatic illusion of pre-modern stages became a topic of new interest. Passing in and out of the dramatic illusion has become an occasion for theoretical reflection, whether our concerns are with alienation or deconstruction or a Pirandellian sense of the theatricality of real life.

Historians of the Elizabethan dramatic illusion (such as Muriel Bradbrook and Ann Righter)[1] see these moments quite differently: they see, not the dramatic illusion being broken down in order to produce a philosophical *frisson*, but a dramatic illusion which is still in the process of formation; not an anticipation of a modern technique, but a relic of the medieval theater. Indeed if one looks at the plays themselves one finds that the revelation of theatricality does not usually come from the actors becoming conscious of themselves as creatures with a metaphysical or ontological problem, but it comes from outside, from the social demands of the audience. The problem is that the dramatic illusion is not being granted its full autonomy; the inductions and prologues and other extra-dramatic moments were attempts to deal with this problem. In what follows I want to hold the philosophical issues in abeyance and handle the question of how the space of the theater is related to the space of real life in social–historical terms.

At the margins of the stage the playing space and the seating space overlapped: not only were the thrust stages surrounded on three sides by the audience, but gentlemen could rent stools on the stage itself at the private indoor playhouses, and at public houses like the Globe they could

---

* A draft of this paper was read at the *Themes in Drama* International Conference held at the University of California, Riverside in February 1985.

sit, if not on the main stage, at least in the 'Lord's room', also used as an upper stage.[2] It is this situation which is the subject of a number of inductions, played at the edge of the stage and at the edge of the dramatic illusion, beginning with Jonson's *Cynthia's Revels* in 1600–1, in which a boy actor mimics the obnoxious behavior of these spectators: smoking tobacco, ostentatiously condemning the actors in word and gesture, and making a series of demands on the playwright.

In part the issue is merely a physical one, Jonson's uncharacteristically polite request in the Prologue to *The Devil is an Ass* that the gentlemen allow the actors enough space to work in being merely a newer form of the cry of 'make room!' which began medieval performances. But something more complex and interesting happens in the 'critical'[3] inductions created by Jonson and Marston and Webster and Beaumont, which are little playlets about the theatrical situation, with actors playing members of the audience and spectators sometimes forced into the fiction. At issue were the autonomy and social nature of the dramatic illusion and its claim on the space of the stage, and finally the rival social claims of aristocratic audience and professional actors and playwrights to the space of the theater. This was a real struggle: we are told of one occasion, from a considerably later period, in which 'a formidable riot broke out when an actor remonstrated with a nobleman for crossing the stage in front of the actors to speak to a friend, while a principal scene of *Macbeth* was playing, and was struck across the face for his pains.'[4] The inductions were functional, as well as being brilliant *jeux d'esprit*, a sort of carapace the plays threw up around themselves to deal with a recurrent set of problems. As these problems remained much the same, the themes of the inductions fell into a formulaic pattern: the war with the gallants on stage – who, as Jonson complained in the Dedication to *The New Inn*,[5] came 'To see, and to bee seene. To make a generall muster of themselues in their clothes of credit: and possesse the Stage, against the Play. To dislike all, but marke nothing . . .' – always had to be fought over again. Typically the worst sorts of disruptive behavior were mimicked and discredited, in the hope that this would preempt such behavior.[6]

Beaumont's *Knight of the Burning Pestle* contains the most extravagant elaboration of these inductions: the induction in fact takes over the whole play. As the actors are beginning to present a play called *The London Merchant* an actor planted in the audience and disguised as a Citizen Grocer interrupts: this looks to him like another city comedy which will insult his fellow Citizens. He clambers up on stage, and his wife is hoisted up after him, and there they sit in all their crass foolishness, soon insisting that their apprentice Rafe be given a part in the play: he becomes The Knight of the Burning Pestle, and gets a subplot of his own which collides with the main one.

This seems novel enough; but the very first secular drama in English, Henry Medwall's *Fulgens and Lucres*, performed about 1497 in the hall of Cardinal Morton, contains a remarkably similar device. Two servants, called A and B, emerge from the audience and begin talking about the play that is about to take place; B has inside knowledge about it and outlines the plot for us, but indignantly rejects the idea that he is an actor. They remain on stage as the play begins. We are still at a point where the dramatic illusion is highly unstable and unsure of itself; so much so that characters in the play never lose the awareness that there is a crowd of people in the hall watching them, and various attempts are made to recognize or integrate the real audience into the world of the play. In one such attempt Cornelius Publius, a Patrician who is a suitor for the hand of Lucres, offers to hire anyone in the audience who can give him advice or assistance. B volunteers, in spite of A's alarm: 'Pece, let be! / Be god thou will distroy all the play' (I, 363–4).[7] B successfully negotiates the barrier between audience and play, and A soon follows suit, becoming a servant to Cornelius' Plebeian rival, Gaius Flaminius. A comic subplot develops as A and B court Lucres' maid, Jone.

This extraordinary instance of formal continuity in the play across the dramatic illusion invites us to notice what has and hasn't changed in the intervening century. In both plays the theater is explicitly a medium for the projection of ideological concerns, and already in *Fulgens and Lucres* this relation is seen to be full of slippages and tensions. Its explicit theme concerns the nature of true nobility, a subject of obvious interest to a late-feudal society, and it has Lucres choose the virtuous Plebeian over the dissolute Patrician, in order, we are told, to convince dissolute gentlemen in the audience to behave themselves. This choice is also clearly designed as a compliment to the low-born Cardinal Morton, seated among his aristocratic guests. But this ethical adventurousness is offset by social caution. A is scandalized when he hears the plot:

> By my fayth but yf it be euyn as ye say
> I wyll aduyse them to change that conclusion.
> What, wyll they afferme me a chorles son
> Sholde be more noble than a gentilman born?
> Nay beware for men wyll haue therof grete scorn,
> It may not be spoken in no maner of case.
>
> (I, 128–33)

Lucres is equally concerned to limit the scandal of her choice – 'It may not be notyde for a generall precedent' – and has to repeat all her hedges and qualifications under interrogation by B before the play ends. A and B thus carry this concern for ideological heresy with them as they leap from the audience into the play; but they are peculiar apologists for the aristocratic party and social conservatism. Their own status is unclear;

both turn out to be masterless servants. B's flashy clothes lead to confusions about his rank and profession.[8] Their raucous subplot is distinctly 'popular' in character, but in spite of its parodies of the main plot it does not subvert or otherwise address those ideological themes. Their own politics seem less ideological than prudential: they look to the play first for entertainment and then for employment, and do not want either disturbed. As in *The Knight of the Burning Pestle*, their conservatism and suspicion turn out to be narrower than the play's vision.

So *Fulgens and Lucres* scatters implications about the ideological character of the relation of audience and play, but the role of A and B is a bit incoherent, and the price it pays for its hypothetical stretching of social norms is the removal of the issue to an ethical utopia – here called, without much conviction, Rome. *The Knight of the Burning Pestle*, on the other hand, both directly represents contemporary social tensions – the Citizen is asking precisely and crudely for an art that serves his social purposes in the class war between citizens and gentry – and responds on behalf of the institution of the theater with wit, equivocation, and a calculated exploitation of the social sympathies and prejudices of the audience. Its strategies are more deliberate, sophisticated, and practiced; they depend on a maturing social conflict and on the institutionalization of the professional theater, and hence a stabilizing of its social role. They depend also on a new social organization of the space of the theater. Altogether Beaumont's theater is capable of carrying a qualitatively new discourse about the social nature and function of art.

I want to try to define some of the prerequisites of this new discourse about the social nature of the theater. I have in mind three, which will turn out to be interrelated: one is a strengthening of the dramatic illusion; the second, a differentiation of the space of the theater – both a differentiation of the space claimed for the dramatic illusion as opposed to that of the audience, and a social differentiation of the space the audience occupied; and the third, the contemporaneity of the satirical realms of city comedy.

First, the strength of the dramatic illusion. Righter talks about the 'tyranny' of the medieval audience over the play, and how the inability to forget the audience limits the depth of the dramatic illusion, makes it shallow and vulnerable, as if it were always about to be squashed flat against the screen in the back of the hall, leaving the actors naked, exposed as poor servants in need of the toleration and co-operation of their masters whom they were seeking to entertain.[9] The inductions of the turn of the seventeenth century, on the other hand, grow out of a sense of security and assertiveness on behalf of a three-dimensional dramatic world: the illusion is deep and resiliant, able to withstand the blows of a hostile audience, even to mount offensive forays of its own, and to grow stronger through this sparring. This confidence had a social, even an economic, base: no longer a fleeting moment in the hall of Cardinal Morton, at the disposal of his guests (with a pause between acts so the company could finish their dinner), the dramatic illusion was now at home, in a commercial theater, entertaining its own guests in a hall its own profits had built. It had produced its own space. To be sure, it still depended on its guests; but the relationship was now one of strong reciprocity.

This sense of security about the dramatic illusion led the players to claim their space with a new confidence. But the gallants did not necessarily acquiesce: their patronage was inflected with aristocratic arrogance, an attitude that they could take or leave the performance as they would a dessert. In *A Midsummer's Night's Dream* Shakespeare remembers the old practices when he has the newly married aristocrats mock and interrupt the rude mechanicals offering their play. Bradbrook tells us the actors did not mind this sort of thing, that disruption by the audience was in itself a mark of acceptance;[10] perhaps; but such was clearly not the attitude of Ben Jonson. The theme of his prologues is the wholeness and autonomy of his plays as art objects; the strategy of his inductions is to isolate those who claimed a social dominance over the play and hold them up to ridicule. The audience could be made to respond together as an audience, to agree that such people were interfering with its collective pleasure, that its interests were with the dramatic illusion rather than with the 'commoning' of a social assemblage in the theater.[11]

Such a reorganization and splitting of the audience was possible because of the celebrated diversity of the Elizabethan audience, and the social tensions that accompanied it. That diversity was much restricted in the private theaters, but still the audience lacked the organizing principle obtaining at performances at court or in the halls of aristocrats, where it would be clear who was the patron of the occasion. Those who used their social prerogative to sit on stage, and then abused it by interfering with the performance, were open to the charge of usurping a patronage that was not really theirs. To sit on the stage was to focus a great deal of social tension on oneself. Strict conventions governed who was eligible – gentlemen in the height of fashion – and if anyone else presumed, like the four Gossips of *The Staple of News*, someone would appear on behalf of the theater management to tell them that the gentlemen would not like it. The dramatists always present sitting on the stage as an act of brazen social ostentation – as Dekker makes clear in *The Gulls Horn-Book*, the gallants expected their presence on stage to provoke a storm of envy, scorn, and resentment, and they reveled in it: let the gallant on stage 'be planted valiantly because impudently, beating down the mews and hisses of the opposed rascality.'[12]

The gallants, then, as Michael Shapiro has pointed out, were putting on a social performance of their own in competition with the dramatic performance;[13] and the quarrel was over the relative importance and interest of these performances. The presence of the gentlemen on stage was a sign not only of the traditional aristocratic dominance over theatrical performances, but also of a situation of social climbing through fashionable behavior, in a context of general social mobility; a situation in which the gallants were basking parasitically in the glamorous aura of the stage.

That the stage was glamorous was new: the commercial stage itself dates only from 1576, and it had only recently become an institution of fashion, in which social styles were set or confirmed, or at least court fashions disseminated. The gallants were regularly accused of stealing lines from plays to be used when they dined out; alternately Jonson defends himself in the Induction to *Cynthia's Revels* and in the Prologue to *Volpone* against the imputation that he gathered his materials from the company he kept: he had been accused of being a 'meere Empyrick.'[14] Socially the world of the plays and that of the audience overlapped: this brings me to my third point, about contemporaneity. It was not until the late 1590s that contemporary London was represented on stage. Plays had been set in all manner of exotic locales, from Scythia to Italy to pastoral Arcadias; comedies were set in the English countryside; chronicle histories presented a realistic England, and sometimes London, but a London of the historical past, the scene also of plays like the ones the Citizen demands to see, celebrating semi-legendary heroes of the city, like Dick Whittington. One might object that given the weakly developed sense of anachronism that obtained, the playwrights had difficulty imagining anywhere besides their own reality: the Roman Senator Fulgens enters giving thanks to an obviously Christian God, and Lucres' maid Jone – not a very Roman name – is said to be the best singer on this side of York. The allegorical tradition fostered, as the complement to its abstraction, an often extreme topicality, which sponsored a kind of realist tradition, and advanced techniques of mimicry: Nashe reports that a Latin Cambridge play carried an impersonation of Gabriel Harvey as far as stealing his gown to play in.[15] But this topicality did not pertain to an extended, secular, social dimension, and so its effects were limited.

The comical satires and city comedies broke with this tradition of merely topical or inadvertent or anachronistic contemporaneity, and became deliberate about it. This event is surprisingly little noticed by literary historians, but it clearly took the theaters by storm. There was a new power on the loose in London, setting off explosions of satiric realism in one neighborhood or social milieu after another, exciting the audience, worrying the authorities, and getting its handlers in trouble. After winning its autonomy from the audience the dramatic illusion returned in triumph to subsume its audience in its subject matter. That the dramatic illusion could stalk unrecognized among the audience was the sign of its new power. As the professional theater produced its own playing place, so did it now produce its own occasions: its sense of its relation to the audience was no longer a response to a festive or aristocratic occasion, calling for ritual behavior or compliment; organized on a commercial basis, the theater could now intervene in Elizabethan society as an institution with its own powers, and it could examine its relation to its audience, and in general comment on the social scene, in social, almost sociological, fashion.

The playwrights had begun to write about precisely the social milieus they themselves inhabited. Ben Jonson in particular liked to set his plays in the neighborhoods of the theaters for which he wrote them. A kind of social realism was born out of this radical continuity between the represented scene and the society which created it: it produced the most thoroughly secular and imminent dramatic space that had yet been seen, expressly social in its intent and implications and interest.

It is precisely these plays for which the inductions are written: the impersonated gallants planted on the stage have counterparts within the plays; and characters in such plays are often avid playgoers and stage-sitters, like Fitzdottrel in *The Devil is an Ass*, who restlessly tries to escape from his scenes so he can appear on stage for the opening of the new Blackfriars play, *The Devil is an Ass*. The inductions are principally concerned with the most immediate social situation on the stage, that concerning the stage-sitters; but this is just part of a larger project of mapping the social space of the theater and, beyond it, of the city. The topic and motive of the realist impulse in city comedy are social competition and conflict (above all around the crucial distinction between those who were gentlemen and those who were not) – the scramble for wealth and status that was taking place from top to bottom of the social hierarchy.

The stage was a center of the social battlefield: the theater was an arena for social display, especially by those sitting on the stage, and the drama was an arena of ideological competition, played out in the rival popular and coterie traditions in the theater.[16] *The Knight of the Burning Pestle* is unusual in that it employs the Jonsonian induction, developed as a skirmishing weapon against the stage-sitters, as a vehicle for representing the wider class war. It is unusual also in that the induction usually served to police the boundaries of the stage and protect the integrity of the dramatic illusion: the induction's origins may owe as much to the actors' improvised reactions to audience meddling as to classical models. In its clearest and most extreme development, in *Every Man Out of his Humour*, Jonson seats two pseudo-spectators on stage to conduct a running critical commentary on the play, and to keep an eye on the rest of the audience to insure their good behavior; the induction serves to guide and control the audience, to extend the dramatist's control of the play's reception.

But *The Knight of the Burning Pestle* is absorptive: it seems to surrender without a fight to the demands of the Citizen and his Wife; it allows the boundary of the stage to dissolve in a way that would be impossible as a practical matter, and socially unacceptable to the aristocratic Blackfriars audience. It is merely ironic towards the intrusion; but the irony is loaded with a specific social and historical meaning.

The Citizen has got the crudest sort of notion about how drama should serve social interests; his Wife, who has never really been to a play before, does not entirely understand how the dramatic illusion works. Like Medwall's audience, she expects to be recognized, to be able to talk directly to the actors, to stand as witness to the events that unfold. Both take up a position that is presumptuously close to the gallants on stage and unbearably close to the drama: he domineers, too violent to be cute, and she indulges herself in a horrid mothering, comforting the imbecilic and debilitated figures they both favor, dispensing candy and sticky embraces. There is a general infantilization of relations. They push and pull at their apprentice Rafe, allowing him no autonomy within the fiction; he declaims a part that is ludicrously old-fashioned.

The old-fashionedness of the citizen party would have been a point the avant-gardist coterie audience would relish: the citizens are not simply dense and crude, but retrograde in their demands. They don't know how to use the advanced sense and techniques of contemporaneity the theater offers them: the Citizen does not want *The London Merchant* rewritten in his interests, he wants it driven off the stage altogether and replaced with a hoary old repertoire of citizen plays, like *The Legend of Whittington*, or *The Life and Death of Sir Thomas Gresham, with the Building of the Royal Exchange*. Through Rafe he introduces into the play the pre-dramatic forms associated with his corporate life (the May-Lord giving a speech from a conduit, and the mustering of the militia at Mile End) and the Quixotic fantasy of knight errantry.

There is a major historical reversal here, which goes beyond a mere competition in stylishness. It had always been the popular element in the theater which stayed in touch with the contemporary reality of the living audience, whatever the setting of the play, from *The Second Shepherds' Play* through A and B's courting of English Jone in *Fulgens and Lucres* to Shakespeare's clowns.

The integration of speech and action into a fully dramatic whole which Bradbrook and Robert Weimann find first in Marlowe's tragedies involved a mode of identification of the entire audience, with those closest to the stage playing no special role. Weimann particularly emphasizes the crucial role of the popular tradition in this evolution, and specifically denies that Elizabethan realism is a realism of subject matter:

> Rather, it is a new sense of the interdependence of character and society, and a fully responsive interplay between dramatic speech and dramatic action in the process of reproducing the cause and effect of human behavior that defines 'realism' in the Renaissance theater.[17]

True; but the satiric realism of the turn of the century *was* a realism of subject matter, a social realism whose direction was guided by the social dynamic in the theater no less than by the moral reaction which L. C. Knights found to be the ideology of drama in the age of Jonson.[18] If *Tamburlaine* is a product of a theater which mirrored the conditions of the Elizabethan settlement, the satirical realism of city comedy was a major instrument of social thought in a period of intensified social competition. It was a sharper realism, the cutting edge of artistic intervention in the social imagination.

And it was being developed to its highest form in the coterie theaters, to which the leading playwrights were shifting their loyalties. This is precisely the period of the King's Men's move into the Blackfriars, which Bentley found so fateful.[19] The rich allusive texture and the condescending irony which saturate *The Knight of the Burning Pestle* declare an assurance of superiority in literary and dramatic resource, and in social initiative.[20] In 1607 the smugness of this assurance was unwarranted and premature; but external social conditions confirmed it during the course of James's reign.

It is a victory whose decisiveness we can find cause to regret. Without the dialectical opposition of the popular element the drama lost its vitality; the naturalistic setting developed by satirical realism was a permanent acquisition of the English theater, but increasingly nothing went on in it except a comedy of manners which grew brittle as its audience contracted to an elite, uniform in manners and outlook. The play with, and revelation of, social space in the theater ceased to be a major instrument of social thought, a wild and exploratory realism, as it was for a while around the turn of the century; and the dramatic space congealed until it could be boxed up by the proscenium arch.

## NOTES

1 Anne Righter, *Shakespeare and the Idea of the Play* (London: Chatto and Windus, 1962); M. C. Bradbrook, *The Rise of the Common Player* (London: Chatto and Windus, 1962).

2 Dekker's *The Gull's Horn-Book* says 'Whether, therefore, the gatherers of the public or private playhouse stand to receive the afternoon's rent, let our gallant, having paid it, presently advance himself up to the throne of the stage.' In *Thomas Dekker: Selected Prose Writings*, ed. E. D. Pendry (Cambridge, Mass.: Harvard University Press, 1968), p. 98. But Webster's Induction to the Globe production of Marston's *The Malcontent* makes it clear that stage-sitting was not permitted there.

3 'The Critical Induction' is the title of chapter 4 in Thelma N. Greenfield, *The Induction in Elizabethan Drama* (Eugene: University of Oregon Press, 1969), pp. 67–95.

4 Irwin Smith, *Shakespeare's Blackfriars Playhouse* (London: Peter Owen, 1966), p. 223.

5 *The New Inn*, ed. C. H. Herford and Percy Simpson (Oxford: Clarendon Pres, 1950).

6 See John Sweeney III, '*Volpone* and the Theater of Self-Interest', *English Literary Renaissance 12* (1982), 230.

7 References are to Henry Medwall, *Fulgens and Lucres*, ed. F. S. Boas and A. W. Reed (Oxford: Clarendon Press, 1926).

8 In *Fulgens and Lucres* actors are already known for the confusing glamor of their dress – see Jackson I. Cope, *The Theater and the Dream* (Baltimore: Johns Hopkins University Press, 1973), pp. 102–3. But without a regular professional metropolitan theater, this fashionableness could not have institutional force.

9 'The Tyranny of the Audience' is the name of part of Righter's first chapter, *Shakespeare and the Idea of the Play*, pp. 31–40.

10 Bradbrook, *The Rise of the Common Player*, pp. 29, 123, 265.

11 See Bradbrook, *ibid.*, pp. 98ff., especially p. 118.

12 *The Gull's Hand-Book*, p. 98.

13 Michael Shapiro, *Children of the Revels* (New York: Columbia University Press, 1977), p. 70.

14 *The Second Part of the Return from Parnassus*, 1, 2, 294, in *The Three Parnassus Plays*, ed. with introduction by J. B. Leishman (London: Nicholson and Watson, 1949).

15 In *Have with you to Saffron-Walden*. Quoted in Leishman's introduction to *The Three Parnassus Plays*, p. 37.

16 I allude, of course, to Alfred Harbage's *Shakespeare and the Rival Traditions* (1952; Bloomington: Indiana University Press, 1970).

17 Robert Weimann, *Shakespeare and the Popular Tradition in the Theater* (Baltimore: Johns Hopkins University Press, 1978), p. 197.

18 L. C. Knights, *Drama and Society in the Age of Jonson* (London: Chatto and Windus, 1937).

19 G. E. Bentley, 'Shakespeare's Theater and After', in *Shakespeare and His Theater* (Lincoln: University of Nebraska Press, 1964), pp. 101–28.

20 'Interplay between the different types of Jacobean theatre depended on recognizing that each was catering for a different type of audience. So different *genres*, already established, could be identified with certain theatres, and parodied at others ... A sharpened awareness of the different responses of different audiences is attested by the inductions and commentaries of early Jacobean theatre, above all by ... *The Knight of the Burning Pestle* ...', M. C. Bradbrook, 'Shakespeare and the Multiple Theatres of Jacobean London', in *The Elizabethan Theatre VI*, ed. G. R. Hibbard (Toronto: Macmillan, 1978), pp. 93–4.

# Minding true things: the Chorus, the audience, and *Henry V**

SHARON TYLER

Even if the phrase is taken only literally, the theatrical space is a paradox, at once a vast arena, of whatever shape, requiring the combined talents of playwright, director, and designer to fill it, and a narrow, arbitrary frame of walls and time into which often recalcitrant material must be confined. Last year the topic of the *Themes in Drama* conference was historical drama, and the historical dramatist, whose material has an independent identity, faces the paradox in its severest form. Robert Bolt 'cursed plentifully' because his play about Elizabeth of England and Mary of Scotland required him to telescope twenty years and two kingdoms, and his two protagonists had never come within a hundred miles of each other. The final *Vivat! Vivat Regina!* he thought a thrilling hybrid:

> I had to adopt a form of play which could leap across both miles and months without a break, without a change of set; an overtly theatrical, highly artificial form . . . The stage . . . is no actual place, the minute that passes is not actual time, it is theatre merely . . . As a playwright I found the form exciting, and it was forced upon me by the historical facts.[1]

Other playwrights have met the same problem with equivalent solutions: Christopher Fry in *Curtmantle*, Maxwell Anderson in *Anne of the Thousand Days* and even in *Joan of Lorraine*, his play about a play about Joan of Arc, recently Peter Shaffer in *Amadeus*.[2] And somewhere far in the background can be heard yet another dramatist muttering to himself, 'May we cram / Within this wooden O the very casques / That did affright the air at Agincourt?'[3]

   But is the dramatist still cursing, or has he moved on to gloating, through the voice of the ultimate mockery that will enable him to represent true things in the only way he can? These words, though ultimately Shakespeare's, are put into the mouth of a puzzling figure, the Chorus, master of ceremonies at the explicit theatre-piece *Henry V*. Various explanations have been offered for this startling personage. He has been seen as a late

* A draft of this paper was read at the *Themes in Drama* International Conference held at the University of California, Riverside in February 1985.

addition, perhaps not even by Shakespeare and probably inserted for a particular performance, because he never takes any action, never speaks to any character, never, in fact, appears to be *in* the play at all.[4] John Dover Wilson, J. H. Walter, and M. M. Reese all associate him with the play's supposed epic nature; he unifies a whole by tying together, to quote Wilson, 'a series of heroic episodes or tableaux,' and is apologetic because, to quote Reese, 'epic and drama are not naturally congenial to one another.'[5] Wilson and Walter both use Sir Philip Sidney's arguments on 'heroical' poetry to defend the play as epic, and Walter further suggests that the Chorus derives from the Nuntius whom Sidney recommends 'to recount things done in former time or other place.'[6] But it is an atypical epic poet who would use his invocation to bemoan the lack of a muse of fire, and an odd Sidnean Nuntius who would spend most of his time recounting what is about to be displayed on stage, and who, far from assisting the unities of space and time, would violate them and then call attention to the fact, sometimes by apologizing for the lack of realism in such dramaturgy. Actually, without the Chorus's repeated references to 'jumping o'er times' and 'th'abuse of distance' (i, Prologue, 29; ii, Prologue, 32), the play would appear far more classically unified than it does. The seven years' campaign is presented as blitzkrieg, and even historically includes nothing like the fifteen-year stretch between the battles of Tewkesbury and Bosworth Field which Shakespeare had without compunction telescoped in *Richard III*. The same, at least once the army has arrived in France, applies to questions of place. There is, for the most notable case, no reason – despite the apologetic and specious reference to those who may have read the book – that the audience needs to know that between Agincourt and the signing of the Treaty of Troyes Henry returned to England and then came back to France, except that the Chorus wants to do a little boasting: 'Myself have played / The interim, by remembering you 'tis past.' And perhaps most seriously, any idea that Sidney influenced *Henry V* must suggest that, however his spectre might have praised the play's subject, it presumably shuddered at the execution. The *Defence of Poetry*, published posthumously in 1595, had excoriated the English stage for its total lack of both verisimilitude and propriety, and besides mixing serious and comic affairs and playing underscored havoc with unities, Shakespeare almost perfectly recapitulates Sidney's own list of horrible examples on how irrationally, illogically, and artificially the theatrical space could be filled:

> You shall have Asia of the one side and Afric of the other, and so many other under-kingdoms, that the player, when he cometh in, must ever begin with telling where he is . . . Now you shall have three ladies walk to gather flowers, and then we must believe the stage to be a garden. By and by we hear news of a shipwreck at the same place: and then we are to blame if we accept it not for a rock. Upon the back of that comes out a hideous monster with fire and smoke:

and then the miserable beholders are bound to take it for a cave. While in the meantime two armies fly in, represented with four swords and bucklers, and then what hard heart will not receive it for a pitched field?[7]

Shakespeare had been successfully committing such excesses for years, and despite the apologies he commits them now. Initially it seems amusingly clear that he either never read or totally ignored this scathing passage. But the numerous and close parallels are certainly incredible irony if they are not conscious allusion. For Asia and Afric Shakespeare has France and England, and the Channel to boot:

> Suppose within the girdle of these walls
> Are now confined two mighty monarchies
> Whose high upreared and abutting fronts
> The perilous and narrow ocean parts asunder.
>
> (I, Prologue, 19–22)

Not only are constant pointed references made (usually by the Chorus) to scene changes, but the epitome of artificiality is achieved when one is announced in advance: the scene in act II, its prologue declares, will shift from London to Southampton as soon as Henry appears – which is a full scene later. Shakespeare does not offer the cave and the monster (however tempted he may have been to equate Henry directly with Saint George), but does include the conversation between two ladies, for which there is no real narrative necessity,[8] the anchorage, though not the shipwreck, and, of course, the battlefield. His deprecatory description of his presumption in depicting Agincourt with 'four or five most vile and ragged foils' is a virtual echo of Sidney's 'four swords and bucklers,' and obviously from somewhere Shakespeare has acquired, for the first and almost the last time in his career, an extreme sensitivity to violations of theatrical unities. But even while he apologizes for it he continues to violate them right and left, showing not only how unlike Sidney's theory his own practice is but that it is based on very different ideas. It is as if Shakespeare had decided, not that epic and drama were totally uncongenial, but that when the historical material he was working with reached the 'heroical' level of Sidney's favorite subject matter, he would prove to Sidney's ghost, on Sidney's own ground, what the English stage could do, and use Sidney's Nuntius to help him.

The Chorus's own explanation for his presence still seems easily the best. He is the audience's guide, their intermediary, their colleague in a necessary creative endeavour. He offers them apologies, of course, but he also jokes with them, assuring them that they will not be seasick crossing the Channel, 'for if we may / We'll not offend one stomach with our play' (II, Prologue, 39–40), and above all he gives them instructions, instructions on how they can and must help by imagination to translate the thin dramatic pretenses and illogical excesses of the form into a play worthy of its subject.

It is largely the Chorus who establishes the rapport which is Shakespeare's demonstrated alternative to Sidney's classically cynical demand for realism in filling without overflowing the stage.

The audience is drawn into its co-operative role more gradually than the immediate request that they assume that role implies. In the first prologue, the Chorus does little more than announce subject, theme, and the crucial limitations of the 'wooden O' in which the players will attempt 'so great an object.' He reminds them that 'a crooked figure may / Attest in little place a million,' and explains that their part is critical: 'For 'tis your thoughts that now must deck our kings, / Carry them here and there, jumping o'er times, / Turning the accomplishment of many years / Into an hour-glass' (I, Prologue, 28–31). But so far he does not require much more than tolerance, and his final plea 'Gently to hear, kindly to judge our play,' is like any number of Elizabethan prologues. To this point, the audience need really only be sympathetic. But a particular sort of sympathy – creative, imaginative sympathy – has already been requested.

Since the Chorus's affiliations are all outward, and the acted portions of the play are perfectly clear without his commentary, it is sometimes easy to overlook the linkages between points made by the Chorus and points made within the action itself. But immediately as the action proper begins, the regular cast moves in to second the Chorus's endeavors. The Chorus has advised the audience that their imagination can and must carry them to France. Westmorland, urging Henry to launch the war, declares:

> Never king of England
> Had nobles richer, and more loyal subjects,
> Whose hearts have left their bodies here in England
> And lie pavilion'd in the fields of France.
>
> (I, ii, 126–9)

The Archbishop of Canterbury immediately chimes in with 'O, let their bodies follow, my dear liege.' The identical expressions not only convey – their respective speakers hope – the level of enthusiasm proper to the venture, but place the audience squarely where it belongs, among the supporters of the enterprise.

The prologue to the second act is a witty speech, full of word tricks. The Chorus triumphantly declares that expectation 'hides a sword from hilts unto the point / With crowns imperial, crowns and coronets, / Promised to Harry and his followers' (II, Prologue, 9–11). But a few lines later he mentions that the French have bribed three traitors 'with treacherous crowns' (i.e., coins), and these traitors have 'for the gilt of France – o guilt indeed! –' planned Henry's assassination. Here Henry is defined as 'the mirror of all Christian kings,' and a brief apostrophe is made to 'England! model to thy inward greatness / Like little body with a mighty heart.' The speech ends with the promise to make a smooth Channel crossing and offend no stomachs with the play. If by the end of this speech the audience cannot think representationally, accept double meanings, and allow the literal and the figurative simultaneous expression, it is not for lack of preparation.

However, still the part demanded of the audience has been largely passive. They are to watch patiently (a frequently repeated word) while the players convey the playhouse (and them) first to Southampton and then to France. By the opening of act III, the audience has to work. The Chorus suddenly breaks into a series of imperatives:

> Suppose that you have seen
> The well-appointed king at Hampton pier . . .
>
> Play with your fancies, and in them behold
> Upon the hempen tackle ship-boys climbing;
> Hear the shrill whistle . . .
>
> O, do but think
> You stand upon the rivage and behold
> A city on th'inconstant billows dancing . . .
>
> Follow, follow!
> Grapple your minds to sternage of this navy,
> And leave your England . . .
>
> (III, Prologue, 3–4, 7–9, 13–15, 17–19)

He no longer claims to set up the picture for the audience; he demands that they do it, though of course it is still his own eloquence which guarantees that they will get it right. He also requires them, members of the enterprise, to manage the practical details of their passage as part of the invading fleet, to grapple on, themselves. Though he concludes with his usual modest appeal ('Still be kind, / And eche out our performance with your mind'), 'work, work your thoughts' better typifies the Chorus's injunctions at this point.

The prologue to act IV, the night before Agincourt, is again a quiet one. Before the series of anxious conversations in the dark, vigor and energetic action like that demanded in act III would be out of place; the audience, like the army, must sit quiet and watchful while Henry moves through the camp exchanging anonymous observations. But when the Chorus says, 'O, now who will behold / The royal captain of this ruin'd band / Walking from watch to watch,' the 'who' he has in mind is clear, and the 'now' seems less likely to mean 1415 than 1599, or 1985 for that matter. As the prologue closes, the Chorus delivers his strongest reminder, daringly at the tensest moment of the play, that it is a play. He is as reluctant as the army for the battle of Agincourt, but for other reasons. He declares that the coming depiction will 'disgrace' the subject, and his reminder to the audience that they must mind 'true things by what their mockeries be' is the most forceful of his many such statements.

And so prepared for, the sequences surrounding the battle of Agincourt are Shakespeare's most defiantly effective use of the very conventions the Chorus ostensibly deplores. The prologue has reminded the audience that the battle will be – very reprehensibly – represented by 'four or five most vile and ragged foils.' Despite the apology – because of the apology – the impression of small numbers, poor condition, an impossible undertaking, becomes inescapable. And what very explicitly makes the French 'confident and overlusty' and the English sleepless with worry is that both sides know that the English are badly outnumbered and in no shape for a battle. When Henry the next day speaks of 'we few, we happy few, we band of brothers,' the point again is reinforced by the so-called weaknesses of the theatre. Assembled to hear the Crispin's day speech, and still looking on as Henry receives the final demand for ransom and angrily rejects it, is the small cast representing the English army – not quite 'four or five . . . foils' or 'four swords and bucklers,' but still few, necessarily but constructively few, and all familiar faces, which have been seen, quite literally, by day and night.[9] The point is representationally made by the unrealistically small group, where it can be obscured when Henry is assigned a supporting cast better designed to represent an army of between five and six thousand. The ultimate supporting cast is seated beyond the stage, and given its cue by the familiar ring of Henry's, 'All things are ready, if our minds be so.'

Historically Agincourt was no disaster, nor despite or because of the Chorus's apologies is its theatrical depiction a failure, and the Chorus who opens act v appears proud of himself. He is very busy, and he requires the audience to be busy 'in the quick forge and working-house of thought' as well. They are fully fellow-artists now, and he can ask for some really strenuous activity:

> Now we bear the king
> Toward Calais: grant him there, there seen,
> Heave him away upon your winged thoughts
> Athwart the sea . . .
>
> (v, Prologue, 6–9)

And so they land him, conduct him through Blackheath to London, and ultimately bring him back to France. The mixture of simple indicative and imperative verifies the new relation of audience and players established by their choric mediator. Where in the early prologues 'we' obviously referred to the players alone, requiring sympathy for their presumptuous enterprise, it now is used for players and audience together; the functional co-operation is assumed to be achieved. The Chorus smugly points out how expeditiously he has disposed of Henry's brief visit home, and he finally asks the audience to return for the final scene with the old reminder that

imagination can conquer all problems of time and space: 'Then brook
abridgement, and your eyes advance, / After your thoughts, straight back
again to France.' And the epilogue, by linking this play not only to history
but to written tradition and to other plays,[10] continues to voice apology at
presumption but hint at pride in daring achievement. Bringing a triple
context, however admittedly 'mangl'd,' to mind here is flexing the walls of
the theatrical space with a vengeance. But after all, the Chorus recalls,
great things can be packed into small space. Henry himself lived 'small
time, but in that small most greatly lived,' and Shakespeare's *Henry V* may
with the audience's help have filled its 'little room' as successfully.

But has it, or has the overtly theatrical presentation been, as it claims,
only conceding the makeshift and mockery which must be apologized for?
Has the audience's only co-operation been the arrogant tolerance of those
who know better? We have clear evidence that it is more, that the Chorus
really does lead the audience to see what is not there. In 1975 the Royal
Shakespeare Company gave a particularly artificial production of *Henry V*,
even to having the preparatory sequences, the first act, performed in
rehearsal clothes. Afterward an interviewer mentioned to Peter Bourke,
who played the camp boy, that the audience remembered his character's
'bloodstained body' as a particularly forceful image. Bourke responded,
'Do they really? That's very good in a way if they do, because there isn't any
blood, we're not using it.'[11] The imaginative response can be even longer-
lasting and survive closer scrutiny of the actual facts. Robert Ornstein, one
of the many critics who find too many disturbing hints and shadows in the
play to be happy with treating it as a patriotic spectacle, points out that
literally speaking it is not at all a series of warlike tableaux:

> Those who think of it as a play of physical action, do so not because its scenes
> are made up of excursions and alarums, but because the Chorus creates such
> memorable word pictures of epic activity and movement – of the preparations
> for war, of the gathering and movement of ships and armies, of the sound and
> fury of battle. Although the Chorus apologizes several times for the author's
> feeble attempts to represent the field of Agincourt with 'four or five most vile
> and ragged foils,' the apology is as sly as it is gratuitous because Shakespeare
> makes no attempt in the play to represent an epic confrontation of armies. The
> war is always offstage.[12]

He is absolutely right; in this triumphant campaign piece the only military
encounter actually depicted is the comic scene in which the cowardly Pistol
captures the even more cowardly LeFer. Ornstein concludes that the play is
really a bleaker work, deliberately undercutting its own brilliant surface.[13]
He may be right, though of course his observation also proves that those
who read the play as a grimly antagonistic account of the horrors of war are
also remembering word pictures, perhaps especially Michael Williams's
musings the night before Agincourt, with the gruesome description of

dismembered bodies and the implication of damned souls, and the classic understatement: 'I am afeard there are few die well that die in a battle.' But it is certainly worth noting that an entire critical school makes, if not the most perspicacious interpretation, the one the Chorus specifically invites them to make.

And the hostile critic as well as the admirer may be led to his conclusions through the Chorus's adroit manipulation. Perhaps because this is a play whose subject responds well to explicitly theatrical representation, it is a play in which representation is a major theme. The entire point of the Chorus's many injunctions to the audience is that truths may, and sometimes must, be known or taught through images and comparisons. But in Renaissance theory the power and importance of exemplary figures goes beyond the theatre and beyond art into life itself, and in this play concern with models and mirrors goes beyond the Chorus's immediate instructions to the audience about 'minding true things by what their mockeries be.' The play is crowded at all levels, literal and figurative, serious and comic, with the terminology of representation, from Henry's orders to 'imitate the action of the tiger' in order to 'be copy . . . to men of grosser blood / And teach them how to war' (a speech which contains what amounts to a set of acting directions on how to depict rage and determination) to Fluellen's gleeful, extended, forced comparison between Henry and 'Alexander the Pig,' delivered with the portentous reminder that 'there is figures in all things.' But it is the listener whose ear has been trained on the Chorus's puns who, even while laughing, will recognize that Alexander the Pig both is and is not Alexander the Great, particularly in a Welsh accent; it is the reader who has become accustomed to weighing analogies who will see another parallel than Fluellen's own between the killing of Cleitus and the rejection of Falstaff;[14] it is the critic who remembers – as the Chorus will not let him forget – that he is only tolerantly allowing an inadequate actor to represent Henry V who will wonder what tolerance it requires to allow Henry to represent the English-soldierly Everyman Harry LeRoy, let alone the mirror of all Christian kings. It is not, however, my purpose here to join the debate about the lustre or tarnish on Henry's armor, but to consider the nature and role of the Chorus. And by whatever logic Shakespeare originally decided to include such a figure and call deliberate attention to the artificial nature of his play, by doing so he made *Henry V* a piece in which, for nearly four hundred years, audiences have been seeing what is described rather than what is staged. This is not gracefully acknowledging difficulty, or even making a virtue of necessity. It is deliberately creating necessity, demanding limitation he habitually ignored, in order to make a virtue of it.

It is tantalizing but pure speculation to see Shakespeare deliberately taking up the artistic gauntlet flung by Sidney. It would be gratifying though probably the wrong side idolatry to see in Shakespeare the man who in the sixteenth century at once predicted and outwitted the entire school of reader-response criticism, acknowledging the importance of the audience's reaction but proving that ultimately it was at his control, not theirs. But the play does prove that, as surely as it rebuts the argument that the theatrical space can only be filled naturalistically or become ridiculous. And the Chorus is both the play's theatrical keystone and, in the wider realm of interpretation, a more critical figure than his almost external position at first implies. If the play is indeed a straightforward rendition of epic action, it is the Chorus, and his skill in playing to the audience's imagination, that makes that action visible. But even if it is something darker and more subtle, whether merely shadowed by events past and events to come or actively hostile to the character and themes it seems to praise, he is still a key figure. It is he who, as the observer unbound by time, takes the last word to mention the future collapse of Henry's achievement, and throughout the play as he holds up the heroic mirror, it is always with the reminder that it is a mirror, which lets audience and critic alike decide whether Henry V and his French campaign accurately repeat its images.

## NOTES

1 Robert Bolt, *Vivat! Vivat Regina!* (London: Heinemann Educational Books, 1971), p. xi. The 'minute' in question is a particular juncture (pp. 64–6) at which literal time appears suspended, and not only do Mary and Elizabeth appear on stage together, but, Bolt explains, 'I brought Spain and Italy on stage as well and represented some months of critical diplomacy in a minute's interchange between the assembled potentates, presided over by John Knox, with the Edinburgh mob as chorus in the wings.'

2 This is not to suggest that the rationale behind the often similar stagecraft is necessarily itself alike. In *Curtmantle*, for instance, Fry explains, 'the stage is William Marshall's mind,' and the omissions and alterations are those which might logically occur in a man's memory (*Curtmantle*, London: Oxford University Press, 1965, p. viii). Shaffer uses costumed extras to arrange and rearrange props, while the fluid action continues around them ('Through a pleasing paradox of theatre their constant coming and going . . . should render them virtually invisible, and certainly unremarkable'), in order to convey the 'sprung line, gracefulness, and energy' of Mozart's music (*The Collected Plays of Peter Shaffer*, New York: Harmony Books, 1982, p. 482). *Anne of the Thousand Days* is also presented as reminiscence (double reminiscence, in this case, with choric commentary by Henry VIII and Anne Boleyn setting the various scenes), while *Joan of Lorraine* is an extended play-within-a-play demonstrating the continuing validity of issues addressed by history. But the original problem in all cases is that of, in Shaffer's phrase, reducing 'a mass of historical material to anything

remotely coherent and yet dramatic' (p. xvi). Anderson later declared that the mental context was the central factor of *Anne of the Thousand Days*, and that as 'a plain historical play' it would have been 'impossible on the current [1948] stage' (*Dramatist in America: Letters of Maxwell Anderson, 1912–1955*, ed. Laurence G. Avery (Chapel Hill, NC: University of North Carolina Press, 1977), p. 237). Fry has perhaps the strongest statement: if the playwright is not prepared at once to offer a story comprehensible to non-historians and to do it without distorting the material, then 'let him invent his characters, let him go to Ruritania for his history' (p. vii).

3  All in-text quotations from *Henry V* are from *King Henry V*, ed. J. H. Walter, the Arden Edition of the Works of William Shakespeare (London: Methuen, 1954).

4  Cf. G. P. Jones, '*Henry V*: The Chorus and the Audience,' *Shakespeare Survey*, 31 (1978), 93–104. Jones reviews previous discussions and argues that both the degree of audience participation requested and the frequent references to the audience as 'gentle' prove that the choral speeches were written for a private performance before a well-born audience, who, being more accustomed to the masque than the playhouse, would expect to be directly involved.

5  Introduction, *Henry V*, ed. John Dover Wilson (Cambridge: Cambridge University Press, 1955), pp. xii–xiii; M. M. Reese, *The Cease of Majesty* (New York: St Martin's Press, 1961), p. 320. Cf. Walter, Introduction, *Henry V* (Arden edn), pp. xv–xvi: 'Shakespeare's task was not merely to extract material for a play from an epic story, but within the physical limits of the stage and within the admittedly inadequate dramatic convention to give the illusion of an epic whole. In consequence *Henry V* is daringly novel, nothing quite like it had been seen on the stage before.'

6  Sir Philip Sidney, *A Defence of Poetry*, ed. Jan van Dorsten (London: Oxford University Press, 1966, reprinted 1978), p. 66. Walter, Introduction, *Henry V*, p. xvi.

7  Sidney, *A Defence of Poetry*, p. 65.

8  III, iv. The setting is normally given as 'Rouen: a room in the palace,' but both are editorial additions (*Henry V*, p. 69n), and the scene is sometimes played out of doors.

9  This is a generalized extension of two observations made by actors in the Royal Shakespeare Company's 1975 production of the play. Barrie Rutter ('Macmorris') points out that the unified nature of the English army was more clearly rendered by the fact that the cast included no extras, and Philip Dunbar ('Nym') notes that since all the characters on stage were familiar the audience saw them as an army of real people – not just 'noblemen and 300 spear carriers' (*The Royal Shakespeare Company's Production of Henry V for the Centenary Season at the Royal Shakespeare Theatre*, ed. and with interviews by Sally Beauman (Oxford: Pergamon Press, 1976), pp. 85, 93–4.

10  Actually the expansion begins in the Prologue to act v, when written source material is alluded to. But it is in the epilogue that the play is itself spoken of as something written 'with rough and all-unable pen,' and here that it is mentioned that what happened afterward were events 'which oft our stage hath shown,' thus making *Henry V* a small part of three broad continua: history as events, history as written material, and drama.

11  *The Royal Shakespeare Company's Production*, p. 78. He adds: 'If they see it, then that's the power and force of the audience's imagination.'

12  Robert Ornstein, *A Kingdom for a Stage* (Cambridge, Mass.: Harvard University Press, 1972), p. 176.

13  He himself uses the Chorus as support for his position, pointing out the juxtaposition of one of the many appeals for gentle treatment with the first blast of the cannon before Harfleur: 'If we have any doubt what kindliness of judgement is we can take our cue from the king' (p. 187).

14  Cf. Lily B. Campbell, *Shakespeare's Histories: Mirrors of Elizabethan Policy* (San Marino, California: Huntington Library Publications, 1968), pp. 304–5. H. M. Richmond (*Shakespeare's Political Plays*, New York: Random House Incorporated, 1967, pp. 177–9) also observes that immediately after Fluellen's speech Henry enters to declare that the killing of the camp boys has aroused his first anger since he came to France – anger to which both Fluellen and Richmond ascribe the killing of the French prisoners.

# A pill to purge parody: Marston's manipulation of the Paul's environment in the *Antonio* plays*

ADRIAN WEISS

When Edward Pearce, Master of Choristers at St Paul's, and William Stanley, sixth Earl of Derby, revived the Paul's choristers as an acting troupe in late 1599, a brief but influential phase in English drama commenced with John Marston as its guiding inspiration. It is not known if Marston was privy to the initiation of the project, but it is certain that he joined the company early on and provided the scripts for its success. Whatever their impact upon contemporary drama, the Induction and the *Antonio* plays have become especially important in recent trends in criticism.

Traditionally, these and other plays written for the boy actors were considered 'straight' plays and accorded the same manner of interpretation as plays written for adult companies. Then in the early 1960s, Anthony Caputi and R. A. Foakes both argued that the comic incongruity of children playing adult roles was the key factor influencing Marston's treatment of his actors and material. Foakes based his argument that the *Antonio* plays were written as parodies upon his perception that a boy-actor 'strutting in a ranting role becomes grotesque'.[1] He presented a collection of self-references from the plays and supposed references to burlesqued plays and adult acting styles as evidence of Marston's burlesque intention. In response, Richard Levin argued persuasively that Foakes and his followers had failed to provide a single scrap of evidence showing that a contemporary audience shared their perception of boy-actors in adult roles, or that the self-references were any clear evidence of intentional parody.[2] However, Levin left unanswered the question: what effects did Marston intend with those self-references, which are found both in the Induction and the *Antonio* plays? Similarly, more recent critics have challenged Foakes' interpretation of specific self-references, but none has suggested an alternate view of their overall function with regard to the dramatic illusion of the plays.

I believe that an examination of the Induction and the *Antonio* plays provides evidence that Marston indeed exploited his boy-actors, but not in

---

* A draft of this paper was read at the *Themes in Drama* International Conference held at the University of California, Riverside in February 1985.

*The theatrical space*

the manner claimed by the parodists. The most important factor overlooked by the parodists is that these plays are integrated with the Paul's
Cathedral environment in a unique manner due to the fact that playwright,
actors, and audience participated in the evolution of this new theater.
Reavley Gair has shown that Marston used the *Antonio* plays to introduce
his select audience to various components of the new theater, including
himself as playwright, the musical talents of the acting company, the
functional properties of the theater, staging effects, and type of dramatic
material to be offered.[3] It is clear from Gair's study that Marston consciously violated the dramatic illusions of the plays by injecting these real-
world references to the theater and St Paul's. What interests us here is one
particular component of the Paul's environment, namely, the multi-
dimensional presence and function of the boy-actors, and the manner in
which Marston manipulated that component in the Induction and the
*Antonio* plays.

It is essential to recognize that the Paul's theater differs from other
theaters in a fundamental way which provided Marston with the potential
for creating a multiple-illusion in the *Antonio* plays. Normally, a theater's
space is 'naked' until setting defines it as a specific locality such as Watling
Street, Bartholomew Fair, the Forest of Arden, Venice, or an indeterminate
point in the dimensionless matrix of an absurdist cosmos. Playwrights of all
periods have capitalized upon this essential feature of theater space by
defining locality in such a way as to evoke associations which in some way
illuminate the world of illusion created in the play. The relatively bare
Elizabethan/Jacobean stage provided Shakespeare and his contemporaries
with a special freedom in using a sense of locality in this manner.[4] In
contrast, the Paul's stage was not 'naked' but came equipped with an array
of associations by virtue of its physical and functional connections with St
Paul's Cathedral. It was part of a self-contained world: the theater shared
not only its space with the Cathedral, but its acting personnel as well. In
addition to performing plays, the boy-actors learned the 'arte and knowledge of musicke' from the Cathedral Master of Choristers, performed as
Cathedral choristers, received their Christian education from a Cathedral
clergyman, studied grammar and rhetoric at St Paul's School, and finally,
lived within the Cathedral precincts. Moreover, the boys occasionally
played a part in the revels of the Inns of Court. Thus the boy-actors of St
Paul's theater carried onto the stage a predefined identity which was
particularly rich in potentially exploitable real-world associations. A Paul's
audience's 'dual consciousness' of actor as separate from role would be
quite different from that evoked by a well-established actor whose previous
performances endowed him with a pre-play identity. Such a consciousness
would include, among other things, an awareness of the contemporary
dramatic milieu of performances by 'scholars' on the grammar school and

university levels. Given this complex interlacing of real-world environment with stage space, it is surprising to find R. A. Foakes, Michael Shapiro and other parodists restricting audience 'dual consciousness' merely to the matter of size-disparity. The boy-actors' self-references could indeed, in Shapiro's words, 'remind' the audience 'of what it already knew,' but a Paul's audience certainly had more to be reminded of than the boys' sizes.[5]

I

Let me briefly review the school performance tradition and its essential features as they relate to Marston's use of his boy-actors. The tradition involved performances by grammar school students for the purpose of practicing the oratorical knowledge and skills related to oral delivery.[6] In his *An Apology for Actors* (1612), Thomas Heywood defended play-acting by boys against Puritan attack by citing the traditional attitude toward the importance of those skills: 'Tully in his boke *ad Caium Herennium*, requires five things in an Orator, *Invention, Disposition, Eloquutien, Memory,* and *Pronunciation,* yet all are imperfect without the sixt, which is *Action*'.[7] Of these six rhetorical processes, the student performances were concerned primarily with *memory* and *pronunciation,* or memorization and recitation of their lines, and *action,* or the gestures necessary for effective delivery.[8] The Induction derives directly from the school performance tradition and exploits the boy-actors' real-world association with that tradition. In a word, the Induction is intended by Marston to play to the elite audience's awareness of school performances. It creates the illusion that his diminutive actors were legitimate actors not merely in that they could mouth lines, but that their *pronunciation* and *gesture* were based upon a sound knowledge of rhetorical theory. If the initial audiences at St Paul's theater were comprised of friends and associates from the Inns of Court as is generally believed, Marston couldn't have chosen a better approach to winning the audience's approval and delight.[9]

This interplay of the Induction, the audience's awareness of the performance tradition, and Marston's use of his boy-actors defines the function of the numerous self-references within the plays, but has gone unnoticed. Hence, the Induction has been the focus of considerable controversy, for it obviously serves the function of modulating audience perceptions of the subsequent dramatic illusion, especially with respect to the presence of the boy-actors. Since Caputi and Foakes, a consensus has emerged that the Induction emphasizes the stature and age of the boy-actors so as to shift the focus to some aspect of the adult theaters. Thus the boys are regarded as vehicles for parody of the outmoded plays and diction of the adult companies, for burlesque of adult acting styles, or for mockery of the crudeness of adult acting.[10] Actually, the purpose is not to direct audience consciousness beyond Paul's to the world of the adult theaters, as these views suggest. Rather, the Induction's parameters are restricted to the Paul's environment itself. When the group of actors appear on stage 'with parts in their hands: having cloakes cast over their apparrell' (Induction, 3–4), neither they nor the stage have been given an identity beyond that which they already possess by virtue of their place in the Paul's environment. The stage, in effect, remains a physical section of the Cathedral precinct, and the actors remain Paul's choristers. The illusion created in the Induction exploits their association with the grammar school performance tradition.

In that illusion, these choristers gather to prepare their homework assignment which, in this case, is the preparation of parts for a school performance. However, this group of scholars has procrastinated to an extraordinary degree, even in the context of the usual juvenile proclivity in that direction. Galeatzo initiates the Induction discussion with a rather alarming temporal reference in addressing the first concern in such an assignment: 'Come sirs, come! the music will sound straight for entrance . . . Are ye ready, are ye perfect?' Piero's response distinguishes the two stages of 'perfecting' necessary. In terms of *memory* or memorization, there is no problem: 'Faith, we can say our parts.' But he hasn't the slightest idea of how to proceed from successful memorization to *pronunciation* and *gesture*: 'but we are ignorant in what mold we must cast our actors.' Marston's flair for shocking an audience is nowhere more apparent and effective. Incredibly, the boys have not yet rehearsed, and are on stage awaiting the opening music! Such a revelation would be enough to shake the confidence of any opening night audience. But this effect is deliberately intended to prepare the audience for the Induction illusion, which reveals that the boys possess a depth and breadth of rhetorical knowledge that guarantee a credible performance despite the feigned procrastination.

Marston's strategy is further clarified by the speech prefixes in the printed text of the Induction, which specifies the actors' roles as opposed to their real names. In many inductions the opposite occurred – as with Will Sly, Sinklow, Cundale and Burbage in the Induction to *The Malcontent*. In such cases, critics generally agree that the purpose of an induction is to remind an audience of the artificiality of the play-world. This is not true of this Induction. Here dramatic identity is to be defined as a combination of the rhetorical style and gesture developed as part of the Induction discussion of a given role. That the speech prefixes of the printed text are not spurious is indicated by the fact that the text itself mentions by name ten roles, including direct addresses to the eight actors on stage in the Induction. Marston's complaint in the 'Letter to the Reader' prefacing *The Malcontent* that 'Scenes invented, meerely to be spoken, should be inforcively published to be read' has obvious relevance. The auditory effect of the rhetorical figures and the visual effect of the accompanying gestures are the identifying features he attempted to manipulate, as the Induction makes quite obvious. Further, the initial stage direction seems to indicate a staging device in which the costumes are revealed as the various roles emerge in their patterns of rhetorical speech and gesture.

Galeatzo, Alberto and Feliche provide commentary and directions in the Induction. In doing so, they call upon relevant components of rhetorical background and display a rhetorical virtuosity that belies their supposedly diminutive talents and sizes. During the course of the Induction, eight roles are described employing standard techniques for the rhetorical figure *descriptio personis*.[11] Four actors call attention to the topics of *invention* employed in their *descriptions*. Feliche concludes his 'draught of the spirit' of his role by indicating that the description is composed of 'native adjuncts' (line 114), referring to the topics 'subjects/adjuncts.' Antonio begins his description of Galeatzo's role: ''Tis to be described by signs and tokens' (line 115), appropriate to a description of a characterless fop/gull. Similarly, 'native adjuncts' 'place of birth' and 'nationality' are employed in Piero's and Alberto's characterization of Matzagente (lines 91–98). Alberto is described from the topics 'fortune' and 'acts' (lines 22–27). Further, three of the roles are classified as stereotypes: Balurdo as 'fool' (line 31), Matzagente as 'Bragadoch' (line 88), and Forobosco as 'parasite-flatterer' (50–51). Galeatzo's 'signs and tokens' identify him as a 'sycophant' (lines 115–125), although this term is not specifically noted by Antonio, who feigns a constant state of anxiety throughout the Induction because of his challenging doubled roles. This comic touch effectively enhances the no-rehearsal illusion.

In addition, dominant rhetorical figures or stylistic traits are added to the stereotype identifications. Parasite Forobosco's language is characterized by 'the titillation of hyperbolical praise' (line 60), and 'servile patches of glavering flattery' (line 55), or, flattering phrases kept on hand for any occasion. Balurdo the fool's language is dominated by the figure *mimesis*,[12] defined here as 'giving an echo to wit' (line 37). Feliche mimics the rhetorical style of Forobosco (lines 45–48) so effectively that the boy playing Alberto 'gets the joke' and interrupts with a reference to the figure that dominates that style: 'What's all this periphrasis?' (line 48).

Of course, there's the much-cited reference 'rampum scampum, mount tufty Tamberlaine' (line 86) applied by Alberto to Matzagente. The reference is not a warning to the audience that the play will burlesque the outmoded fare of the adult theaters, but works within the Paul's environment as do the rest of the references. For Alberto follows up immediately with the note that Matzagente's archaic high style 'is native to his part. For acting a modern Bragadoch . . .' (line 88). The point made by the complete reference is that the Matzagente role is a particular stereotype which can be defined partially in terms of a rhetorical style. It creates the impression that this group of grammar scholars has learned to identify styles by their labels.[13]

Furthermore, the definition of role by rhetorical style is complimented by references to gesture and costume. Hence, Piero is told to 'grow big in thought' (line 11), that is, to make his delivery conform to the weighty passions and matter which the rhetoric of his ornate high style expresses, and gesture is specified as well as language: 'then thus frame your exterior shape to haughty form of elate majesty' (lines 7–8). Alberto presumably provides a sample of the gesture corresponding to the easily recognized 'mold' of 'elate majesty,' a reference repeated later in the Induction by Antonio (lines 119–120). After he's been given his directions, Piero confidently exclaims: 'If that be all, fear not, I'll suit it right.' Supposedly he knows enough from Galeatzo's brief demonstration to create a credible role. Piero's pun reveals the interplay between the appearance of the actors 'having cloakes cast over their apparrell' and the emergence of their play-world identities. The implicit stage direction 'I'll *suit it* right' signals the removal of Piero's cloak to reveal the ducal costume beneath, an essential part of the 'mold' which Piero then demonstrates as he proclaims: 'Who cannot be proud, stroke up the hair and strut?' Forobosco's punning reference 'I but dispose my speech to the *habit* of my part' likewise appears to perform the same function. A more complicated manipulation of cloak and costume seems intended in the interaction between Antonio-Florizel and Alberto (lines 65–80). Beneath a hooded cloak ('two subtle fronts under one hood'), the Florizel disguise (a long buckler or a loose toga?) covers most of the basic Antonio costume but allows Antonio to point to the exposed portion ('I shall grow ignorant . . . how but to truss my hose'). Alberto's quip 'Tush, never put them off; for women wear the breeches still' capitalizes upon the fact that both costumes can be seen simultaneously, providing a visualization of this trite aphorism.

One of the more interesting aspects of the illusion created in the Induction is the boy-actors' consciousness of their distinct function as actors performing an illusion, and their awareness of the audience's critical expectations and potential response to their performance. In regard to the first, their awareness of their acting function is evoked through repeated use of the terms 'play' (seven occurrences), 'act' (three times), and more significantly, the earliest use of the word 'personate' (line 5) with acting as its specific referent, a use firmly established by Heywood's *Apology*.[14] With respect to awareness of the audience's expectations, Antonio expresses two concerns about his doubled roles, and fears that 'I shall be hiss'd at' (line 66). When he doubts his appropriateness for the role of Florizel: 'I a voice to play a lady!' (line 72), Alberto reassures him: 'O, an Amazon should have such a voice, virago-like' (line 73). Assuming that this exchange is 'straight', it literally indicates that the voice of the boy playing Antonio-

Florizel has deepened and is 'man-like'; hence the boy doubts that the audience will believe his female personation.[15] The second problem involves the dexterity required in switching male and female roles. Antonio explains: 'Ay, but when use hath taught me *action* to hit the right *point* of a lady's part . . . I will be ignorant when I must turn young prince again' [emphasis added] (lines 75–76). He uses the term *action* exactly as does Heywood's comment quoted earlier, and his comment is well-taken if the female 'pointing' in delivery is as different as he suspects.[16] In a second instance, Alberto corrects Forobosco's inflated perception of his acting abilities by reference to the audience's critical expectations. When the latter boasts that 'Ho, I will so tickle the sense of *bella graziosa madonna* . . .' (lines 59–60), Alberto undercuts him by replying 'Thou promisest more than I hope any spectator gives faith of performance'(lines 62–63). The effect of this type of interplay between actors and audience is to establish a bond of mutual respect that is quite unlike the antagonism generated in the majority of the inductions written for the boys.

In short, Marston demonstrates that his boy-actors know what acting is all about from their grammar school study of rhetorical theory and practice. Or, it is more correct to say that in the Induction, Marston creates the illusion that the choristers of St Paul's are quite impressive rhetorical scholars, able to engage in a rapid roundtable of rhetorical criticism, spot a figure when they hear one, compose extemporaneous descriptions of persons, mimic the rhetorical style of a colleague's role and judge audience perceptions. The cumulative effect of the Induction is not, as generally thought, to reinforce the theme of inexperience or inadequacy. Quite the contrary; the boy-actors, Antonio excluded, exude a self-confidence grounded in their mastery of rhetoric which tempts them to undertake a performance with no more rehearsal than a brief discussion of the rhetorical principles which define their respective roles. It is amusing to speculate about how the boys' schoolmaster would have reacted to the illusion of the Induction had he been standing in the wings. Probably something like: ''sfut, 'tis all but feigned.' To the Paul's audience, however, it must have been a delightful and reassuring spectacle, and this group of students probably appeared extremely sophisticated, compared to the usual grammar school actors.

II

Moreover, Marston extends the illusion of the Induction into the play proper. Within this play, the remarkable incidence of references to acting and various aspects of language seems intended to reinforce the illusion that the Induction creates about the boy-actors. Rhetorical terms (for example, *synecdoche*) are noted about thirteen times. Character stereotypes ('sycophant') or types of language ('groping flattery') are mentioned about a dozen times. In addition, characters comment upon their own or another's language almost twenty times. Language's inadequacy for the expression of heightened passion is noted four times. Several characters repeat words and phrases which they used in their Induction roles, thereby establishing a strong reminder of their Induction identities. The play is laced with these verbal reminders, and Marston sets many of these scenes either with Feliche or other Induction characters on stage to engage in Induction-like critical commentary which doubly reinforces the intended reminder (for example, Forobosco at II, i, 104–124, Matzagente at II, i, 178–187, and Balurdo's numerous examples of self-affectation.) The *description of persons* techniques likewise are duplicated in the play (Rossaline on Matzagente, I, i, 116–139). The Induction concern for gesture reappears: at one point, Flavia requires three lines to list Rossaline's acting accomplishments while the latter displays his mastery of feminine gestures (III, ii, 149–51). Similarly, Balurdo practices facial expressions for twenty-five lines (III, ii, 119–44), a reminder of extensive commentary in *Ad Herennium* and *Institutes* on the subject. In addition, Marston may have added a new reminder of the boys' real-world roles not seen previously in the Induction. The declamatory nature of Antonio's opening speech and many other speeches throughout both plays, with their sophomoric use of alliteration, assonance and contorted syntax, may be intended to evoke the association with the school performance tradition, where 'musty fopperies of antiquity' were the standard fare.

Furthermore, the Induction concern with audience response extends into the play. The Prologue apologizes for any 'rude scenes' that might result in the performance because of the actors' pretended procrastination, requesting that the 'respected auditors' respond leniently with 'dimpled smiles' rather than 'bended brows.' After the so-called 'operatic duet' in Italian in IV, i, the Page steps out of role to deliver an extended nine-line critique to the audience which is directly in the vein of Induction commentary. Like Antonio in the Induction, the Page expresses concern that the efforts of the boy-actors will meet with disapproval through no fault of their own – difficult doubled roles and questionable scenes are to be blamed on the author, not the actors. The intended effect, I believe, is to elicit audience approval for the talented actors, who are able not only to create their roles without rehearsal but also to engage in sophisticated critical commentary about their material, seeing it from the perspective of the audience. Likewise, Alberto's explicit exit from the play's illusion: 'Here ends my part in this love's comedy' (v, i, 66), evokes the Induction illusion of students consciously playing dramatic roles guided not only by their knowledge of rhetoric, but by their knowledge of literary genre as well. Antonio's reference to the world of illusion within the play: '. . . here a pleasing stage / Most wished spectators of my tragedy' (v, ii, 214–15) has a similar effect.

These and other aspects of the boy-actors' Induction illusion appear with equal frequency in *Antonio's Revenge*.[17] Although he is a new character not encountered in the Induction, Pandulpho exhibits the same complex consciousness created there for the boy-actors. His references to rhetoric and acting are doubly revealing in his struggle with rising passions, for his role is imbued with an awareness of the relation of acting to feeling: 'Woulds't have me cry, run raving mad up and down / for my son's loss? Would'st have me turn rank mad, / Or wring my face with *mimic action*,[18] / Stamp, curse, weep, rage, and then my bosom strike? / Away, 'tis *apish action, player-like*' (i, ii, 312–16).[19] Here, consciousness of *gesture* or *action* on the stage as distinct from self-expression are added to the sophisticated awareness created in the Induction. Again, it is a boy-actor in the illusion generated by his real-world grammar school identity. Similarly, when Pandulpho later 'breaks out': 'Why, all this while I ha' but play'd a part, / Like to some boy that acts a tragedy . . .' (iv, ii, 70–71), the reference directly evokes the grammar school tradition as a foil. 'Like to some boy' is not self-reflexive in the least, but differentiates between this particular actor and the general class of boy actors. Here, as elsewhere, Marston's efforts are consistently directed at showing that the Paul's boy-actors are sophisticated and capable of carrying an adult illusion.

In fact, Antonio's closing speech, framed as an Epilogue, is based squarely upon the assumption that the audience would find the boys successful in carrying their adult roles. Otherwise, his wish that a muse 'engage his pen to write' the tragedy of Mellida's death could only remind the audience of the boys' inadequacies. For that 'black tragedy' would consist of 'scenes suck'd up / By calm attention of choice audience' from whom the Epilogue would 'Instead of claps . . . obtain but tears.' If the *Antonio* plays were meant *or played* as parodies, Antonio's comments could only be taken as self-mockery following two hours of burlesque humour generated by the boys' inability to have such an effect upon an audience. That Antonio's plea is 'straight' and is intended to evoke 'tears,' and not laughs, is obvious from the tone of the passage, which is muted and grief-laden, quite unlike Marston's usual fare. There is no real reason to doubt the seriousness of the plea. It would be entirely in keeping with the judgment voiced by Jonson in his famous 'Epitaph on Saloman Pavey,' the only contemporary extra-dramatic evidence of the boys' ability to evoke such reactions. In the conceit of the 'Epitaph,' Pavey is credited with personating an aged man so effectively that the Fates were deceived into taking him although he only was 13 years old. It is no wonder that Caputi, Foakes, Shapiro and the rest of the parodists are totally silent about the evidence of the 'Epitaph,' especially since we have long known that Pavey was a member of the Paul's company when the *Antonio* plays were performed.

Overall, Marston interlaces the illusion of the Induction with the illusion of the plays, where the boy-actors continue to play the roles of grammar school students performing a play. Elizabeth M. Yearling has suggested that Marston's creation of the rhetorical awareness exhibited in these plays is intended to imbue his characters with a heightened self-awareness and thus distinguish them from the stock characters of the public theaters.[20] Her point is well-taken, so long as we remember that the rhetorical awareness is carried into the plays as part of the illusory identity created for the boy-actors in the Induction.

Finally, Marston's manipulation of the cathedral environment includes the other aspect of the boys' real-world identities as choristers. Gair has detailed the extensive use of music in the *Antonio* plays.[21] The distinction between real world and stage illusion virtually collapses in this context. Cornets sound 'florishes' and 'sennets' at least a dozen times. In addition to the numerous songs, including the singing contest in v, ii, the text calls for music from 'all the pleasing instruments of joy,' 'Lydian wires,' and 'still flutes.' According to Gair's estimate of the company's size, some of the instrumental music in the plays would have been performed by one or more of the actors, still in costume. If this innundation were not present within the plays, the nature of the evening's entertainment at Paul's would have provided a reminder of the boys' real-world identities. The *praeludium* preceding the performance as well as the *entr'act* musical interludes changed the stage space from its play-world illusion back to a showcase for the choristers performing, presumably, in costume.[22]

III

In short, if we 'try to get inside these plays as pieces for the theater,' as Foakes suggests, it is impossible to forget they are performances by boys. It seems to be begging the question to attribute anything but minor localized significance to those few scattered self-references which could possibly evoke size-disparity, given the nature of the Paul's performance and Marston's manipulation of the environment of the theater. The stage of Paul's, as I noted earlier, is not naked. A play written for the Globe can be produced by any troupe in any location without loss of intentional real-world associations – such plays are not rooted to their original playhouse. But it seems clear that the *Antonio* plays are. The only stage capable of supporting the multiple illusion of these plays is Paul's, nestled in the cloisters, with all the associations occasioned by that environment. To view them as unidimensional dramatic attempts at parody ignores not only the fundamental uniqueness of the theater, but of the audience's consciousness as well. A modern director attempting to produce the Induction with adult actors, it seems, would have to strain in order to make it relevant. This is perhaps the reason for the omission of the Induction in Peter Barnes' revival of the plays at the Nottingham Playhouse in 1979, where reviewers were unanimously enthusiastic about the success of the production. Moreover, Marston's manipulation of the boy-actors' real-world environment does not undercut the seriousness of the plays, as is frequently claimed. If anything, it enhances the credibility of the boy-actors and invites the audience to view the plays unrestricted by any sense of the actors' inadequacies in playing adult roles. Surely Marston's experimentation with the revenge tragedy convention suggests that he intended the *Antonio* plays to be taken seriously.[23]

However, the plays have their lighter side in the amusing spectacle performed by the boy-actors, whose identities are defined by the Paul's environment and the illusion of the Induction. In this context, they are not unlike the Inns' entertainments, where the complex nature of the dramatic illusion was quite similar. The Prince of Purpoole, however attired and bespeeched, derived his dramatic existence from Gray's Inn, the real-world space within which the pageant was played. Further, the real-world space subsumed in the dramatic illusion of the *Gesta Grayorum* of 1594 included the real-world identities and talents of the 'actors' in the form of their lengthy orations, the list of mock statutes of the Prince's realm, and of course, in their real-world absorption in the courtship of the opposite sex and bawdiness. The audience, moreover, was comprised (among other 'respected auditors') of Inns' colleagues equipped by training and vocation to appreciate the displays of oratory and pageantry which were the stuff of the revels. Beyond that, the illusion spilled into the space surrounding Gray's Inn, converting into tributaries of the Prince's illusory realm such locales as Tottenham, Clerkenwell, Paddington, Holborn, Islington and St Giles. Finally, it is worth noting that his 'progresse' wound through 'St Paul's Church-yard; where, at St Paul's School, His Highnesse was entertained with an Oration, made by one of the scholars of the School'.[24] The oration runs to some sixty lines of Ciceronian Latin, is laced with rhetorical figures, and undoubtedly was accompanied with appropriate *gesture*. For his incorporation of his real-world identity in the illusion of the Prince's 'progresse', the scholar received 'much thanks' for the 'entertainment' he provided. It does not seem far-fetched to assume that the *Antonio* performances were attended by some of those present at the 1594 revels. My discussion of the Induction and the *Antonio* plays could as easily have begun at this point in the Prince's 'progresse', for here we see the roots of Marston's use of the Paul's environment as an integral element of theatrical illusion.

## NOTES

1 See his 'John Marston's Fantastical Plays: *Antonio and Mellida*, and *Antonio's Revenge*', *PQ*, 41 (1962), 229–39: 'By the end of the Induction, in fact, it is clear that the play to follow will parody old ranting styles, make the children out-strut the adult tragedians, who were still performing the plays of Kyd and Marlowe, and burlesque common conventions,' and *Shakespeare: The Dark Comedies to the Last Plays: From Satire to Celebration* (Charlottesville, VA: University Press of VA, 1971). It is interesting to note that Kyd's *Spanish Tragedy* is a major target of the supposed parody of 'old ranting styles.' That this was still a popular play, and moreover, that Jonson wrote additions about this time to be performed along with the 'old ranting style' raises serious question as to whether it actually was seen by audiences as outmoded and as fruitful a butt of parody as Foakes claims. The reinterpretation of the boys' plays has led to their use as the basis for defining contemporary acting styles, an approach begun by Caputi. He argues that in the Induction, 'Marston unequivocally outlines an acting style weighted heavily with burlesque intention,' a conclusion which he supports by a 'heap' of conditional premises: 'If we grant that the sophisticated turn-of-the-century audience probably felt a disparity between what the children pretended to be and what they obviously were, surely it is not rash to assume that not only the audience, but the producers, the playwrights, and the actors as well were aware of this disparity. From this it is but a short step to conclude that they exploited this disparity not only for the "charm of the masquerade," but also for its inherent comic and satiric effects,' *John Marston, Satirist* (Ithaca: Cornell University Press, 1961), p. 103. Such 'short steps' produce a 'grand leap' and obscure the fact that the major premise itself is an assumption ungrounded in facts. For an even more astounding 'heap', see Michael Shapiro, 'Children's Troupes: Dramatic Illusion and Acting Style,' *Comparative Drama*, 3 (1969), p. 42.

2 'The Proof of the Parody,' *Essays in Criticism*, 24 (1974), 312–17. Levin's point is: 'Moreover, the Prologue and the Epilogue to *Antonio and Mellida* and the Prologue to *Antonio's Revenge*, all of which contain the conventional admission of 'imperfections' and plea for indulgence, never relate this to the youth of the actors (which is not even hinted at), let alone to any intention to exploit their youth' (313).

3 See 'The Presentation of Plays at Second Paul's: the Early Phase (1599–1602) [hereafter 'The Early Phase'], *The Elizabethan Theater VI*, ed. G. R. Hibbard (Toronto, 1977), pp. 21–47; 'Second Paul's: Its Theater and Personnel: Its Later Repertoire and Audience (1602–6), in *The Elizabethan Theater VII*, ed. G. R. Hibbard (Toronto, 1978), pp. 21–45; 'Introduction,' *John Marston: Antonio's Revenge*, ed. W. Reavley Gair (Revels Plays, Manchester, 1978), pp. 27–34; and Chapter 4 especially, *The Children of Paul's: The Story of a Theater Company, 1553–1608* (Cambridge: Cambridge University Press, 1982), pp. 113–46. In addition to describing the evolution of Paul's, he notes that Marston attempted 'to offer intimate glimpses of the organization, structure, and operational pattern of the choristers,' 'The Early Phase,' (p. 34).

4  See Clifford Leech, 'The Function of Locality in the Plays of Shakespeare and his Contemporaries,' in *The Elizabethan Theater I*, pp.103–16.

5  The concept and terms are introduced by Michael Shapiro, 'Children's Troupes: Dramatic Illusion and Acting Style,' *Comparative Drama*, 3 (1969), pp. 42–53, in his curiously circular argument about acting styles which echoes Caputi's (cited in note 1).

6  The details of the tradition are documented in Richard Brinsley, *Ludus Literarius* (1612); C. W. Wallace, *The Children of the Chapel at Blackfriars, 1597–1603* (Lincoln, 1908); and especially, H. N. Hillebrand, *The Child Actors: A Chapter in Elizabethan Stage History* (reprint, New York: Russell & Russell, 1964), pp. 1–39. In his necessarily brief but insightful summary, Andrew Gurr aptly describes the tradition: 'Acting in plays was customary in many schools in the sixteenth century as a tail on the necessary dog of oratory' (94), although he might have added that it was required statutorily in some schools, *The Shakespearean Stage, 1574–1642* (Cambridge: Cambridge University Press, 1980).

7  *An Apology for Actors (1612)* (New York: Scholars' Facsimiles & Reprints, 1941), Sig. C3, 9–12. He refers to Cicero, *Ad C. Herennium libri IV de ratione dicendi*, III, xi, 19 – III, xv, 27. A more extensive treatment of the subject is found in Quintilian's *Institutio oratoria*, book XI, where many comments comparing the orator's and stage-actor's delivery and gesture must have influenced acting styles in Marston's day, especially in the school performance tradition. Heywood's argument implies the importance of the tradition, for it is the basis of his defense of play-acting not merely by students, but by boys in the adult companies as well, where the presence of an educational motive is dubious at best. It is worth noting that in the famous oration scene in *Julius Caesar*, Marc Antony supports his claim to be 'a plain blunt man' who 'only speak[s] right on' by denying his oratorical skills specifically in terms of these rhetorical divisions: 'I am no orator, as Brutus is . . . and that they know full well that gave me public leave to speak . . . For I have neither wit [*invention*], words [*elocution*], nor worth [*disposition* in the sense of the judgment necessary to organizing matter], Action [in Heywood's sense], nor the power of speech [*pronunciation*] to stir men's blood' (III, ii, 218–224). Significantly, Antony's claim links a stereotype ('plain blunt man') with specific rhetorical traits and language, the formula Marston uses in the Induction.

8  Delivery was the ultimate goal toward which study of rhetorical theory was directed. Central to the process was the ability to match *pronunciation* and *gesture* to the matter (*logos, pathos*) of a speech as suggested by the figures used to express it. Heywood expresses the idea thus: 'It [playing] instructs him to fit his phrases to his action, and his action to his phrase, and his pronuntiation to them both' (Sig. C4, 7–9). The extent of knowledge required for effective delivery can be sensed from the discussion in book XI of the *Institutio Oratoria*.

9  Philip J. Finkelpearl, *John Marston of the Middle Temple, an Elizabethan Dramatist in His Social Setting* (Cambridge, Mass: Harvard University Press, 1969), reveals the emphasis upon matters rhetorical that permeated the Inns' environment and entertainments (see especially pp. 32–69). Similarly, Gair suggests that 'the audience was, if Marston can be trusted, "choice" and "select" – perhaps even personally invited. Certainly they were knowledgeable in contemporary theater

and familiar enough with Marston and Stanley to recognize them,' 'Second Paul's: Its Theater and Personnel: Its Later Repertoire and Audience (1602–6)', p. 33. The close connection between Inns' entertainments and the *Antonio* plays in their rhetorical inclinations and manipulation of environment makes Gair's suggestion highly probable.

10 A major portion of the parodist position is grounded in assumptions about the styles of acting utilized by both the adult and the child actors. The problem is that little or no evidence exists to support such assumptions. Shapiro admits as much in remarking that 'The paucity of external evidence makes it difficult to assess these conjectures about the acting style of the chorister troupes' (49). Lacking such evidence, he nonetheless proceeds to classify the probable acting styles for the boys' plays according to three types of formalism on the basis of 'the suitability of the particular style' to the plays. However, his 'suitability' criterion is developed without a single reference to the principles advanced in the rhetorics (and studied by the boys) regarding delivery, a flaw in methodology which is characteristic of the parodists in general. While this approach produces interesting reading, its results are mere conjecture and not historical demonstration.

11 See Cicero's discussion of this type of composition, *De Inventione*, I, xxiv, 34–7, and *Ad Herennium*, III, vi, 10 – III, ix, 15, the sources of Renaissance school-text material about stereotypes, relevant figures and techniques for descriptions of persons, and the thirteen attributes of persons which provide matter for *invention* (name, nature, manner of life, fortune, habit, feeling, interests, purposes, achievements, accidents, and speeches).

12 See Henry Peacham, *The Garden of Eloquence* (1593) (Scholars' Facsimiles & Reprints, Gainesville, 1954), pp. 138–9. Peacham is unique among Renaissance rhetoricians in choosing his term from the Greek rather than Latin sources. Marston is credited (*O.E.D.*) with the first use of the Greek derivative 'mimic' in place of the Latin 'imitation' in 1598 (*The Scourge*) to denote dramatic 'representation' of feigned persons (see note 18).

13 Rhetoricians commonly identified a recognizable style by noting its most famous proponent or originator, as in 'Lipsius his hopping style.' John Hoskins, with whom Marston was associated at the Inns, quite frequently uses this type of stylistic labeling in his *Directions for Speech and Style* (ed. Hoyt H. Hudson, Princeton: Princeton University Press, 1935), which he wrote for his nephews (who were about the same age as these actors). Marston's term 'tufty' very likely echoes Hoskins' 'tuftaffeta orators' (p. 17), a term commonly applied to the type of style used by Matzagente. 'Tufty' in the sense of 'short outbursts' (*O.E.D.*) simply doesn't make sense in this context.

14 In discussing *action* and *gesture*, terms which he uses interchangeably, Heywood cites a list of criteria to be followed, which he summarizes: '. . . to qualifie euery thing according to the nature of the person personated . . .' (Sig. C4, 26–27). The rhetorical principles employed in the Induction closely parallel Heywood's list, although both are derivative from the Latin rhetorics noted earlier. The introduction of the term 'personate' was intended to shift emphasis from the more mechanical 'acting' to the essence of effective representation of character on the stage, namely, the actor's imaginative experience of the emotions he

attempts to arouse in the spectators. So Hamlet, in the 'Hecuba' speech, is impressed that the player 'But in a fiction, in a dream of passion . . . .' Cicero praised the effectiveness and difficulty of personation: '. . . morum ac vitae imitatio vel in personis vel sive illis, magnum quoddam ornamentum orationis et aptum ad animos conciliandos vel maxime, saepe autem etiam ad commevendos; personarum ficta inductio, vel gravissimum lumen augendi . . .' (*De oratore*, III, 53, 204–5). Quintilian groups both *prosopographia* and *sermocinatio* under *fictiones personarum*, for 'certe sermo fingi non potest, ut non personae sermo fingatur' (*Institutio oratoria*, IX, ii, 32), and agrees with Cicero: 'Mire namque cum variant orationem, tum excitant' (IX, ii, 29). Hence, Heywood's defense of the moral benefits of acting is made specifically in terms of the actor's power to move through personation: '. . . what English blood seeing the person of any bold English man and doth not hugge his fame . . . as if the Personator were the man Personated, so bewitching a thing is liuely and spirited action, that it hath power to new mold the harts of the spectators and fashion them to the shape of any noble and notable attempt' (Sig. B4).

15  In Foakes' view, this interchange (Induction, lines 68–80) is somehow supposed to remind the audience that 'a lady was the appropriate part for a boy to play on the public stages, and strutting in a ranting role becomes grotesque in a child,' 'John Marston's Fantastical Plays,' p. 229. The logic of this leap has always eluded me, since the exchange calls attention to the inappropriateness of this boy's voice for a lady's role. Beyond that, there is no evidence that this group of boys 'strutted' and 'ranted' in performing the *Antonio* plays. In fact, the criticisms of exaggerated acting styles voiced in the Induction and the plays obviously prohibit such gesture and pronunciation.

16  In *An Apology*, Heywood notes that playing 'not onely emboldens a scholar to speake, but instructs him to speake well, and with judgement, to obserue his commas's [sic], colons, & full poynts, his parenthesis, his breathing spaces . . .' (Sig. C3v, 31–4), listing some of the usual basics of *pronunciation*. In one of the many references to *pronunciation* in the *Antonio* plays, Marston transforms these into an amorous context in the reunion of Antonio and Mellida (IV, i, 213–214), where Mellida describes their hoped for future: 'we'll point our speech / With amorous kissing, kissing commas . . .' Rossaline ends her lengthy 'grocery list' descriptions of suitors with: 'and there's the full point of my addiction' (v, ii, 43–68). Her 'pointing' is a good example of Marston's syntactical formula for representing the discourse of women as loosely related concatenated clauses lacking underlying logic. Macquerelle furnishes the classic example of this formula, especially act v, scene 2 of *The Malcontent*, where Malevole ends his mimicry of her style in exasperation: 'I can hunt the letter no farder: o God, how loathsome this toying is to me, that duke should be forc'd to foole it . . .' Indeed, the marked difference of syntactical structure in Marston's depiction of female speech confirms Antonio's fears.

17  The exact temporal relation of *Antonio's Revenge* to *Antonio and Mellida* is a disputed matter, as is the question of whether the two were conceived as a single work in a two-part structure. However, the Induction makes absolutely clear that a 'second part' is a possibility, depending upon audience receptiveness: 'Therefore I have heard that those persons, as he and you, Feliche, that are but

slightly drawn in this comedy, should receive more exact accomplishment in a
second part; which, if this obtain gracious acceptance, means to try his fortune'
(134–8). However, Feliche's role of 'firking satirist' is subsumed conventionally
in the figure of the revenger in tragedy; hence his role evaporated. That Feliche
is dismissed between the two plays seems clear evidence that Marston wrote and
played the Induction before writing *Antonio's Revenge* and quite possibly before
he had a clear concept of the sequel's plot, especially with regard to its impact
upon the Feliche role. Otherwise, the comment is inaccurate. That does not,
however, deflect credence from the intention of a second part. In any event, the
existence of the sequel clearly suggests that 'gracious acceptance' was forthcoming from audiences of *Antonio and Mellida*, and that the multiple-illusion
formula was a success. Gair's argument that audience reaction was negative and
his curious dating of the four early plays simply don't make sense either logically
or empirically (see 'The Early Phase,' 27–30). Furthermore, G. K. Hunter's
analysis of the parallel plot structures of the *Antonio* plays lends support to
arguments by earlier critics that the two plays probably were writen sequen-
tially (see his '*Henry IV* and the Elizabethan Two-Part Play,' *Review of English
Studies*, 19 (1954), 236–48).

18 Lost in the stampede to condemn Marston for his coinages, critics have
overlooked the possibility that, at least in some cases, Marston was making a
critical statement. His use of 'mimic' and 'personate' is a case in point. He may
have been the type of fellow who struggled through the *Poetics* and the Italian
literary critics for a deeper understanding of the dramatic art, despite Jonson's
depiction of him as Crispinus, a superficial faddish fop whose love of language is
equatable with that exhibited by Sir Jeffrey Balurdo.

19 Foakes believes that this is one of the references which suggest burlesque of the
exaggerated acting styles of adult common players, 'John Marston's Fantastical
Plays,' pp. 233–4. However, this is clearly impossible. Pandulpho specifically
rejects such gesture and certainly doesn't use it here, unless perhaps to illustrate
the gestures noted. Such an illustration would duplicate those seen in the
Induction. Further, the 'Ha, ha, ha' (line 310) of his previous speech indicates
the gesture he has used, and Alberto confirms that: 'Uncle, this laughter ill
becomes your grief' (line 311). Where is the burlesque if the gesture is lacking?

20 'These examples do not seem ironic pointers to dramatic unreality, but attempts
by Marston to render his characters more solid and lifelike by pointing out how
their demeanor contrasts with the usual behavior of stage tragedians. The effect
is quite sophisticated: we know we are watching a play, we are warned against
the melodramatic clichés of the stage, and then we are invited to see these people
as somehow different,' '"Mount tufty Tamberlaine": Marston and Linguistic
Excess,' *Studies in English Literature*, 20 (1980), 257–69.

21 See 'The Early Phase,' pp. 26, 37.

22 See *The Children of the Chapel*, pp. 106–18, regarding the format of the
performance.

23 Charles A. and Elaine S. Hallet, *The Revenger's Madness: A Study of Revenge Tragedy
Motifs* (Lincoln: University of Nebraska Press, 1980), provide the first detailed
analysis of Marston's use of the tradition. In their view, his treatment fails in
part because it is so accurate a portrayal, and because he attempts to integrate

two contradictory modes of the tradition – the revenging hero and the retribution of a tyrant motif – in a single character and action. Their point is that the modes are irreconcilable. The parodist approach denies the element of seriousness since, in Foakes' terms, 'The plays work from the beginning as vehicles for child-actors consciously ranting in oversize parts, and we are not allowed to take their passions or motives seriously. Their grand speeches are undermined by bathos or parody, and spring from no developed emotional situation, so that we are not moved by them, and do not take them seriously enough to demand justice at the end,' 'John Marston's Fantastical Plays,' p. 236. While the moral indignation of modern critics at the conclusion of *Antonio's Revenge* proves nothing about an Elizabethan audience's reaction, the unanimity of that critical response certainly suggests that they have indeed taken the play seriously enough to demand justice at the end.

24 *Gesta Grayorum (1688)* (Malone Society Reprints, 1914), 55. Hillebrand notes that 'learned orations in Latin' were standard entertainments for dignitaries visiting grammar schools (see *The Child Actors*, p. 33).

# Philippe James de Loutherbourg and the early pictorial theatre: some aspects of its cultural context*

CHRISTOPHER BAUGH

When Philippe de Loutherbourg replied to David Garrick by offering his proposals for scenic and administrative change at Drury Lane in 1772, the English theatre had been operating an elegant, highly workable and architecturally sound compromise for a little over one hundred years. The essence of this compromise concerned the relative space allocated to audience, actors and scenery. It was a compromise which took into account the well-established conventions of acting developed by the theatre prior to 1642, the excitement and novelty of perspective scenery and also the demands of an audience for a clearly defined relationship with the events witnessed and their social expectations about theatre-going.

My aim will be to suggest that the proposals of de Loutherbourg herald the collapse of this compromise and imply a radical re-evaluation of the theatre space. It will not be my intention to try to confer upon de Loutherbourg the status of a conscious theatre revolutionary; information about his theatre career is sparse and he left no body of theoretical writings. Further, as Sybil Rosenfeld has amply proved,[1] almost all the scenic innovations sometimes credited to his decade in the theatre had appeared in one form or another upon the London stage before his arrival in England. The theatrical significance of de Loutherbourg is twofold. First, his letter to Garrick and his practice in the theatre brought together effects and techniques which had hitherto had an occasional or sporadic existence within scenic practice. Second and more important, the bringing together of these techniques constituted a coherent new vision of the theatre space; a vision which represented a distinct turning point in performance convention and which was to have major effects upon the theatre for the next one hundred years. It was, I believe, a vision which was anticipated and significantly paralleled by cultural prerogatives outside the small world of eighteenth-century theatre. A new language of theatre emerged whose grammar dominated the theatre until its syntax was mercilessly exposed as being false by the twin onslaught of three-dimensional realism and the

* A draft of this paper was read at the *Themes in Drama* International Conference held at the University of London, Westfield College in March 1985.

glare of electric lighting during the last years of the nineteenth century.

David Garrick's action in requesting new scenic ideas in the early 1770s may be described as either an action fully in keeping with his managerial role as arbiter of theatrical taste and also with his personal development as a man of his time, or as giving in to pressure from Covent Garden and performing a theatrical *volte face* upon his initial manifesto so clearly stated in Johnson's well-known inaugural prologue of 1747:

> 'Tis yours this night to bid the reign commence
> Of rescu'd Nature, and reviving Sense;
> To chase the charms of Sound, the pomp of show,
> For useful mirth, and salutary woe;
> Bid scenic virtue form the rising age,
> And truth diffuse her radiance from the stage.

Of course, as the conscientious manager which his letters show him to have been, Garrick could not ignore the competition. Through John Rich, Covent Garden had some years before nailed its colours firmly to the spectacular mast and regularly imported foreign scenic talent to provide specific scenes for that theatre. But, although never shying away from a Thespian battle, Garrick does seem to move towards a new relationship with 'the charms of Sound, the pomp of show', gradually and in his own good time.

The first trip to France in 1751 shows him to have been impressed with the scenic effects which he saw, but he appears to be in two minds about the staging arrangements at the Comédie Française:

> the Appearance of y$^e$ house was not so bad as I expected from y$^e$ report of others, y$^e$ glass branches gave it a rich look, but y$^e$ candles instead of lamps at y$^e$ front of y$^e$ stage are very mean & y$^e$ building on y$^e$ stage wholly destroys all *vraysemblance* (as y$^e$ french call it) & with all their perfection, occasions ten thousand absurdities –

and adds,

> I am not certain there is not an advantage to y$^e$ actors & audience from y$^e$ shape of their theatre.[2]

I assume that Garrick's doubts refer to the audience structures built on either side of the stage which would indeed have hampered scenic illusion. But for a performer, the proximity of this audience and their location upon three sides would be attractive. Whatever Garrick's doubts may have been, it is generally concluded that this first overseas excursion not only increased his confidence but also widened his appreciation of theatre as a multi-faceted art. Perhaps he also felt that he could one day reconcile 'sense' and 'show'.

Before his next, more extended, European travels, he mounted his elaborate *Antony and Cleopatra* early in 1759 and before the end of the same

6 David Garrick's house at Hampton, Middlesex. From William Watts, *Seats of the Nobility and Gentry*, in a collection of the most interesting and picturesque views, London, 1779.

7 James Thornhill, design for *Arsinoe, Queen of Cyprus*, Act II, sc. iii, Drury Lane Theatre, 1705. (Victoria and Albert Museum)

year he challenged Rich on his own ground by giving 'sense' to pantomime dumb show in introducing the first speaking Harlequin in *Harlequin's Invasion*. The tour of 1763–5 shows another aspect of Garrick's personality which adds to the feeling that by 1772 he and Drury Lane were 'ready' for the ideas of de Loutherbourg. Although by no means possessing the antiquarian fervour of a Kemble, Garrick's letters home are filled with reports of his keen interest in landscape and location. 'I am antiquity-hunting from Morning to Night', he reported from Rome.[3] Throughout his travels he was an avid collector of books and prints as well as practical scenic ideas for immediate implementation at Drury Lane.[4] The timing of this tour is apt since *Herculaneum* (1738) and *Pompei* (1748) had just been published in *Le antichita di Ercolano* in 1757 and John Winkelmann published the enormously influential *History of Ancient Art* in 1764. Garrick's lifelong friend, Robert Adam, had just returned from his three-year study of antiquity in 1757 and, of course, Lessing's *Laokoon* was to come in 1766.

During the season following his return in 1765, his modifications to theatre practice take on a greater significance. He had already cleared the stage of audience by the season of 1762–3. He now removed the overhead candelabra as a main source of stage lighting and counterweighted the footlights so that a lowering of the entire trough of lamps below the stage could effect a dimming of the stage light.[5] He also introduced, as an important source of light, upright battens of lampholders which were hung behind wing shutters. Whilst the removal of on-stage audience can be seen as a measure to help maintain the actors' oft-threatened dignity, bearing in mind Garrick's response to practice at the Comédie Française, it may also be interpreted as a desire to remove an anomalous visual element even though it meant the sacrifice of a degree of intimacy with the audience. The concomitant reduction in the depth of the forestage, usually interpreted as placating his partner Lacy in the treasury and the actors' benefit takings, may also be seen as the early stirrings of the desire to perceive the theatre event as a whole, complete image – to maintain *vraysemblance*. Alien to such an image would have been the glaring presence of the overhead lighting and it is symptomatic of a changing theatrical sensibility that the response was universally favourable:

> The public were agreeably surprised on the opening of Drury Lane theatre, to see the stage illuminated with a strong clear light, and the rings removed which used to supply it.[6]
> ... the disposition of lights behind the scenes ... cast a reflection forwards exactly resembling sunshine.[7]

During the subsequent seasons before his engagement of de Loutherbourg, Garrick can be seen committing himself more and more to such 'charms of Sound' and 'pomp of show'. Regularly increasing the number of dancers and musicians in the company, spending more upon new scenes

8 Artificial ruin of a Roman arch, Kew Gardens, engraving, ca. 1776. (Victoria and Albert Museum)

9 de Loutherbourg, scene model for *Omai, or a Trip Round the World*, Kensington Gardens, Covent Garden Theatre, 1785. (Victoria and Albert Museum)

and costumes, he devoted more time and energy to producing his 'entertainments'. In this context, entertainment is as elusive a term as 'burletta'. D'Archenholz describes it later in the century and ties together for us several aspects of this changing taste:

> Among the number of *peculiarities* belonging to the English Playhouses, may be reckoned the afterpieces called ENTERTAINMENTS. These for the most part, consist of a happy mixture of dialogue, song and dance; the decorations are amazing; and the machinery is carried to the most astonishing perfection. The people are uncommonly attached to this kind of diversion. All the great events that occur to the nation are dramatised and represented on the stage.[8]

Bowing out of really serious competition with Covent Garden over the staging of the Coronation of George III in 1760, Garrick now forced the competition by following up the 'great event' of the Stratford Shakespeare Jubilee of early September 1769 by his 'entertainment' called *The Jubilee* with its spectacular procession of Shakespeare characters. This played ninety times during the 1769–70 season and must have done something to recoup the expensive disappointments of the real event. George Colman at Covent Garden hastily put out his *Man and Wife; or, The Shakespeare Jubilee.*

Although still the undisputed monarch of the acting profession, Garrick actually performed less and less; fewer than twenty times during the 1771–2 season. His energies became more and more concerned with devising new material and directing the company whose numbers had risen to ninety-five performers by 1770. Jean Monnet's letter of introduction on behalf of de Loutherbourg ('un de nos plus grands peintres, et garçon fort aimable') could well have fallen upon an aesthetically prepared and sympathetic potential employer. Critical tradition, at this point, usually lays stress upon Garrick importing some fashionable scenic talent, mounting a popular and lucrative 'entertainment' and being left with the scene-room well stocked with useful scenery for future use. Although it was indeed fashionable to import talent, it is unlikely that de Loutherbourg's artistic reputation had spread to England.[9] It has been suggested that he might have known Servandoni and perhaps have worked in the French theatre,[10] but there is no evidence to suggest that he met Garrick with a substantial record of theatrical success behind him. The letter of introduction and the evidence of easel paintings and sketches which de Loutherbourg must have brought over with him or done as a trial for Garrick, seem to have been sufficient to commit the cautious and astute manager to the enormous salary of £300 which de Loutherbourg requested for the first three months' work at the close of the 1771–2 season.

De Loutherbourg's letter to Garrick (see Appendix p. 000) is brief, self-assured and very much to the point. Judging by its opening remarks it was written at Garrick's request for further information. It is made clear from the opening lines that what is being proposed is a new approach to scenic

10 Fireplace designed by Robert Adam for Garrick's house at 4 Adelphi Terrace, ground floor, front room, 1772. (Victoria and Albert Museum)

decoration with all its necessary machinery. This is not a letter from a painter asking that he may design a single production or set of scenes. It is worth quoting the short central section of the letter in which de Loutherbourg gives specific details of his approach.

. . . I must make a small model of the settings and everything which is required, to scale, painted and detailed so as to put the working painters and machinists and others on the right track by being able to faithfully copy my models, and, if I deem it necessary to retouch something in the final display, to enhance the

11 de Loutherbourg, *Smugglers Landing in a Storm*, oil.on canvas, 1791. (Victoria Art Gallery, Bath)

12 de Loutherbourg, *Lake Wynandermere*, engraving by William Pickett. From *The Romantic and Picturesque Scenery of England and Wales*, London, 1805: reprinted by The Scolar Press, Ilkley, 1979. (Ironbridge Gorge Museum Trust)

effect, then I must do so. I shall draw in colour the costumes for the actors and the dancers. I must discuss my work with the composer and the ballet-master.

The letter continues by requesting complete control over the Drury Lane work force, suggests his fee of £300, informs that there are seven models ready to be painted and concludes by asking Garrick to name the day and time when they may meet and go into further detail. In such terse, confident and almost arrogant terms, a theatrically untried easel painter puts forward the job description of the modern scenographer.

It has already been noted that Garrick's thinking may well have been moving him towards such a position before he received de Loutherbourg's letter. I believe, however, that there are other factors which may act as corollaries to help us to understand the extent and implications of this break with tradition. Henceforward the stage could be viewed as a harmonious and completed vision into a world not participated in by its immediate audience – a 'window on the world' for an essentially passive spectator. This is the aesthetic culmination of the monoscenic vision of the Italian Renaissance; the logical conclusion of Inigo Jones's introduction of the proscenium arch, not only as an apposite frontispiece and masking device but as the architectural expression of an entire concept of theatre.

In the latter part of the eighteenth century this must be seen as a perfectly 'harmonious' step for the theatre to take whether de Loutherbourg had appeared on the scene or not. As such it is worth considering it alongside other cultural activities of the period. The ordered 'composing' of the English landscape by the great gardeners; the authority and unifying control given to a Capability Brown or a Humphrey Repton are neatly paralleled by de Loutherbourg's requests. Brown had already laid out the grounds of Garrick's house at Hampton in 1754 (plate 6), being initially called upon to unify with his 'comprehensive eye' the two halves of the estate.[11] He seems to have met a kindred sensibility in the actor who said:

> I own I love a good Situation prodigiously, & I think the four great Requisites to make one are, Wood, Water, Extent & inequality of Ground.[12]

These great gardeners' rejection of the formal gardens with their symmetrical borders, avenues of trees and topiary hedges where:

> lions and unicorns guard the corners of his parterres, and a spread-eagle of remarkable growth, has his wings clipped and his talons pared the first Monday of every month during spring and summer[13]

may be compared with the theatrical rejection of the *à volonté* formality of the French theatre or the scenic style represented by Thornhill's designs for *Arsinoe* (1707) (plate 7), in favour of the looser compositions of John Inigo Richards or de Loutherbourg (plate 9). Many a mid-to-late eighteenth-century country villa provided itself with windows like proscenium arches

13 de Loutherbourg, *Llanberis Lake*, oil on canvas, ca. 1786. (Musée des Beaux-Arts, Strasbourg)

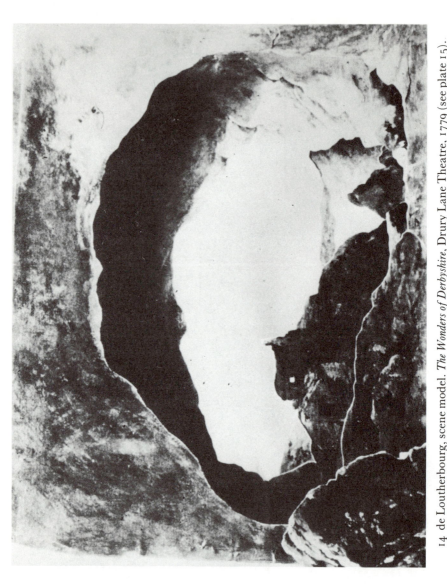

14 de Loutherbourg, scene model. *The Wonders of Derbyshire*, Drury Lane Theatre, 1779 (see plate 15). (Victoria and Albert Museum)

15  de Loutherbourg, *Peak's Hole Derbyshire*, engraving by William Pickett. From *The Romantic and Picturesque Scenery of England and Wales*. (Ironbridge Gorge Museum Trust)

through which to view the unified picture of the designed landscape with its created irregularities and uneven ground, scenically planted 'dead' trees and distant hermitage or temple to 'close' the prospect. Whilst employing Brown and actively participating in the taste for 'improvements', Garrick could still make stage capital out of such 'garden-mania'. Act II, scene 2 of Garrick and Colman's *The Clandestine Marriage* shows Mr Sterling contemplating his ruins which have cost him £150 to put 'in thorough repair', his spire 'built against a tree a field or two off, to terminate the prospect', and his 'little gothick dairy' where his sister wishes Lord Ogleby to 'take a dish of tea' or 'a sullabub warm from the cow'. The theatrical parallel is clear, between the contrivance of the scene designer and the landscape gardener clumping his trees, arranging his hills, digging his 'ha-has', laying out his serpentines, constructing the cascades of 'tin' water and building his ruins (plate 8) to create 'natural' scenes which could play upon the emotions of the spectator. As such they are both, in their ways, ingenious stage managers, carefully studying and arranging their effects.

The unifying process moved indoors and when the Garricks left their Southampton Street house and moved into the Adam brothers' newly built Adelphi Terrace in February 1772, the actor had the entire interior designed and furnished under the Adams' unifying supervision (plate 10). Pleased with the effects of this work, he commissioned Robert Adam to design a classical façade for the villa at Hampton two years later.

Although the etymology of the word 'picturesque' is varied and complex, its accepted meaning during the eighteenth century seems clear. It denotes an object or view worthy and reminiscent of a painted picture. Judgement of such views was initially based upon a similarity to the paintings of Claude Lorrain, Nicolas Poussin and Salvator Rosa. The wild mountain scenes of the latter with their implications of extreme human activity have been noted as a possible influence in de Loutherbourg's work (plate 11).[14] Closer to home, by the last decades of the century, tourism and antiquity-hunting flourished all over the British Isles. This was considerably aided by improvements in the stage-coach network and the turnpike roads were accounted the best in Europe. The Rev. Gilpin in his *Three Essays* (1792) gives us a clear picture:

> But among all the objects of art, the picturesque eye is perhaps most inquisitive after the elegant relics of ancient architecture; the ruined tower, the Gothic arch, the remains of castles and abbeys. These are the richest legacies of art. They are consecrated by time; and almost deserve the veneration we pay to the works of nature itself.

The romantic concern with the relationship between human emotion and natural phenomena; the seeking for scenic and locational equivalences to mental states, begins a long tradition of theatrical meteorology, shipwrecks and stormy seas, volcanoes and earthquakes, fires and avalanches. Add

16 Drottningholm Court Theatre, stage-setting, ca. 1785. (Drottningholm Theatre Museum, Stockholm)

such phenomena to Gilpin's list and we have almost the entire vocabulary of the melodramatist's scenic vocabulary. The inevitable excesses of the picturesque are instantly recognizable as those which befell the theatre. Performance conventions are neatly catalogued by William Beckford in his 'Captivating Scenery' from *Modern Novel Writing, or the Elegant Enthusiast* (1796):

> Round this cave no gaudy flowers were ever permitted to bloom; this spot was sacred to pale lilies and violets . . . Here stretched supinely on a bed of moss, the late Lord Mahogany would frequently pass the sultry hours of the day, and here its present worthy possessor Lord Charles Oakley would sometimes also indulge himself . . . Here he formed schemes of delusive joys, stifling the rising sigh, stopped the flowing tear, and in social converse with his dear friend Henry Lambert would oftentimes smoke a comfortable pipe, when the soft radiance of the moon played upon the pearly bosom of the adjacent waters.

The ardent tourist combing the Lake District[15] and mountains of Wales or Scotland in search of the picturesque (plates 12, 13), would frequently carry along with them a series of devices which could assist in the framing, composing and lighting of the real world. The 'Claude' glass,[16] named after the painter, seems to have been the most popular. It consisted of a slightly convex mirror, tinted smoky grey and mounted in a folding case. Standing with his or her back to the real view, the spectator watched the scene, composed and unified in the glass and looking like a painting or a well-lit stage picture. The tinting of the mirror helped to light the scene atmospherically and render the distant hills suitably misty and 'romantic'. Amongst the guidebooks and viewing glasses of the really dedicated seeker after such 'shows', there would be found sketchbooks and tiny boxes of the newly invented moist cakes of watercolour. It is, of course, no coincidence that the medium of watercolour should flourish in this environment and that the necessary pigment technology should appear. The rapidity of its technique and its essential translucency made it an ideal, portable medium to capture the fleeting light, the random view or unique location. De Loutherbourg received some training in chemistry and is reputed to have made innovations in pigment- and paint-making.[17] Paint quality was to become an increasing concern of both easel and scene painter. New colours and manufacturing processes were a regular by-product of the Industrial Revolution and, by the early years of the nineteenth century, this technology was to make available to the scene-painter colours which hitherto had only been available in the quantities needed by the easel painter.[18]

The words 'location' and 'locational' have appeared several times and it is clear that interest in and demand for topographical recognizability – both easel and theatrical – was manifest. Paintings begin to appear with very detailed titles: Richard Wilson's *Llyn-y-Cau, Cader Idris* (1774), Wright of Derby's *Cromford Mill, Matlock by Moonlight* (1782–3), Girtin's *The White*

17 de Loutherbourg, model pieces for a sea-coast scene: *Robinson Crusoe*, Drury Lane Theatre, 1781. (Victoria and Albert Museum)

*House, Chelsea* (1800) exemplify much of the atmospheric and locational qualities which were in demand. Neatly linking for us several themes of contemporary taste, Elizabeth Montagu visited Vauxhall gardens in July 1754 'where Mr. Tyers has had the ruins of Palmyra painted in the manner of the scenes so as to deceive the eye and appear buildings'.[19]

It would seem only natural, therefore, that de Loutherbourg's theatre work should receive consistent reference and praise for atmosphere and recognizability. The *London Magazine* (November 1774) reports on the production of Burgoyne's *The Maid of Oaks*:

The most remarkable scenes were Mr. Oldsworth's mansion, which we are informed is taken from a view of Lord Stanley's house and improvements: the portico is in an imitation of the temporary building at the late celebrated Fête Champêtre; the magnificent scene of the saloon is also similar to that noble-man's apartment, which changes to one of the most beautiful scenes ever exhibited, representing a celestial garden, terminated by a prospect of the Temple of Love, in which the statue of the Cyprian goddess appears in the attitude of the Venus of the Medicis. The background is illuminated by the rays of the sun, which have a most splendid and astonishing effect.

For Garrick's many social acquaintances this must have offered an extra pleasure since, on the 20th of August in the same year, the Garricks held what the *London Chronicle* called 'a splendid entertainment or Fête Champêtre at [their] gardens at Hampton'[20] to celebrate their twenty-fifth wedding anniversary. After a concert of music there was shown the 'Temple of Shakespeare and the gardens were illuminated with 6000 lamps, and the forge of Vulcan made a splendid appearance'.[21] This latter was the work of another of Garrick's 'imports', the French pyrotechnist Torré,[22] who arrived with de Loutherbourg also carrying a letter of introduction from Monnet.

Location and recognizable topography could obviously feature as the subject matter of theatre. In 1778 the astute and tightfisted Sheridan paid out £35 expenses to de Loutherbourg to make sketching trips to Kent and the Derbyshire Peak district to prepare for forthcoming Drury Lane attractions. One of the results of this summer research was perhaps the theatre's first travelogue and ancestor of the panoramas and dioramas of the nineteenth century. *The Wonders of Derbyshire* (January 1779) would seem to encapsulate so much of the cultural context to which I have referred (plates 14, 15).[23]

Given that Garrick's personal taste, his theatre practice and the sensibility of the audience were all, in some way, already moving towards de Loutherbourg's ideas, what are the implications in terms of the theatre space? Practical solutions to de Loutherbourg's scenic vision are based upon an extension, and a more thorough use of the laws of perspective. The real world of three dimensions is broken up into a series of two-dimensional planes. By carefully placing these, one behind the other, *and* illuminating them with equal care so that the individual planes might merge into one another, the original three-dimensionality could be reconstituted within the mind of the spectator. Such illumination was essential, otherwise a dark shadow would outline each plane and separate it from the next upstage surface. Photographs of the surviving contemporary scenes at Drottningholm, excessively lit – presumably for photographic purposes – clearly show the dangers (plate 16). And of course, the floor surface must be similarly treated. Although ground-rows[24] were in use during the earlier years of the eighteenth century and indeed had been used by Jones and

18 de Loutherbourg, *The Needles, Isle of Wight*, engraving by William Pickett. From *The Romantic and Picturesque Scenery of England and Wales*. (Ironbridge Gorge Museum Trust)

Riot at Covent Garden Theatre, in 1763, in consequence of the Managers refusing to admit half-price in the Opera of Artaxerxes.

19 L. Boitard, interior of Covent Garden Theatre, the 'Fitzgiggio' riot in progress, 1763.

Webb for their 'scenes of relieve', the stage floor of the late seventeenth and early eighteenth century was essentially flat, featureless and dramatically neutral. As the surviving designs and model fragments show, de Loutherbourg consistently 'orchestrated' the floor surface – treating it scenically as much as he treated the sides, back and upper surfaces of the stage space (plates 17, 18). The stage floor becomes an area capable of being as visually committed as the wings, backshutters or cloths and the 'cloudings'. The logic of such a commitment achieves its fullest architectural and structural expression in the sloats, bridges and trapwork of the nineteenth-century mechanized stage-house.

A considerable theatrical and ultimately architectural problem now occurred which neither Garrick nor his designer was to resolve during their theatre practice. This was, of course, the crucial relationship between the performers on their traditionally neutral forestage and the on-stage, increasingly complete, scenic world. Hitherto the balance had been maintained by the elegant compromise of a tripartite theatre space: a place for the audience, a place for the performer and a place for a scenic statement (plate 19). The scenic statement was a decorative, locationally apposite backing against which the dramatic action was played. Obviously there are countless plays prior to this period which demand physical contact between the player and the scenery.[25] Opera also, with its traditionally heavy reliance upon spectacle, frequently called for close interaction between performer and setting. But the use of the locationally neutral proscenium doors as the principal means of entrance and exit from the stage, maintained a just and delicate relationship between actor and scene. The frequently re-occurring locations of pre-romantic drama allowed for a stock scenic system kept justly 'in its place' by performer and theatre architect. The well-known passage from *The Case of the Stage in Ireland* is worth quoting here since it provides such a clear feeling for the place of scenery before the time of de Loutherbourg:

> The stage should be furnished with a competent number of painted scenes sufficient to answer the purpose of all the plays in the stock, in which there is no great variety, being easily reduced to the following classes, 1st, Temples, 2dly, Tombs, 3rdly, City walls and gates. 4thly, Outsides of palaces, 5thly, Insides of palaces. 6thly, Streets. 7thly, Chambers. 8thly, Prisons, 9thly, Gardens. And 10thly, Rural prospects of groves, forests, deserts, &c. All these should be done by a master, if such can be procured; otherwise they should be as simple and unaffected as possible, to avoid offending a judicious eye. If for some particular purpose, any other scene is necessary, it can be got up occasionally.[26]

The full implications of de Loutherbourg's proposals, the unity, the control, the suggested harmony (*résonner*) of all the elements, run counter to this practice and the sensibility which animated it. It must, however, be stressed that the stock system did not disappear overnight; that de Loutherbourg and his immediate scenic successors were primarily concerned with pantomime, musical theatre and 'entertainments', and that it was not really until the close of the century that the 'legitimate' drama was to use scenery as one of its leading characters.

The main features of the architecture, established by Wren in the 1670s, had changed little. But now, the still extensive forestage was becoming something of an anomaly when set against the more fully realized image of a, perhaps recognizable, picturesque world beyond. This forestage, set firmly within the same architectural volume and, until the 1760s, lit by the same candelabra, allowed and demanded a very special relationship between performer and the audience. For example, this 'being one' with the audience made the practice of wearing contemporary clothes utterly logical and right for the shared space. Token aspects of 'period' or character were acceptable and allowable as they still might be in the drawing-room charade. Indeed, fully realized and researched costume for all characters would have appeared positively out of keeping with the theatre space. Ultimately, the performer just had aesthetically and physically to 'fit in' and be unified – perhaps even controlled – as another element in the pictorial world created in the theatre. It is significant, I think, that in such a short letter, de Loutherbourg should lay such stress upon costume design and its harmonizing with other elements. The theatrical and dramaturgical conventions of which the forestage was an expression, could have no future relationship with the controlled visions now beginning to appear upstage.

Whatever might have been the real reasons for de Loutherbourg's early retirement from the theatre – moving on to what he considered higher things, financial problems with Sheridan – it is true to say that the theatre, whilst welcoming him for what he had to offer, was not yet ready to accept the full consequences of his proposals. The *Eidophusikon* offered him a small-scale opportunity to further his techniques (plate 20). The real theatre had to await the huge theatre buildings of the 1790s, the antiquarian concerns of Kemble and his designer, Capon, and the full dramatic consequences of a pictorial sensibility. Sheridan's *Pizarro*[27] meets this sensibility and the player, often complaining and resisting, is pulled away from his tradition-blessed place with the audience into the box of tricks behind the proscenium arch.

Although I have referred to the audience as essentially passive within this new theatre relationship, tourism, the rage for seeing spectacular sights and their attendant literature, clearly show the emotional relationship between spectacle and spectator. As the tourist, Mr Ockendon, and his party, approached the southern shore of Innisfallen by boat in 1760, they were:

> quite transported with a marvellous scene of pure nature . . . more exquisite than any I had ever seen, either in France, Italy, or England: . . . we rested

20 E. F. Burney, *The Eidophusikon of de Loutherbourg*, ca. 1782. (Trustees of the British Museum)

upon our oars within the bowery bosom of this sublime theatre . . . and
remained enraptured with the beauties we beheld.[28]

The witnessing of visual spectacle as an aid to emotional escapism would
seem to have strong eighteenth-century roots. The emotional power and
attraction of such pictorialism was to create a theatre form which could –
within the subsequent one hundred years – be strong enough to create its
own material, its own unified product which the writer would merely serve,
in Rowell's term, as 'handyman' to the needs of the theatre.[29]

Demographic and social reasons are usually cited as the principal agents
in the formation of this new theatre:

> The rowdy, illiterate new audiences crowded into the theatres, requiring their
> interest to be roused by vigorous action, their emotions moved by pathos, and
> their troubles soothed by a happy ending. Forced to reject much of the
> Georgian repertory, the new theatre found itself without a drama and had too
> often to substitute spectacle. In these hand-to-mouth conditions manager,
> actor and author were content if their public was caught and briefly held by a
> new offering. There was no time or occasion to question the standards of that
> offering.[30]

The reasons for the lack of so-called 'literary' quality within the theatre of
this period obviously lie much deeper than Rowell suggests and it is clearly
wrong to charge the first-generation urban working class, important
though this factor is, with such complete responsibility for this change. I
have tried to suggest that delight and concern for the spectacular and the
pictorial have much deeper roots which cut across the classes in which the
theatre played its traditional leading and following role. It may also be true
that the forces which energized and rejuvenated the visual imagination
during the latter half of the eighteenth century were perhaps not of a kind to
have a corresponding influence upon dramatic literature. B. Sprague Allen
concludes his study of antiquarian classicism:

> The greater knowledge of antiquity that accompanied more systematic arch-
> eological research and the excavation of seats of ancient culture, as well as the
> measured drawings and study of buildings . . . stimulated the sense of beauty
> and invigorated architecture, interior decoration, and other formal arts. But
> such activities were not likely to affect literature as would undoubtedly have
> been the case if, as in the Italian Renaissance, precious Greek and Roman
> manuscripts had come to light and amazed mankind.[31]

Responding to antiquarianism, classicism, landscape, tourism and the
picturesque, the theatre found a new, radically different voice. This voice
initially reflected the concerns and interests of all classes. Demographic
change and urban conditions quickly allowed this voice to become a
proletarian voice and, for the first time in English theatre history, took
control of that voice as patron. Within the continuum of this cultural
reaction, de Loutherbourg is to be seen as a major catalyst. His proposals to

Garrick and his short theatre career organized the practice of the stage to respond more closely to this movement and his work implies the spatial, architectural and performance conventions which the theatre subsequently adopted.

## NOTES

1 See Sybil Rosenfeld, *Georgian Scene Painters and Scene Painting* (Cambridge, Cambridge University Press, 1981), pp. 42–3 *et passim*.

2 Ryllis C. Alexander (ed.), *The Diary of David Garrick, Being a Record of His Memorable Trip to Paris in 1751* (New York, 1928, Blom, 1971), p. 5. Garrick would have seen at least four rows of audience ranged on either side of the forestage separated from the performers by iron railings. Up to fifty people as audience may also have been forming a semicircle behind the performers, in the wings, etc., *ibid.*, pp. 58–9.

3 D. M. Little & G. M. Kahrl (eds.) *The Letters of David Garrick*, 3 vols. (London: Oxford University Press, 1963), I: letter 329, 11th April 1764, to George Colman.

4 Little & Kahrl, *ibid.*, letter 329 concludes: 'I have sent the plan of a fine Scene & colour'd, . . . it is in several parts & wrote upon $y^e$ back which is 1st 2d &c (I will send a further explanation of it, but any Italian & our Saunderson will understand it – they $sh^d$ go upon it directly, it will have a fine Effect.' Saunderson (Saunders, Sanders, Sanderson) was the carpenter at Drury Lane.

5 Richard Leacroft suggests in *The Development of the English Playhouse* (London: Eyre Methuen, 1973), p. 118, that the 'counterpoize to front lamps 170lbs' included in the *Covent Garden Inventory* (1743) implies that Covent Garden already operated this practice. This may be the case; or Garrick may have introduced a new method of doing this; or the Covent Garden 'counterpoize' may well have been used to assist in the raising and lowering of the forestage candelabra for candle-changing purposes. The 'front lamps' of the *Inventory* could refer to either foot- or overhead lights.

6 Gösta Bergman, *Lighting in the Theatre* (Stockholm, 1977), p. 216, quoting *Universal Magazine*, September 1765.

7 *Annual Register*, September 1765.

8 Cecil Price, *Theatre in the Age of Garrick* (Oxford: Blackwell, 1973), p. 76, quoting D'Archenholz, *A Picture of England* (Dublin, 1791), p. 236.

9 Almost every entry in Garrick's diary of his 1751 visit to Paris (see note 2) contains references to his abiding love of pictures and galleries. It is possible that on his later visit to Paris in 1765 he may have encountered the young de Loutherbourg who was busy building his easel reputation.

10 P. H. Highfill, Jr, K. A. Burnim, E. A. Langhans, *A Biographical Dictionary of Actors, Actresses, Musicians, Dancers, Managers & Other Stage Personnel in London, 1660–1800* (Carbondale: Southern Illinois University Press, 1978). Hereafter *B.D.*, vol. IV, p. 300.

11 See Edward Hyams, *Capability Brown and Humphry Repton* (London: Dent, 1971), p. 49.

12 Little & Kahrl, *The Letters of David Garrick*, vol. I, letter 126, 4th July 1753.

13 B. Sprague Allen, *Tides in English Taste 1619–1800* (New York: Pageant, 1958), vol. II, p. 194, quoting *The Mirror*, nos. 61–8.

14 See Sybil Rosenfeld, *A Short History of Scene Design in Great Britain* (Oxford: Blackwell, 1973), p. 87.

15 The taste of the preceding generation had been decidedly different. Guy Miège in *The New State of England* (London, 1691), vol. I, p. 236, describes Westmorland as 'one of the worst Counties in England', preferring the more southerly counties because they were 'generally a flat and open Country, not over grown with wild and unwholsom Forests, nor dreadful high Mountains'.

16 For a full account of this and similar devices, see Michael Clarke, *The Tempting Prospect: A Social History of English Water Colours* (London: Colonnade, 1981), p. 33.

17 See *B.D.*, vol. IV, p. 30.

18 For a full treatment of innovation in pigment technology, see R. D. Harley, *Artists' Pigments c. 1600–1835*, 2nd edn (London: Butterworth Scientific, 1982); see also John R. Wolcott, 'The Scene Painters' Palette: 1750–1835', in *Theatre Journal*, Dec. 1981, pp. 477–88.

19 Emily J. Climenson, *Elizabeth Montagu, the Queen of the Blue-Stockings* (London: Murray, 1906), vol. II, p. 52.

20 See *B.D.*, vol. VI, p. 56.

21 *Ibid.*, p. 57.

22 *B.D.*, vol. VI, p. 56, refers to 'The eminent French pyrotechnist at Ranelagh, Morel Torré', and says that Garrick had been responsible, on Monnet's recommendation, for Torré's immigration and prosperity. *B.D.*, vol. IV, p. 300, says that de Loutherbourg arrived in London in 1771 accompanied by Giovanni Battista Torré, a pyrotechnist who later became a London print dealer.

23 *The London Packet* (8–11 January 1779), gives a good impression and plot summary of this pantomime and is, perhaps, typical of similar 'entertainments', quoted in *B.D.*, vol. IV, p. 307.

24 See Richard Southern, *Changeable Scenery* (London: Faber & Faber, 1952), p. 70.

25 Chapter 8 of Southern, *ibid.*, is still the most thorough exploration of this topic and of the use of scenery generally during the Restoration period.

26 Quoted in Sybil Rosenfeld, *Georgian Scene Painters and Scene Painting*, p. 24.

27 It would be good and appropriate to believe that de Loutherbourg came out of retirement to design this play. The evidence to date is very slight, see A. Oliver & J. Saunders, 'De Loutherbourg and Pizarro', *Theatre Notebook*, 20 (Oct. 1965), 30–2.

28 Samuel Derrick, *Letters* (Dublin: 1767), no. XXXVII, quoted in B. Sprague Allen, *Tides in English Taste 1619–1800*, p. 203.

29 George Rowell, *The Victorian Theatre 1792–1914*, 2nd edn (Cambridge: Cambridge University Press, 1978), p. 1.

30 *Ibid.*, p. 31.

31 B. Sprague Allen, *Tides in English Taste 1619–1800*, p. 241.

## APPENDIX

To Mr. David Garrick
Adelphi Buildings in the Strand, London.

[Mr Louterbourg's Propositions to y<sup>e</sup> Managers (in a different hand)]

Sir,

You wish to know clearly my ideas about the scheme of scenery which I proposed to undertake for your theatre.

The following is what I think.

I do not want to do for you a commonplace thing such as has already been done in some other places, but really something which will do me honour, and profit (both) you and me.

In order to achieve this, I must invent scenery which will have the effect of creating a new sensation upon the public. To this end, I must change the method (manner) of lighting the stage so as to serve the effects of the painting. I should also change the method of pulling off simultaneously an entire scene (set of scenes) – and generally, alter such machinery as might be necessary to the aspiration of my talents, such as I have. Having a zealous regard for a reputation which has taken eighteen years for me to acquire, I certainly would not wish to risk it upon something which I did not believe to promise a success as assured as anyone may have in any of his endeavours. Furthermore, I must make a small model of the settings and everything which is required, to scale, painted and detailed so as to put the working painters and machinists and others on the right track by being able to faithfully copy my models, and, if I deem it necessary to retouch something in the final display, to enhance the effect, then I must do so. I shall draw in colour the costumes for the actors and the dancers. I must discuss* my work with the composer and the ballet-master. In this way, you may see that I will spare nothing for the success of a project to which I have committed my reputation. If you were to give me full authority over all of your workers, I would use this trust as an honest man and would treat your interests as my own. You will bear the necessary charges for all the materials for this work and you will pay the young painter, who I recommended, only as you are accustomed to pay your other scene-painters. I will vouch for his conduct and that he is very hardworking and diligent, which is important to you; moreover you will see for yourself.

For my own part, in consideration of three months of my time and all that I shall have to do, I believe that you will not find too much my requesting 300 pounds sterling. Once the machines are installed, this will be a great improvement for all succeeding scenery. Moreover there are seven model scenes to be painted.

These, my dear Sir, are my thoughts. If you would care to indicate to me a precise time, I will explain to you more clearly that which would take me too long to write.

---

* In the original *res*fonne. There are two justifiable possibilities for the translation of this. (a) *résonner*, to echo and (b) as a form of *raissonner*, to discuss. I am grateful to E. L. Stockwell of London University, Goldsmiths' College for most valuable advice upon matters of French usage during the Eighteenth Century.

Certainly, Sir, I dare give you my word that you will be surprised at the effect of my work and the quantity which I shall achieve.

I beg you to assure Madame Garrick of my respects and remain,
Sir,

Your servant and friend de Loutherbourg.

# The space of discourse and the discourse of space in Jacques Ancelot's *Louis IX**

## BARBARA T. COOPER

At first glance, there might seem to be something almost perverse about a study that proposes to examine the use of space in an early nineteenth-century French neoclassical tragedy, for in such works there is rarely more than a single, unchanging decor about which the characters, once on stage, move relatively little. Indeed, as Victor Hugo so pertinently observed in the 'Preface' to *Cromwell* (pp. 81–2), in these tragedies, 'tout le drame se passe dans la coulisse. Nous ne voyons en quelque sorte sur le théâtre que les coudes de l'action; ses mains sont ailleurs. Au lieu de scènes, nous avons des récits; au lieu de tableaux, des descriptions' (all of the drama takes place in the wings. On stage we only see as it were the elbows of the action; its hands are elsewhere. Instead of scenes, we have narrative accounts; instead of tableaux, descriptions).[1] Hugo, of course, was opposed to the concept of the stage as the space of discourse. Other writers, however, felt that the concrete representation of setting and action was less important than their poetic evocation in the dialogue. These critics, partisans of the unities of time, space, and action, considered tragedy to be the genre of the ideal rather than of the real and held the discourse of space in greater esteem than its visual presentation. The study of space in a neoclassical tragedy cannot then be reduced to an examination of its concrete, tangible manifestations. The dimensions of the question are far more vast and more complex than they might at first appear. Jacques-Arsène-Polycarpe Ancelot's *Louis IX* (Théâtre-Français, 1819), written in strict conformity to the rules of French neoclassical dramaturgy, revolves almost entirely around the principle of being true to one's word (respecting treaties and the code of chivalry; honoring one's promises and one's oaths to God and king) and seemingly typifies the claustrophobia and inaction Hugo denounced as characteristic of early nineteenth-century French tragedy. It should thus prove to be an ideal vehicle for the analysis of the stage as the space of discourse and of tragic drama as the *locus* for the discourse of space.

---

* A draft of this paper was read at the *Themes in Drama* International Cor.ference held at the University of California, Riverside in February 1985.

### 1   The space of discourse

'La scène est à Memphis dans le palais du soudan. Le théâtre représente
une partie de ce palais' (The action takes place in Memphis [Egypt] in the
sultan's palace. The scene is set in a part of that palace). As summary as
they are, these liminal stage directions – the only concrete indication we
have concerning the way the stage might have been set for Ancelot's
tragedy – nonetheless provide important clues regarding the use of space in
*Louis IX*.[2] Of the two sentences that make up this description of the decor, it
is in fact only the second that is of any operative significance for the
production of the play. This second sentence – 'the scene is set in a part of
that palace' – is, however, notable for its vagueness. It fixes the drama in an
undefined part of a palace, providing no specific information regarding the
configuration or decoration of that space. Indeed, such a description would
seem to justify Hugo's characterization of the decor of most neoclassical
tragedies as (p. 81) a 'lieu banal' (an unmarked (that is, lacking distinctive
markings) space). Still, we should not underestimate the importance of the
physical restriction of the playing space ('une partie de' – a part of) this
sentence calls to our attention. On the one hand, of course, this limitation
signals to the reader or viewer of *Louis IX* that the tragedy he is about to
discover is a 'regular' drama, that is, written in accord with the established
norms of neoclassical composition (the unities of time, space, action, etc.).
On the other hand, considered within the context of the complete description of the set – a grammatical necessity given that the 'ce palais' (that
palace) of the second sentence has as its antecedent the 'le palais du soudan'
(the sultan's palace) of the first sentence – one can observe that the space in
which the drama will unfold figures is at the end of a list of increasingly
closed settings (Memphis, the sultan's palace, a part of that palace), each of
which fits neatly inside its predecessor rather like a Russian doll. What this
means for the confrontation of opposing forces that the tragedy sets forth is
a subject to which we shall return later. For now, we must examine the
initial sentence of the stage directions more carefully and consider what it
contributes to the definition of space in *Louis IX*.

Unfamiliar with the conventions of stagecraft at the Théâtre-Français in
the early decades of the nineteenth century and unmindful of the universal-
ist bias inherent in the neoclassical aesthetic, the naive student of Ancelot's
tragedy might assume that the references to Memphis and to a sultan's
palace in the first sentence of the play's stage directions mark the dramatist's concern for what is commonly called 'local color.'[3] As we have seen,
however, the progressive narrowing of the playing space all but erases the
distinctive characteristics of the exotic oriental setting. The theater-goer
does not see Memphis nor the unique architectural design of the Egyptian
palace; he sees only an unspecified interior space whose configuration and

decoration – as we have already observed – are left undefined. What is more, we know that at the Théâtre-Français the usual decor for tragic drama was the 'palais à volonté' (standard palace), used indiscriminately for works set in any and all historical periods or geographical locations. It would nonetheless be premature to conclude that this invisible setting served no purpose, for as we shall see in a moment, it is densely woven into the fabric of the play's dialogue. There it poetically evokes a socio-historical context that weighs heavily on the meaning and evolutions of the drama.

All is not said about the physical space in which Ancelot's tragedy unfolds in the two-sentence description of the decor, however. One must also consider the way in which the play's characters move about the space defined at the beginning of the work.[4] *Louis IX*'s single stage setting suggests a certain fixedness, a stasis that seems to be in harmony with the characters' status as prisoners and jailers. (Defeated in a battle that would have led to the eventual liberation of Christ's tomb in Jerusalem, the French are being held for ransom by their Muslim captors.) The sense of confinement that emanates from the unchanging decor is nonetheless apparently belied by the freedom with which the characters enter and exit from the stage. Aware that he would surely be called to task for these improbable comings and goings, Ancelot was careful to justify them by having a character observe that Louis and his followers were prisoners of their word of honor and that as knights and Christians faultlessly faithful to their oath, they had been given free rein of the palace (II, vii, p. 28). What is more, the characters' arrivals on and departures from the scene are always announced in the dialogue by references to the sound of approaching footsteps or off-stage voices, to sightings, and to those circumstances which explain their movements.[5] In virtually every instance, the characters' wanderings are clearly motivated by a need to engage in conversation. Such an observation makes it clear that in *Louis IX*, the stage is indeed the space of discourse and that all visible action in this play is verbal.[6] In some ways, however, this finding is less significant, and certainly less surprising, than our discovery of the pattern of movement and confinement – movement in confinement – that appears so persistently throughout the play. We shall want to examine this aspect of the drama again in the second part of our study. Our analysis of the space of discourse must, in the meantime, continue along one final path before it can be said to be complete.

Our discussion of the characters' movements on and off the stage suggests that the wings, although invisible to the eye, are not a void into which the actors fall when they leave the playing space. On the contrary, to the great displeasure of thinkers like Victor Hugo, all of the physical action in *Louis IX* occurs in settings the spectator cannot see. The theater-goer is nonetheless provided with ample information to help him to imagine the spaces which extend beyond and encompass the visible stage. We thus

come back to that first sentence in the play's stage directions which told us
that the action takes place in Memphis, in the sultan's palace. That edifice
and that city are physically contiguous to the part of the palace represented
on stage and are constantly made present by their inscription in the
dialogue.[7] The language used to describe these places is, to be sure, poetic
and thoroughly conventional, but to the extent that it creates a picture in
the listener's mind, such discourse must also be considered dramaturgically
functional. The palace is evoked by repeated references to its doors, prisons,
walls, and ramparts ('portes,' 'cachots,' 'murs,' 'remparts'). It is, of course,
a matter of no little interest and importance that all of these metonymical
fragments of the palace intensify and underscore a sense of enclosure and
containment.[8] Beyond the palace lies Memphis, a city variously described
as African and Asian, Egyptian and Syrian, a city located on the banks of
the Nile and the Jordan in the torrid climes of the Muslim empire. It would
be a mistake to laugh at this imprecise geography, for its purpose is not to
pinpoint a specific site, but rather to establish the context, the framework,
and the confines of a drama played out in space.[9] Thus the words 'bord,'
'rivage,' and 'plage' (edge, shore, beach) which recur in almost every
description of the local setting and which might otherwise bring to mind an
image of evasion and openness, instead come to signify boundaries and
barriers to a passage that cannot yet be made.

   The series of circumscribed spaces that moves outward from the stage to
the horizon quite naturally creates in the hearts and minds of the Christian
prisoners an intense longing for their native land. In their conversations,
they conjure up the vision of a distant France lying far beyond and
unconnected to the space contiguous to the stage. The words 'loin' and
'lointain' (far away, far off) attach themselves with pitiable regularity to the
fields, the skies, and the paternal dwellings the crusaders recall with infinite
nostalgia and regret. Their exile, their radical separation from this space of
sustenance, love, and comfort is further highlighted by the repeated
characterization of the setting in which they find themselves as 'étranger'
(foreign, totally alien). It is not surprising, then, that this tragic drama
which opens (I, i, p. 1) with all the pathos inherent in the question: 'Dans les
murs de Memphis les chrétiens enchaînés / A d'éternels malheurs seraient-
ils condamnés?' (Within the walls of Memphis are the subjugated (literally,
in chains) Christians to be condemned to eternal misfortunes?) should end
(V, iv, p. 64) with Louis' joyous affirmation: 'Compagnons, votre Dieu
comble votre espérance: / Nous saluerons bientôt les rives de la France'
(My companions, God rewards your hope in Him: Soon we shall salute the
shores of France).

   The dialogue of *Louis IX* thus communicates, via immaterial, verbal
signs, the information contained in the stage directions.[10] Although the
spectator actually sees only the smallest of the three concentric circles

mentioned in the description of the decor, his mind is given the means to conjure up not only those spaces adjacent to the stage, but also a third space from which the imprisoned characters are seemingly forever cut off. If the visible space of discourse achieves a vast horizontal extension and a sense of depth by means of the omnipresent discourse on space, that poetic effect in no way diminishes the sense of confinement and the limited freedom of movement which mark the characters' destiny. On the contrary, although Louis and his followers enter and exit from the playing space with no apparent difficulty, they never lose their status as prisoners and exiles. It is simply that they adventure into another part of their jail.

## II   The discourse of space

What does it mean to place before an audience a group of characters whose voices echo forth from prison – albeit a prison without bars? Is this setting, even in the absence of a realistic decor, truly a 'lieu banal' (an unmarked space) as Victor Hugo would have it? Clearly not. As Anne Ubersfeld has already observed in her study of 'Le Lieu du discours' (p. 12): '[L]e discours d'un homme en prison, c'est d'abord le discours de la situation de parole *je – en prison*' (The speech of a man in prison is first of all an enunciation of the linguistic context *I – in prison*). In addition to our analysis of the space of discourse, then, we must also examine the discourse of space in *Louis IX*. As we shall see, however intangible it might be, the setting of this drama is clearly essential to Ancelot's tragic project.

If the stage does not show itself to be a prison either by means of its decor or its hermetic separation from all annex spaces, then the spectator must be told that he is viewing a space of confinement. It is not surprising, therefore, that the dialogue of *Louis IX* is liberally sprinkled with allusions to the crusaders' status as captives and prisoners and to their prolonged detention in the sultan's palace. Most likely metaphorical rather than real, the chains ('les chaînes,' 'les fers') by which the prisoners are bound ('enchaîner,' 'lier') resound more loudly in the dialogue than they do on the boards, yet they contribute significantly to the atmosphere of terror and desolation that is meant to spark the viewer's sympathy for the plight of these more or less undeserving victims of God's disfavor.[11] Furthermore, Egypt and the palace are routinely qualified as 'fatal rivage' (fateful shore), 'murs odieux' (odious walls), and 'funeste lieu' (deathly place) in phrases where the conventional adjectives of French neoclassical vocabulary bear down with all their tragic weight. If these observations bring to mind the name of Aristotle, that is as it should be, for the first speech of the prison-decor might roughly be translated: 'I inspire terror and pity.' Ancelot was certainly not the first – nor the last – dramatist to be aware of this message and to exploit it.[12]

A second message the decor might be said to announce is: 'I am a place where power subjugates all men – kings as well as commoners.' The sultan of Egypt not only labels himself (III, iii, p. 34) the master of the space in which Louis and his followers have been confined ('Seul je suis maître ici' – I alone am master here), but also affirms (II, ii, p. 20) his mastery over their fate ('Je peux tout, j'ai vaincu' – I can do anything; I was victorious). The prisoners, on the other hand, see their detention as an enslavement ('esclavage') and themselves as slaves ('esclaves') of a situation over which they have no control. (The frequent use of the verb 'entraîner' – to carry, lead along – is indicative of the passive posture that is theirs.) The master–slave relationship the text would at first have us accept is ultimately belied by the evolution of the action, however. In the final act of the drama, in an ironic reversal of fortunes, the sultan who had boasted of his mastery of space becomes a prisoner in his own palace while Louis, who had been his captive, is offered control of the Egyptian's realm.[13] The French king's generous refusal of the offer does not mitigate the impact of the lesson that the play seems to set forth. The palace is a space in which captives and captors alike are held prisoner. Human power is an illusion and the outcome of the conflicts between men locked within the closed arena of their ambitions depends not so much on their individual forces as on those extra-human agencies which impinge on their destiny.

These extra-human agencies also find their expression in the discourse of space. We have already seen how the constellation of contiguous enclosed spaces (Memphis, the sultan's palace, a part of that palace) stands in radical opposition to the far-off land of France, as if the decor were saying: 'I am the here which is not the there.' Examined from another angle, however, the dichotomous pairs Occident/Orient, Africa–Asia/Europe, Egypt/France, Memphis/Paris not only announce the theme of exile, but also set forth a socio-historical context. This can perhaps be seen more clearly if we observe that there is another set of geographical co-ordinates embedded in the text of *Louis IX* which we have not yet examined. In Ancelot's drama Egypt is set in contrast not only to France but also to Zion; Memphis is placed opposite not only Paris but also Jerusalem (see, for example, II, i, p. 16). When coupled with the references to the 'lessons of the past' (II, i, p. 15), these new co-ordinates make it clear that the conflict between Louis IX and the sultan is part of a larger battle between Christians and Infidels, between true believers and those unfaithful to God's Word. If there is no concrete action on the stage, then, it is because the real motors of History are not the men who play out the drama of individual events, but the invisible, impersonal forces that move them about the chessboard of life.

The final message of the decor of Ancelot's tragedy might thus be translated: 'I am the space of illusion.' The illusion that men are free to influence the course of History is, as we have just seen, implicitly denied by

21 Jacques Ancelot's *Louis IX* IV, vi. (Photo, Bibliothèque Nationale, Paris)

the drama. Surely the movement in confinement – that movement which is neither truly free nor liberating – takes on its full symbolic significance in this context. Men may move about, they may act, they may believe they have power, but none of these things signals any real control over the course of their own destinies.

On another level, the schematic, non-representational decor of the play may also be considered to stand as a rejection of the facile confusion of the space of real life with that of drama, as an affirmation of the tragic stage as the space of an ideal (that is, intellectual, created by the mind) vision. The spectacle of tragedy, as our study of Ancelot's *Louis IX* has by now made evident, does not require the services of a set designer and a machinist to be compelling; it can be seen clearly with Œdipus's blinded eyes.

In acknowledging the tragic stage as the space of the ideal, we must not however lose sight of the ideological vision that underscores the aesthetic construct that is *Louis IX*. It was not, in all likelihood, a disinterested appreciation of the artistic merits of Ancelot's tragedy that prompted Louis XVIII to reward the dramatist for his work. It is rather more probable that the restored monarch perceived in Ancelot's play, and meant to recompense, a view of the world and of the historical process that confirmed his right to rule.[14] The story of a king defeated, exiled on foreign shores, and prevented by an infidel from returning to his rightful place in France contains, after all, too many parallels to the life of Louis XVIII to have escaped royal – and audience – attention.[15] The tragedy of *Louis IX* could, then, be considered a metonymy for royal destiny. That destiny – based on a compact with God – always involves, or so Restoration tragedy seemingly would have one believe, a temporary fall from grace and a period of exile from Eden–France followed by a redemption, a restoration.[16] Viewed in this light, Louis XVIII's return to power becomes 'natural,' an inevitable event in a History of France modeled by extra-human agencies.

The question of theatrical space in Ancelot's *Louis IX* is thus far more complex than an initial appreciation of the problem might lead one to believe. However immaterial it might be, the setting of this drama is clearly essential both to the tragic dimensions of the play and to the ideological message it communicates.

## NOTES

1 The quotation is from the edition of Victor Hugo's *Cromwell* by Anne Ubersfeld (Paris: Garnier-Flammarion, 1968). All translations are my own. Research for this study was completed with the help of grants from the French Government and from the University of New Hampshire Central Research Fund.

2 Quotations are from the edition of Ancelot's *Louis IX* published by Mme Huet (Paris, 1819). Contemporary drama critics make no allusion to the set in their

published reviews of Ancelot's play and the library of the Comédie-Française contains no documents recording the details of the work's *mise en scène*. For an indication of the importance such paratextual information as this can have for the analysis of a drama, see Jean-Marie Thomasseau, 'Pour une analyse du para-texte théâtral: quelques eléments du para-texte hugolien,' *Littérature*, 53 (1984), 79–103, who asserts (p. 83) that it can be '. . . fortement révélateur des armatures secrètes de l'oeuvre et des projets d'écriture scénique de l'auteur' (highly revealing of the secret structure of the work and of the author's staging intentions), and Michel Corvin, 'Contribution à l'analyse de l'espace scénique dans le théâtre contemporain,' *Travail théâtral*, 22 (1976), 62–80, pp. 64–7.

3  On these conventions, see Germain Bapst, *Essai sur l'histoire du théâtre: la mise en scène, le décor, le costume, l'architecture, l'éclairage, l'hygiène* (Paris: Lahure, 1893), pp. 528 and 533 and Marvin Carlson, '*Hernani*'s Revolt From the Tradition of French Stage Composition,' *Theatre Survey*, 13 (1972), 1–27.

4  See Régina Yaari's observation, 'L'Espace dans *Woyzeck* de Büchner,' in *Le Texte et la scène: études sur l'espace et l'acteur*, ed. Bernard Dort and Anne Ubersfeld (Paris: impr. F. Paillart, 1978), pp. 11–42 (p. 15) that: 'En dernière instance c'est le personnage, les personnages, par leur façon d'investir [un] lieu, qui en déterminent le caractère, qui en feront un lieu ouvert, un lieu de passage ou un lieu fermé, un lieu d'interiorité' (In the last analysis it is the character, the characters, by the way they invest [a] space, who determine its nature, who make it an open space, a passage or a closed space, a space of interiority).

5  See Jacques Scherer, *La Dramaturgie classique en France* (Paris: Nizet, 1983; 1st printing, 1960), part II, chapter V, who calls such links 'liaisons de présence.'

6  For positive judgments of the absence of what some early nineteenth-century French critics disparagingly characterized as 'adventures' or 'incidents,' see the review by A. Martainville, 'Théâtre Français', *Le Drapeau blanc*, 147 (9 Nov. 1819), 3–4, and C.'s *feuilletons* of 7 and 10 Nov. 1819 in the *Journal des Débats*, 1–4, 'Théâtre Français: première représentation de *Louis IX*,' and 'Théâtre Français: seconde représentation de *Louis IX*.'

7  On the concept of contiguous space, see Steen Jansen, 'L'Espace scénique dans le spectacle dramatique et dans le texte dramatique,' *Revue romane*, 17 (1982), 3–21, p. 16.

8  For a discussion of similar practices in other early nineteenth-century French neoclassical tragedies, see Barbara T. Cooper, 'Canvas Walls and Cardboard Fortresses: Representations of Place in the National Historical Dramas of Early Nineteenth-Century France,' *Comparative Drama*, 17:4 (1983–4), 327–47, pp. 328–34.

9  Jacques Scherer makes a similar point in *Racine et/ou la cérémonie* (Paris: Presses universitaires de France, 1982), p. 197.

10  The stage directions thus have the status of what Tadeusz Kowzan, 'Signe zéro de la parole,' *Degrés*, 10: 31 (1982), a–a16, calls in his discussion of Racine's *Athalie* and *Bérénice* (p. a15), the 'signes zéro du décor, c'est-à-dire, [des] signes implicites dont le signifiant n'a pas de réalité matérielle, visuelle, et dont le signifié se dégage du contexte sémantique, notamment à travers les signes verbaux' (zero signs of the decor, that is to say, implicit signs whose signifier has no material, visual reality and whose signified is derived from the semantic context, notably via verbal signs).

11 J. B. Colson, *Répertoire du Théâtre Français, ou Détails essentiels sur trois cent soixante tragédies et comédies*, 2 vols. (Bordeaux: chez l'auteur, 1819), refers (1, p. 186) to the chains used in staging Raynouard's *Les Templiers* (1805). It is unlikely, however, that Louis and his followers were actually encumbered by chains during the production of Ancelot's play. Certainly the lithograph of Mme Ancelot's pathos-filled portrait of the actors playing Louis and his family (plate 21) does not provide evidence of the presence of chains on stage.

12 See Scherer, *La Dramaturgie*, pp. 167–8 for earlier examples of this.

13 This is even more obvious in a ms version of Ancelot's play conserved at the Archives Nationales, Paris (F[18] 616). There the sultan reappears on stage in the final scene of the drama bound in chains.

14 Indeed, according to Henri Frère, *Ancelot: sa vie et ses oeuvres* (Rouen: Le Brument, 1862) (p. 29), 'Emu de la glorification de sa race et de l'éloquent panégyrique de saint Louis, heureux de rencontrer un poëte prêt à populariser son règne et digne de lutter contre le succès moins royaliste des *Vêpres siciliennes*, Louis XVIII annobilit Ancelot, accepte sa dédicace et lui fait une pension de 2 000 fr.' (Moved by the glorification of his race and by the panegyric of St Louis, happy to encounter a poet ready to popularise his reign and worthy to combat the less royalist success of the *Vêpres siciliennes*, Louis XVIII enobles Ancelot, accepts his dedication [of *Louis IX*] and accords him a pension of 2,000 fr.). Frère goes on to say that Ancelot refused the title and the pension offered him.

15 In this case, Egypt would become a cipher for England. The drama critic for the *Journal de Paris* notes in his *feuilleton* of 7 Nov. 1819: 'Une circonstance que nous aimons à remarquer, c'est que les nombreux passages de cette tragédie qui fournissent des allusions si naturelles à la sagesse et aux vertus d'un monarque, digne descendant de S. Louis, ont été saisis avec le plus vif enthousiasme, et qu'elles n'ont pas peu contribué à exciter et à soutenir la bienveillance des spectateurs pour l'ouvrage qui leur donnait l'occasion de faire éclater l'expression de sentimens toujours prêts à s'épancher de tous les coeurs français' (A circumstance that we are pleased to note is that the many passages of this tragedy which furnish such natural allusions to the wisdom and virtues of a monarch [who is the] worthy descendent of St Louis, were seized upon with the greatest enthusiasm, and that they contributed in a not insignificant way to excite and sustain the kindly disposition of the spectators for a work which gave them the opportunity to allow free rein to those sentiments which are always ready to burst forth from French hearts).

16 Alienation from power – whether it is seemingly the result of mental incompetence (Charles VI), political weakness (*les rois fainéants*), or foreign occupation (Charles VII and Jeanne d'Arc) – is a frequent theme in Restoration tragedy. Beneath the diversity of historical accident, the same cause (ambition, division among the nobility) always has the same effect (loss of royal control) in these tragedies. Such plays generally conclude with the prospect of a return to power of the legitimate ruler – a prospect validated by historical fact and repeated in the re-establishment of the Bourbon monarchy after the Revolution and the Napoleonic era.

# 'Put into scenery': theatrical space in Byron's closet historical dramas

## JOHN SPALDING GATTON

The theatre and history enthralled Lord Byron in his youth and held him in their sway throughout his life. A dedicated patron of the playhouse from approximately the age of five, he claimed that he 'could not resist the *first* night of any thing.'[1] For a year in 1815–16 he served on the Sub-Committee of Management at the Theatre Royal, Drury Lane. In his journal he recorded that from the moment he could read his 'grand passion was *history*.'[2] Between April 1820 and July 1821, while resident in Italy, he integrated these interests by writing three historical dramas along neo-classical lines. *Marino Faliero* concerns the Doge of Venice executed in 1355 for plotting with the oppressed plebeians to overthrow the oligarchical Republic. *Sardanapalus* recounts the final hours of the quasi-historical last king of Assyria, a pacifist who avoids capture by his rebellious subjects through self-immolation. In *The Two Foscari*, a sense of duty compels a fifteenth-century Doge to sentence his son to torture and perpetual exile for crimes against the State.[3]

In correspondence and in prefaces to the blank-verse tragedies, Byron maintained that he had written them, not for the stage, but for the study. To his publisher John Murray he insisted that he wished 'to steer very clear of the possibility of being put into scenery.'[4] Only *Marino Faliero* was acted in his lifetime, and, then, without his permission; 'coldly received' at Drury Lane in 1821, the production was withdrawn after seven nights.[5]

Scholars have generally taken Byron at his word, reading the histories as closet pieces.[6] But even apologists for the plays' dramatic merits seem to have scanted internal evidence that Byron (whatever his comments to the contrary) designed these dramas for performance.[7] For, while observing the neo-classical unity of place, he tailored his scripts to the physical disposition of contemporary English playhouses, specifically, of London's major theatres, Drury Lane and Covent Garden, exploiting the machinery that made possible swift, imaginative scene changes; filling the large stages with spectacle; and creating declamatory dialogue appropriate to the vast auditoria.

Rebuilt in the early nineteenth century after devastating fires, Drury

22 Theatre Royal, Drury Lane, auditorium, 1813.

Lane and Covent Garden had similar interiors. A proscenium divided the stage into two sections: a forestage or apron on which most of the action occurred; and a deeper rear space framed by the arched opening and given over mainly to scenic backgrounds, although the actors, who could enter and exit through its side scenes, moved with increasing freedom and frequency into this area.[8] Proscenium doors provided direct access to the forestage. Drury Lane, which reopened in 1812 to Benjamin Wyatt's design, had an apron approximately 70 feet wide at its front edge and 20 feet deep, backed by an opening 33 feet wide and 30 feet high. The upstage portion continued another 48 feet, for a total stage depth of 68 feet. Wyatt maintained that, 'excepting in cases of Spectacle,' the scene 'seldom extended, in depth, beyond 30 feet from the front line of the Stage.' In an attempt to place the actors permanently behind the arch, within a picture frame, Wyatt eliminated the proscenium doors, but the players' objections forced their restoration. They had disappeared for good by the 1822–3 season, during drastic interior alterations designed by Samuel Beazley. In Robert Smirke's Covent Garden (1809), the forestage, 10 feet deep, measured some 42 feet across at the front, narrowing to 38 feet 6 inches at the opening. The arch was over 30 feet high, with a backstage 56 feet deep. Covent Garden preserved its proscenium doors until 1813.[9]

According to his biographer John Galt, Byron professed to be ignorant of 'how to make the people go on and off in the scenes.'[10] Proscenium doors, however, would permit him to indicate a direction in *Sardanapalus*: '*Exit PANIA. Enter ALTADA and SFERO by an opposite door*' (III, i, 301). Their use later in the play would prevent the king's wife Zarina from encountering his mistress, as described by an embedded direction. He tells Myrrha that it was 'well' she 'entered by another portal,' else she had met the Assyrian queen (IV, i, 450–5). Other characters are conducted '*off the stage*' (IV, i, 411, 422) or pass '*over the stage*' (*The Two Foscari*, I, i, 55, 280).

Theatrical conventions limited extensive movement in space. To tell his stories, Byron championed the neo-classical unities above all other dramatic tenets. 'With any very distant departure from them,' he declared in the Preface to *Sardanapalus*, 'there may be poetry, but can be no drama.'[11] By compressing events and eliminating subplots he sought to honor the unities of time and action. He treated the unity of place with greater flexibility. In *Marino Faliero*, Byron purposely transferred certain of the incidents out of the ducal palace, their historical setting, into other sections of Venice, 'to produce the Doge in the full assembly of the conspirators, instead of monotonously placing him always in dialogue with the same individuals.'[12] *Sardanapalus* is confined to a single royal chamber, while *The Two Foscari* unfolds in a hall, a prison cell, and in the Doge's private apartment.

In the text, action moves smoothly from place to place, as shown to advantage in *Marino Faliero*. At the end of the first scene, set in a palace antechamber, an official hastens to the Doge with a message; scene ii opens with Faliero, in his quarters, anxiously awaiting the document. Act III, scene i concludes with Faliero being led from an outdoor location to a meeting with the conspirators; they are revealed assembled in a house in the next scene. Such swift transitions have prompted A. N. Vardac to observe, without elaboration, that Byron's plays are cinematic in construction.[13] In the lap dissolve, one image on the screen blends gradually into another. Machines that altered and defined theatrical space in the Regency theatre allowed Byron to realize a similar visual effect on the stage.

Increasingly in his day, painted canvas drops furled on rollers, and scenery raised and lowered through cuts in the floor helped change settings. But the rapid spatial transformations Byron described could best be achieved by using backshutters (also known as 'scenes' or 'flats'), a device popular since the Renaissance. These pairs of framed scenery formed a single painted background when they came together in the middle of the stage. The shutters moved in grooves fixed to the floor and to the stage superstructure at some half-dozen positions behind and parallel to the proscenium arch. Depending on the grooves used, the set on the stage could vary greatly in depth. To change the place, the halves of the joined shutter were drawn off to either side of the stage in full view of the audience, to reveal a second pair, depicting another locale, already in place in other grooves. Shutters were also pushed on to cover the previous setting. Thus, an antechamber could be transformed quickly into the Doge's chamber, and a Venetian piazza could dissolve into an interior. In theatrical parlance, the flats 'opened' and 'closed,' and their movements were so marked in a play's stage directions. Changeable wing pieces, sliding in separate grooves, masked the outer edges of the shutters. In a variation on the grooves, wings were mounted on frames projecting through long slits in the floor and fastened to wheeled carriages running on rails beneath the stage. A system of ropes, barrels, and shafts ensured that as one set of wings rolled off the stage, another pair moved on. Covent Garden was equipped with grooves, among other machines. Drury Lane possessed six pairs of carriages which, at some time prior to the 1822–3 season, were replaced by grooves.[14]

In addition to routine scene changes, *Marino Faliero* offers the opportunity for two striking uses of shutters. In deference to the neo-classical convention of *bienséance*, which relegated violence to the wings, Byron could not represent on the stage the Doge's beheading (v, iii). Therefore, at the crucial instant when the executioner raises his sword above the kneeling Faliero, Byron must suspend the action. A total blackout was not possible, as the auditorium remained illuminated during the performance, and the main curtain descended only at the end of the play (Byron's histories conclude with the direction '*the curtain falls*'). Nor could the actors simply troop off the stage in plain view. Byron consequently specifies that as the blade rises, '*the scene closes*' (v, iii, 104). The movement of the shutters provides an easily effected climax to the action and prepares for the theatrical use of the flats in the next scene.

To suggest the setting for v, iv, the shutters just closed – ideally, in grooves immediately inside the arch – would represent '*the grated gates of the Ducal Palace, which are shut,*' as called for by the text. The majority of scene iv, involving plebeians excluded from the beheading, would be played on the forestage, the actors entering through the proscenium doors. When the stage direction reads, '*The gates are opened; the populace rush in*' toward the place of execution at the Giants' Staircase, the flats would be pulled back in their grooves, giving the illusion of the opening of the barriers. The palace exterior from scene iii would still be in place upstage. This technique would adapt a convention of the Restoration theatre: when a character knocked on a door painted on shutters closed near the proscenium, the scenes parted to reveal a room beyond.[15]

The placement of a conversation between two conspirators (II, ii) and of the Doge's farewell to his wife (v, ii) likewise testifies to Byron's astute understanding of the workings of the physical theatre. Each of these scenes is followed by one with elaborate sets. Act III, scene i requires the façade of a church, an equestrian statue, and a gondola lying in a distant canal. The Giants' Staircase dominates v, iii. To allow for the arrangement of large sets during an actual performance, a scene of suitable length was customarily played before shutters closed in downstage grooves.[16] Meanwhile, the concealed upstage area would be prepared with backscenes or drops, wing flats, and larger set pieces – in *Faliero*, either the property statue or the practicable steps. A succeeding scene, played on the apron, could hide the dismantling process. The dialogues of the conspiring plebeians, of Faliero and the Dogaressa, and of the entire cabal (III, ii) provide the necessary cross-over or cover scenes, important both to the exigencies of the plot and to the more prosaic demands of setting the stage.

*Sardanapalus* requires the most complicated set piece in the histories – an imposing funeral pyre. And only in this play did Byron faithfully observe the unity of place, restricting the action to '*A Hall in the Royal Palace of Nineveh.*' In a letter to John Murray, Byron cautioned, 'Mind the *Unities* – which are my great object of research.'[17] Consequently, he could not write a scene, set in a different locale and acted in front of downstage shutters, that would hide the arrangement of the pyre. But another convention offered a solution. To dress the stage, actors often carried in or wheeled on furniture and small properties in view of the audience, such as the table in *Faliero* (I, ii), the banquet in *Sardanapalus* (III, i), and the desk and chair in *Foscari* (II, i).[18] In this manual fashion Byron provided for the erection of the pyre. According to the scripted directions, at the king's command, '*Soldiers enter, and form a Pile about the Throne, etc.,*' which he encourages them to make 'Higher . . . / And thicker yet' (v, i, 275–81, 357–8). Byron thus transformed routine stage business into a theatrical effect that preserved spatial integrity while heightening tension and visually enhancing the scene.[19]

To help realize the 'Simplicity of plot' that was his avowed intention in *The Two Foscari*,[20] Byron dispensed with complex set pieces. Nevertheless, the action requires scenery for three locales. As in *Marino Faliero*, flats sliding in grooves could produce these settings on the stage with the speed with which they appeared on the page. In the final line of act II, Doge Francis Foscari, in conversation with his daughter-in-law in a Palace hall, determines to visit his imprisoned son; in the next scene the young man is presented in his cell. At the end of the fourth act, the leader of a deputation intends to call on Foscari; a change of shutters immediately transports the audience from a hall to the Doge's apartment, where he awaits the group.

The physical dimensions of the stages familiar to Byron permitted, even encouraged, scenes of enormous spectacle, featuring masses of people, often exotically costumed, pyrotechnics, and re-creations of natural disasters. Such displays proved immensely popular with audiences. To a point, Byron's histories indulged the contemporary taste for extravaganza. The scene culminating in Marino Faliero's death (v, iii) opens with elaborate pageantry capable of filling both the apron and backstage with crowds, pomp, and color, all dominated by the massive set pieces depicting the court of the Ducal Palace and the Giants' Staircase. The Doge in his robes of State enters in solemn procession with the Council of Ten, patricians, and guards. All mount the steps, at the top of which waits the executioner with his sword. Early in the play Faliero threw down his bonnet in disgust at his political impotence (I, ii, 87). Now, on the site where he had assumed the cap and with it the office of Doge, this symbol of his station is ceremoniously removed. He is Doge no longer. Even before the first line is spoken, these rituals, played out in dumb show on several stage levels, dramatically set the tone for the beheading. The play concludes with a spectacle worthy of the Grand Guignol: a Chief of the Ten exhibits the bloody sword to the people, the plebeians swirl about the staircase, and Faliero's 'gory head rolls down the Giants' Steps' (v, iv, 27–9).

In his second Venetian tragedy, *The Two Foscari*, Byron again dressed the stage with foreign color, in the persons of senators, guards, and palace functionaries. Given his quest for simplicity in design, however, absent are those shows of Renaissance panoply that distinguished *Marino Faliero*.

In this century, Squire Bancroft and William Archer, professional men of the theatre, declared that *Sardanapalus* was 'more fitted' for public performance than any of Byron's tragedies.[21] This fitness derives, in part, from the numerous effects Byron included that add variation to the play's single interior setting: the procession of Sardanapalus and his '*Train of Women and young Slaves*' (I, ii); a lavish banquet in the '*illuminated*' Hall, the ominous rumblings of a thunderstorm, an on-stage battle between the king and the rebels (III, i); and the erection and lighting of the funeral pyre (v, i). The final picture of Sardanapalus atop the ignited pile and of Myrrha springing forward '*to throw herself into the flames*' (v, i, 498) assures a thrilling finale. The playhouse could produce a conflagration with special scenery, chemicals, and fireworks, but Byron claimed to scorn the 'taste of the day – for extravagant "coups de theatre" [sic],'[22] and thus he brought down the curtain in the first moments of the holocaust. Later nineteenth-century productions of the drama invariably expanded the fire to give literal meaning to Sardanapalus' vision of the 'blazing palace, / And its enormous walls of reeking ruin' (v, i, 480–1).[23] If such additions exceeded Byron's intentions, emphasizing spectacle at the expense of the poetry, they nevertheless bore witness to the theatrical potential of his original script, with its attention to the demands of large stage spaces.

Auditorium size also influenced Byron's histories. At Drury Lane the actors faced a nearly circular auditorium, with an overall diameter of about 75 feet and with the back wall of the boxes at a distance of 53 feet 9 inches from the edge of the apron. The ceiling was 48 feet above the floor of the pit. Covent Garden's horseshoe – with four tiers and an upper gallery – had a diameter of 51 feet 6 inches, the same dimension as the auditorium well from the front of the forestage. Each house held approximately 3,000 people.[24] Only a declamatory delivery complemented by rhetorical gestures and striking tableaux could hope to penetrate such areas.

Byron successfully met the vocal and visual challenges of the playhouse by suiting the dialogue of his protagonists to those actors who had mastered the space. In the Preface to *Marino Faliero* he stated that he could 'conceive nothing better' as performers than John Philip Kemble and Edmund Kean 'in their very different manners.'[25] For these historical pieces ostensibly not meant to be staged, he crafted speeches that neatly fused key elements from the contrasting acting styles of the principal contemporary tragedians, whose work he knew well.[26] Kemble's technique combined nobility of bearing with frequent pauses, resulting in a more studied, less spontaneous performance. Still, according to John Taylor, '. . . with dread pauses, deepen'd accents roll, / Whose awful energy arrests the soul.'[27] Sir Walter Scott explained that an 'asthmatic tendency' forced Kemble 'to husband his efforts, and reserve them for those bursts of passion to which he gave such sublime effect.'[28] Where Kemble cultivated a deliberateness in word and action to command the stage, Kean relied on grotesque posturing, spasmodic gestures, and what John Keats termed a voice of 'indescribable gusto.'[29] Opportunities for histrionics designed to fill the space abound in Byron's plays. Orations on such themes as liberty, revolution, patriotism, and death figure prominently in the plots. Action must perforce come to a standstill whenever a Byronic character in effect strikes a pose in which to pronounce an opinion or react to a situation, be it Faliero's appeal for membership in the conspiracy (iii, ii, 130–210); his self-exhortation to remain firm in his resolve (iv, ii, 131–99); his address 'to Time and to Eternity,' climaxing in a curse on Venice, the 'Sea-Sodom' (v, iii, 26–104); or his kneeling defiance of the executioner (v, iii, 104); Sardanapalus' defense of pacifism (i, ii, 386–419); or his graphic narration of a nightmare (iv, i, 78–165); Doge Foscari's dissection of 'that loathsome volume – man' (ii, i, 332–66); or his sudden prostration by the body of his son (iv, i, 214).

Even as he discouraged any production of *Marino Faliero*, Byron suggestively linked these actors with the title role: 'the play is *not for acting* – Kemble or Kean could *read* it – but where are they?'[30] Byron hoped that the manager of Drury Lane would 'have the grace to wait for Kean's return' from America 'before he attempted it – though *even then*,' the playwright claimed he would be 'as much against the attempt as ever.'[31] Living in Italy, Byron was personally unable to prevent *Faliero* from opening at

Drury Lane in April 1821, with Cooper as the Doge. In its review, the *Times* of London observed that 'the character is decidedly Kean's. Had he played it, the *Doge of Venice* would not have been so coldly received; he would have given life, and spirit, and energy, to every scene.'[32] Byron commented pointedly – and confidently – to Thomas Medwin that had Kemble appeared in the piece, 'its fate would have been very different.'[33] That the actor had been retired since 1817 in no way affected his opinion. Byron drew in Sardanapalus and Francis Foscari protagonists as heroic and alienated as those Kean impersonated, notably, Richard II and Richard III. He introduced into Sardanapalus a note of irony that Kean made a trademark in his delineation of Richard III. In a telling observation, Byron described the Assyrian king as 'almost a comic character – but for that matter – so is Richard the third,' a remark that glances at Kean's acting as much as at Byron's perception of the monarch.[34] The inescapable conclusion is that, despite his own defensive rhetoric, Byron fully intended his dialogue to be spoken –and heard – in an actual theatre.

Byron's express mission for his historical verse plays required that they conform to the physical playhouses of the day. These works are nothing less than clarions for revolution in drama and politics. As a theatre-goer, a manager of Drury Lane, and its script reader, Byron was acutely aware of and distressed by the rant, the Gothic melodramas, the child-tragedians, and the performing animals that increasingly dominated the English stage and dimmed its luster. In the poetic 'Address' he wrote for the opening of the new Drury Lane in 1812, he prayed, '. . . may our stage unfold / Scenes not unworthy Drury's days of old' (lines 70–1).[35] Expressly to combat current excesses and thus to reform the drama, Byron modeled his historical plays on the conventions of neo-classical theatre. He adopted a severity of style for the language, evolved a simplicity of plot, moderated spectacle, and, whenever possible, observed the unities. As a champion of liberty, Byron grieved to see his beloved Italy languishing under Austrian control, and Greece, the birthplace of democracy, oppressed by the Turks. In the historical dramas, as in other of his writings, he urged the Italians – indeed, all subjugated peoples – to practice self-preservation, to unite against the common foe, and to cast off the tyrant's yoke. He might assure his cautious, conservative publisher John Murray that, despite appearances, *Marino Faliero* was 'not a political play,' but to his more liberal friend Douglas Kinnaird, Byron frankly admitted that the work was 'full of republicanism.'[36] *Sardanapalus* and *The Two Foscari* permit a similar interpretation.

Byron clearly intended his plays to serve in the vanguard of an assault on the abuses rampant in the British theatre and to sound a call to arms in international political struggles for freedom. The most effective way for him to disseminate the ideas contained in these dramas was through performance, wherein the directness of his plots could be seen and their rallying cries heard to advantage. His deprecating comments about their dramatic merits may be taken as examples of the defensive pose he frequently adopted to forestall anticipated criticism of a new work. Even as he railed against their production, he endeavored to make the pieces attractive to theatre managers, to players, and to audiences, as if to ensure their presentation. Thus, the works, for their inherent radicalism, contain no theatrical innovations, but rely instead on traditional staging methods, current acting styles, and popular taste in spectacle.

By carefully suiting his historical tragedies to the mechanical, visual, and aural capabilities and limitations of contemporary theatrical space, Byron gave the lie to his claim in the Preface to *Marino Faliero* that he could not write a 'stage-worthy' play.[37]

## NOTES

1 Leslie A. Marchand (ed.), *Byron's Letters and Journals*, 12 vols. (Cambridge, Mass.: The Belknap Press of Harvard University Press, 1973–82), IV, p. 290; hereafter, *BLJ*.

2 *BLJ*, VIII, p. 108.

3 Quotations from the plays are from *The Works of Lord Byron: Poetry*, ed. Ernest Hartley Coleridge, 7 vols. (London: John Murray, 1898–1904); hereafter, *Poetry*.

4 *BLJ*, V, p. 238.

5 *The Times*, London, 26 April 1821, p. 3.

6 Scholars who view Byron's historical dramas as closet plays include: Samuel C. Chew, Jr, *The Dramas of Lord Byron: A Critical Study* (1915; rpt, New York: Russell & Russell, 1964); M. K. Joseph, *Byron the Poet* (London: Victor Gollancz, 1966), p. 110; Leslie A. Marchand, *Byron's Poetry: A Critical Introduction* (Cambridge, Mass.: Harvard University Press, 1968), p. 102; and William Ruddick, 'Lord Byron's Historical Tragedies,' in *Essays on Nineteenth-Century British Theatre*, ed. Kenneth Richards and Peter Thomson (London: Methuen & Co., 1971), pp. 83–94.

7 Among proponents of the plays' dramatic qualities are David V. Erdman, 'Byron's Stage Fright: The History of His Ambition and Fear of Writing for the Stage,' *ELH*, 6 (1939), 219–43; G. Wilson Knight, 'The Plays of Lord Byron,' *TLS*, 3 Feb. 1950, p. 80; Jerome J. McGann, *Fiery Dust: Byron's Poetic Development* (Chicago and London: University of Chicago Press), pp. 205–44; Boleslaw Taborski, *Byron and the Theatre* (Salzburg: University of Salzburg, 1972); and Peter J. Manning, 'Edmund Kean and Byron's Plays,' *Keats–Shelley Journal*, 21–2 (1972–3), 188–206.

8 For his *Treatise on Theatres* (1790) George Saunders designed an ideal playhouse with a shallow forestage that would, he said, force the actor to 'appear (as he

certainly should do) among the scenery'; quoted in Richard Leacroft, *The Development of the English Playhouse* (Ithaca, NY: Cornell University Press, 1973), p. 162.

9 For plans and measurements see the *Survey of London*, gen. ed. F. H. W. Sheppard, vol. xxxv: *The Theatre Royal Drury Lane and the Royal Opera House Covent Garden* (London: The Athlone Press, University of London, 1970), pp. 59–65, 94–7; and Leacroft, *The English Playhouse*, pp. 166–88.

10 John Galt, *The Life of Byron* (1830; rpt, Philadelphia: R. West, 1973), p. 333.

11 *Poetry*, v, p. 9.

12 *Poetry*, iv, p. 340.

13 A. N. Vardac, *Stage to Screen: Theatrical Method from Garrick to Griffith* (Cambridge, Mass.: Harvard University Press, 1949), pp. xxii, 234.

14 *Survey*, p. 63, and Leacroft, *The English Playhouse*, pp. 168–9, 176–8.

15 Lee J. Martin, 'From Forestage to Proscenium: A Study of Restoration Staging Techniques,' *Theatre Survey*, 4 (1963), 12–13.

16 Martin, 'From Forestage to Proscenium,' pp. 10–11.

17 *BLJ*, viii, pp. 155–6.

18 Martin, 'From Forestage to Proscenium,' pp. 25–6.

19 To allow for the placement of trick flats for the fire, Macready, who originated the role of Sardanapalus in 1834, stipulated that the pyre was to be built behind a curtain, 'out of sight of the audience'; quoted in Alan S. Downer, *The Eminent Tragedian: William Charles Macready* (Cambridge, Mass.: Harvard University Press, 1966), p. 236.

20 *BLJ*, viii, p. 218.

21 Squire Bancroft and William Archer, 'Byron on the Stage,' in *Byron, the Poet*, ed. Walter A. Briscoe (1924; rpt, New York: Haskell House Publishers, 1967), p. 169.

22 *BLJ*, viii, p. 156.

23 For examples of spectacular renderings of the fiery conclusion to *Sardanapalus*, see Downer, *The Eminent Tragedian*, pp. 236–7; J. C. Trewin (ed.), *The Journal of William Charles Macready, 1832–1851* (Carbondale and Edwardsville: Southern Illinois University Press, 1967), pp. 24–8; Martin K. Nurmi, 'The Prompt Copy of Charles Kean's 1838 Production of Byron's *Sardanapalus*,' *The Serif*, 5 (1968), 3–13; and Margaret J. Howell, '*Sardanapalus*,' *The Byron Journal*, 2 (1974), 50–2 (on Kean's 1853 mounting of the play).

24 *Survey*, pp. 59–60, 96–7; Leacroft, *The English Playhouse*, pp. 172–4, 180–5.

25 *Poetry*, iv, p. 338.

26 Both actors made favorable impressions on Byron. In 1811 he judged Kemble as Coriolanus to be 'glorious,' having 'exerted himself wonderfully'; *BLJ*, ii, p. 149. Kean's interpretation of Richard III in 1814 merited an enthusiastic review in Byron's journal: 'By Jove, he is a soul! Life – nature – truth – without exaggeration or diminution. Kemble's Hamlet is perfect; – but Hamlet is not Nature. Richard is a man; and Kean is Richard'; *BLJ*, iii, p. 244.

27 John Taylor, *The Stage*, quoted in Joseph W. Donohue, Jr, *Dramatic Character in the English Romantic Age* (Princeton, NJ: Princeton University Press, 1970), p. 251.

28 Sir Walter Scott, review of *Memoirs of the Life of John Philip Kemble*, by James Boaden, *Quarterly Review*, 34 (June 1826), p. 215.

29 John Keats, *Poetical Works and Other Writings*, ed. Harry Buxton Forman, rev. edn Maurice Buxton Forman (New York: C. Scribner's Sons, 1938–9), vol. 5, pp. 227, 229–32.

30 *BLJ*, VIII, p. 60.

31 *BLJ*, VIII, p. 112.

32 *The Times*, London, 26 April 1821, p. 3.

33 Thomas Medwin, *Medwin's Conversations of Lord Byron*, ed. Ernest J. Lovell, Jr (Princeton, NJ: Princeton University Press, 1966), p. 135.

34 *BLJ*, VIII, p. 155; see also Manning, 'Edmund Kean.'

35 *Poetry*, III, p. 55.

36 *BLJ*, VII, pp. 168, 190.

37 *Poetry*, IV, p. 337.

# Fixed, floating and fluid stages*

STANLEY VINCENT LONGMAN

Of necessity, the stage is a confined space. Moreover, its confines normally remain constant: the limits of its area are fixed. The idea of a confined, isolated area gathering the focus and energies of the play lies at the base of the theatrical experience. It is one of those things which distinguishes stage from screen. The screen, to be sure, is also a confined space. It, too, focuses attention and concentrates energies, but it does so with a fundamental difference: the confinement is variable and shifts with the camera. Entering on to stage or exiting means crossing a barrier by an act of volition; being on screen or off depends on the eye of the camera. When it looks at an actor he is on screen. The cinematic experience implies that the fictional world is all there awaiting the camera's pleasure. The theatrical implies that the fictional world is all here, encapsulated by the stage. This does not prevent the fictional world from extending beyond the confines of the stage, but it does give focus and power to on-stage activity and a curious dramatic value to any off-stage activity that remains 'out there' and unseen.

The stage is not only a confined space; it is also tacitly a metaphor for a much larger world. By virtue of the sense of occasion or festival created by the social act of theatre, a moment on stage assumes a weight beyond all proportion to the significance a similar moment might have in everyday life. A cough on stage is something more than a cough. A crossing is more than a matter of getting from here to there. The stage is expected to stand for more than itself. Almost by definition, it stands for the larger world, which in a way we occupy out in the auditorium.

These two circumstances, the inevitable confines of the stage and its insistence on standing for something more than itself, pose a considerable challenge to the playwright. Faced with an empty, confined space, available only for a span of time, he must define and characterize it with considerable care. That space is a literal, physical confined area, while being simultaneously an imagined realm.

This paper explores the various ways of characterizing stage space. As

* A draft of this paper was read at the *Themes in Drama* International Conference held at the University of California, Riverside in February 1985.

the title suggests, this exploration breaks stages into three types according to their dramatic use. Faced with accepting and using the stage's confines, the playwright may take them for what they are and incorporate them into the play's fictional world, as in early Realism or much of Neo-classical drama. This is the 'fixed stage.' The action of the play occurs within a closed space which remains the same throughout. The edges of the stage stand for the limits of the immediate fictional world and do not vary from the beginning of the play to the end. At the opposite extreme, the playwright may seemingly overleap the confines of the stage, shifting at will the virtual world of the play on and off stage, letting the confines stand for virtually the whole world, an inversion of Shakespeare's 'All the world's a stage.' This is the mode of action in Elizabethan drama and Epic Theatre, making the stage a constantly changing, fluid place. Still another alternative is to use the stage as encapsulating a generalized locale and several places within it and so producing the feeling that the stage is a sort of island. This is the 'floating stage.'

These three types of stages, fixed, fluid and floating, serve to describe the basic alternatives in defining and characterizing stage space. They are not of course the only ways of doing so. One way is to see stage use as 'representational' or 'presentational,' in accordance with the degree to which we are made aware of the fictional world of the play as against the stage as its platform for presentation. In other words, the more closely the stage is made to correspond to the appearance of the fictional world, the more representational the play is, while the more openly and frankly the play treats the stage as mere stage, the more presentational it is. Naturally, this calls for a sort of spectrum, placing a play's stage use somewhere closer to the one extreme or the other. The polarity itself is a just recognition of the double existence of the dramatic stage as itself and a fictional world simultaneously. By virtue of this condition, too, there can be no such thing as a purely representational or purely presentational stage. Plays can only tend in one direction or the other.

Nevertheless, the representational/presentational polarity seems to have less and less relevance to the ways in which the stage is really used. The distinction mattered in the earlier days of Realism and the various revolts against it, but nowadays no one is much interested in that battle. Representationalism stood for Realism and Naturalism, and presentationalism for all forms of anti-Realism. Placed against the whole history of drama, the theatre proves to have tended always towards the presentational until the days of Ibsen and Antoine. And now, in the last quarter of a century, the question of how closely the stage matches objective reality does not seem particularly indicative of anything that matters.

What is an interesting issue is the kind of consciousness applied to the stage. The confines of the stage, after all, impinge not only on off-stage space, but also upon the audience's space, and hence upon their collective consciousness. Seen this way, some uses of the stage are distinctly self-conscious, others merely conscious. The presence of the stage *as* stage is made to assume an aesthetic importance. We are then being continually reminded of its presence. The stage *as* stage, of course, always does matter to a play, but some of its uses are merely conscious, not self-conscious. Accordingly, one may remind the audience of the stage's existence while creating illusions. One may also fix once and for all the nature of the stage space in accord with the fictional world. Doing so does not deny the stage's existence, and may even depict the world in a distinctly unrealistic way. Samuel Beckett's *Endgame*, for example, is not representational nor certainly realistic, and yet its use of the stage is conscious, not self-conscious. Thornton Wilder's *Our Town*, to cite a very different (and much older) example, is essentially realistic, but its stage use is self-conscious.

Dividing stages into the fixed, the fluid and the floating, bears this idea in mind. The question of conscious or self-conscious stage use is not the only factor, however. Use of one or another of the three types of stage depends not only on consciousness, but also on how the terms of the play incorporate the conditions of the stage. The distinctions between these types of stages cut the matter a different direction. A fixed stage may be conscious or self-conscious. Jason Miller's *That Championship Season* uses a fixed and conscious stage, for example, while Luigi Pirandello's *Six Characters in Search of an Author* uses a fixed, self-conscious stage. Floating stages likewise may be conscious (as in the case of *The Crucible*) or self-conscious (as in the cases of *Mother Courage* or *The Visit*). The same holds true of the fluid stage: *King Lear* is conscious, while *The Good Woman of Setzuan* is self-conscious.

Perhaps somewhat closer to the three types listed is the idea of concentrated action as against comprehensive action. Again a spectrum between two extremes is involved. At issue is the degree to which the dramatic action adheres to the crucial moments of the play. If concentrated, the play employs a late point of attack and presents only those moments central to the dramatic issue at stake. The play then also represents a very restricted space. The unities of time and place are natural to such a play. Greek tragedy, Neo-classical drama and early Realism all tend to the concentrated. They tend also to the fixed stage. The comprehensive approach puts before the audience all actions relevant one way or another, even if to a mere subplot. Such a play would employ an early point of attack, rich and varied action that may take place over months or even years, and in many different, even widely separated locales. Elizabethan drama, Romantic drama, and Epic Theatre tend in this direction. And such plays tend to employ fluid stages.

The comprehensive/concentrated polarity draws distinctions based on either the economy and focus of the dramaturgy or its richness and variety.

They are worthwhile, revealing distinctions. There are two problems with this approach when we apply it to stage space. The first is that it does not apply specifically to the stage as space. Somehow, the space dimension of the theatre has lacked a vocabulary to help describe the various uses to which it may be put. The second is that there are no pure versions of either comprehensive or concentrated plays. All plays fall somewhere on a spectrum closer to the one extreme or the other. One that is closer to the concentrated always makes some use of comprehensive techniques, for, to be significant at all, stage action must be freed of the normal restraints of mundane time and space. Likewise, comprehensive drama requires some concentration or it would fly apart like a released spring. There are no purely presentational or representational plays, either. But there are fixed, fluid and floating stages. They really do exist.

Seeing stage use in accordance with these three types may help us more accurately to describe how plays use their medium. The enormous variety of ways a playwright may define and characterize stage space requires flexibility in analysis. Isolating three types would not at first seem to be a way of attaining that flexibility. Accepting three basic types, however, does not preclude recognizing the multiple ways in which they may be implemented. There are an infinite number of ways in which a play may assume a fixed stage. To designate it as a fixed stage is to recognize that the playwright then faces the issues inherent in such a stage. Moreover, there are ways in which the stage may adopt a double character, as both fixed and floating, or mix the types, characterizing one area of the stage one way, another, another.

To begin, the fixed stage translates the boundaries of the stage into virtual terms, and frequently derives dramatic values from the isolation thus produced. What these dramatic values may be and how they are created are never the same from one play to another. The natural confines of the stage serve not only in defining the immediate world of the play's fiction, but also imply an extension of that world beyond our view, a world beyond. If we are inside a room, what is in the next room, or outside, or in another distant town may assume dramatic importance. If we are before the palace in Thebes, what happens in Corinth across Mt Kithaeron matters, even (or especially) if it is beyond our view. Moreover, the many ways in which the audience is made to relate to the realm of the stage makes a difference. A fourth wall is vastly different from an orchestra in which a chorus dances and sings in a Greek theatre. Still, *A Doll's House* uses as fully a fixed stage as *Oedipus Rex*.

By way of illustration, here are three very different versions of the fixed stage: Harold Pinter's *The Room*, Anton Chekhov's *On the Harmfulness of Tobacco*, and Luigi Pirandello's *Six Characters in Search of an Author*. Each uses the boundaries of the stage in an unique way.

While *The Room* is the most recent of these plays, it is perhaps the most traditional in the manner in which it defines and characterizes stage space. The play nevertheless applies some novel and bizarre values to these boundaries, values that are distinctly 'Pinteresque.' Pinter himself has spoken about the unsettling feeling one has upon walking into a room and abruptly encountering persons engaged in an activity of an unknown nature or purpose. Most of Pinter's plays deal in this sensation, the audience itself feeling it on encountering any one of his many 'rooms.' For the characters, the sensation is in a sense reversed, especially in the earlier plays, so that the characters in the room take comfort from being here instead of 'out there' where activities of 'unknown nature or purpose' are going on. This is certainly the case in *The Room*, as well as *The Dumb Waiter* and *The Birthday Party*. It is cozy here, it's 'all right with me,' as Rose says. Outside it is 'murder,' cold and windy and the roads are covered with ice. Then, someone has moved in down in the basement: a Negro who must have some purpose in being in this house. After all, it is damp down there, and one would not want to be there if it were possible to avoid it. There are other rooms, other apartments, after all. Yet old Mr Kidd, the caretaker, who ought to know about them, has forgotten how many there are, or even how many floors the building has. The Negro, Riley, has been asking about Rose and has instructed Mr Kidd to let him know as soon as her husband Bert leaves. Meanwhile, Mr and Mrs Sands investigate the room with the idea of moving in, although clearly the place is not to let. The whole outside world carries a sense of threat and menace. Thus, the natural confines of the stage become not only the literal confines of the room, but a source of palpable comfort for its inhabitant as well.

Anton Chekhov's *On the Harmfulness of Tobacco*, too, is a play about a frightened character. Instead of paranoia, however, self-hatred propels the play forward. The sole character, Nyukhin, is not holed up in a room against the outside world; rather he is trapped in his own skin and has come on stage not so much to give the promised lecture as to get away from himself. And, all alone on stage, he makes a spectacle of himself. The normal confines of the stage expand to incorporate the whole theatre, and with it, the audience. The play develops out of the encounter between Nyukhin and us. We take a role in the play, as an audience gathered to hear Nyukhin's lecture on the harmfulness of tobacco. We assume, thus, the double identity of lecture audience *in* the play and audience *of* the play. Nyukhin takes a certain comfort from being on stage, even if he is a nervous wreck, for it means that, at least for the duration, he is away from his wife and his miserable life at the boarding school she runs at Dog Alley, 13. So the stage is a lecture podium from which he hopes to inspire companionship and compassion in his audience. The lecture on tobacco never occurs. Instead, we are treated to a desperate, buffoonish appeal for sympathy as

Nyukhin paints a picture of his henpecked misery. All this would make us intensely uncomfortable if it were a real lecture, but aesthetic distance and our other role as play audience lets us enjoy the spectacle. As lecture audience, we nevertheless reject him and his appeal for sympathy, simply by doing nothing. In desperation over our recalcitrance, he projects himself on to a hillside under the moon, a pole or scarecrow at peace with himself and the world. At the crisis moment in this spectacle of self-hatred, Nyukhin yanks off his frock coat that he wore thirty-three years ago at his wedding and that he still wears when his wife sends him out to give lectures for charity. He throws it to the ground and stamps on it. He virtually splits himself in two in order to provide his own effigy and do violence to it. Suddenly, he is aware that his wife is waiting for him in the wings of the theatre. He puts his coat back on, speaks a few words on the dangers of tobacco, and meekly exits to return to Dog Alley, 13, and his miserable life.

Space in this case is fixed, yes, but it takes on an intriguing configuration. The stage, Nyukhin's podium, is set over against the auditorium populated by the lecture audience. These two realms constitute the fixed, physical space, with a double existence: actor/speaker, stage/podium, audience/audience. The world beyond is split in two directions, Dog Alley pulling in one direction and the hillside under the moon in the other. Finally, all these tensions are brought to bear in the crucial moment when Nyukhin stamps on himself.

*Six Characters in Search of an Author* also expands its boundaries out into the house, although this time we are treated as if we did not exist. The actors have gathered at the beginning of the play to rehearse a 'hopeless' play by that perversely bewildering Pirandello. As in a fourth-wall play, we are Toms peeping in on the rehearsal, except that our space is not only acknowledged, the action spills into it: the Director, the Leading Lady, and even the Six Characters make their way through the auditorium in the early moments in the play. During the play, the Director often descends into our space to watch the 'show.' And at the end the Stepdaughter runs laughing out through the auditorium. For the duration of the play, however, the Characters are virtually confined to the stage. This is most graphically illustrated when the Son, who wants nothing to do with the play, attempts to leave the stage, only to find himself trapped. The Characters can only leave the confines of the stage to consult with the Director on the scenario for their play. They must stick together until that moment when the play's events liberate three of them: the two children die and the Stepdaughter runs from the theatre, leaving the Father, Mother and Son in lonely tableau. Despite the momentary release, all the Characters are doomed to repeat endlessly the effort to realize the play, always with the same result: the play fails to materialize and they are thrown back into their eternal search for an author. The theatre as a fixed space is clearly their trap.

The fluid stage is the diametrical opposite. If the fixed stage maintains its confines inviolate throughout the play, the fluid stage deliberately shatters them, so that the time and place of the action are in constant flux. We are now here, now there. The fluid stage is essentially a *platea*, a generalized acting area. The principle behind the *platea* is the collaboration of the audience in ascribing an imaginary place to the acting area. In its medieval version, the entrance of the actors through one mansion, or scenic piece, and their making their way to the *platea* invited the audience to transpose the mansion's depicted location to the *platea*. In the Elizabethan version, the mansions themselves became generalized in the form of various entrances: doors, windows, traps, discovery spaces, inner alcoves, and so forth, each serving to alert the audience to a change in place. Naturally, the fluid stage lends itself as readily to comprehensive dramaturgy as the fixed does to concentrated dramaturgy.

Despite the flow of action bounding over time and space, the stage retains its sense of confinement. The stage may enlarge or contract to encompass now a Senate chamber, now a bedchamber, but it remains a distinct place within boundaries. Entrances and exits still matter, and of course they always imply a world beyond. 'Noises off' still have impact. And frequently a distant land exerts a force or influence, as Norway upon Hamlet's Denmark, England on Macbeth's Scotland, or Venice on Othello's Cyprus. 'Suppose,' says the Chorus at the outset of *Henry V*, 'that within the girdle of this wooden O lie two mighty monarchies,' France and England. That may be a broad expanse, but it is still confined. And the individual scenes telescope much closer.

While the Elizabethan playhouse represents the epitome of the fluid stage, it is not the only version of it. With the advent of more and more thrust stages in the modern world and the influence of cinema, we encounter more and more plays employing fluid stages. Moreover, many of the unstageable plays out of the Romantic era have held stage after all on stages made fluid: *Goetz von Berlichingen*, *The Prince of Homburg*, or *Peer Gynt*, for example. Berthold Brecht, pronouncing himself the inventor of the only new dramaturgy since Aristotle, also rediscovered the fluid stage and made it integral to the idea of Epic Theatre.

The charm of the fluid stage derives from its playing upon our imagination. The stage, the actors, the properties do not disguise themselves, but simultaneously they conjure in our imagination a whole other world as we watch. Three vivid examples are Berthold Brecht's *Caucasian Chalk Circle*, Dario Fo's *Isabella, Three Ships and a Teller of Tall Tales* and the British National Theatre's production of *The Passion Play* as directed by Bill Bryden. In the case of the first, years pass and the stage moves wherever Grusha goes until it takes an interest in Azdak, whom it then follows until it meets Grusha again. Platforms on stage may become the walls of the palace in Grusinia's capital city, or mountains, or peasant huts, or the sides of a great chasm. The latter refers to the scene of the rotten rope bridge, where Grusha finds herself trapped by the pursuing ironshirts. She is in no real danger, obviously, for she is only a few feet from the stage floor, but the chasm is very real for all that.

In Fo's play, the stage contains a changeable platform equipped with several staffs. Easily and quickly, the platform transforms from throne room, with heraldic banners hanging from the staffs, to a gallows with nooses hanging, to Christopher Columbus' ship with sheets hanging. When Columbus sets sail on this platform, a rolling wagon is placed in front of it. Lords and ladies of Ferdinand and Isabella's court stand on this wagon waving handkerchiefs while stagehands pull them off stage by means of a great rope. Once 'at sea,' the ship encounters a great storm, created by lighting, sound and a great sheet stagehands shake in front of the platform, suggesting enormous, towering waves. Sailors on board are tossed about violently, and some are even thrown off into the surging brine, where they drown and crawl off stage on hands and knees below the shaking sheet.

Finally, in the case of *The Passion Play*, a modern adaptation of the English mystery cycle plays, the audience finds itself witnessing the whole story of the *Bible* from the Creation through the Last Judgement, the scenes taking place in their very midst. God rises up out of the crowd on a fork-lift and casts Lucifer into Hell and creates the world. Noah appears walking through the crowd in squeaking shoes, and has us help build the ark. We become the crowd witnessing Christ's persecution and calling for Barabbas, and so forth. It is environmental theatre in the full sense of the term. The action takes place in our very midst, and we walk to meet it, turn and find it behind us, and the next moment perhaps at our side. Still it operates within confines, and for the duration of any one scene we know where the focus of attention lies. This, too, is a fluid stage.

Finally, the floating stage falls somewhere between the two extremes of fixed and fluid. It respects the confines of the stage and maintains them throughout the duration, but they correspond to the boundaries of a generalized locale. This gives it the floating quality, for it stands as a sort of island removed from its normal surrounding: it is a relatively neutral stage made to represent a limited number of specific places within the general locale. That general locale is usually a town, as in Grover's Corners, New Hampshire in *Our Town*, Salem, Massachusetts in *The Crucible*, Solon, Michigan in *The Runner Stumbles*, Güllen, Switzerland in *The Visit*, or Eldridge, Iowa in *The Rymers of Eldridge*. If the fluid stage maintains the *platea* principle, the floating maintains Pierre Corneille's '*lieu théâtrale*.' Faced with the French Academy's rigorous requirement to adhere to the unities of time and place, Corneille declared, in essence, that if you do not tell the audience where exactly the action is, they will never know you moved, and of course if you do not tell them what time it is they'll never know how much later it may be at the end of the play. This is Corneille's '*lieu théâtrale*,' or 'theatrical place.' 'In and around the palace' became a favored setting for such Neo-classicists. Indeed, many ancient Greek plays are floating stage plays, plays such as *The Bacchae* or *The Birds* in which the exact location shifts about within a general one.

A peculiarity of the floating stage is that it takes advantage of qualities derived from both the fixed and the fluid stages. It maintains the confines of the stage, translating them into dramatic terms, and at the same time it invites the audience's imagination to collaborate in filling out the world of the play. In doing so, the play sometimes involves the audience in curious ways. Two good examples are Douglas Turner Ward's *Day of Absence* and Friedrich Dürrenmatt's *The Visit*.

Ward bills his play as a 'reverse minstrel show,' the actors being black in whiteface. We first encounter two Southern crackers sitting half asleep under signs saying 'store,' conversing languidly and waving lethargically to various imaginary passers-by. Two fundamental conditions are laid down by this opening: one is the play upon the minstrel show tradition, turning it topsy-turvy, and the other is the establishment of a whole town through the signs and the imaginary passers-by. In the course of the play, we are treated to scenes of growing frenzy all over town as the realization sets in that all the blacks in the community have disappeared. As these white folk turn frantic, the satire gains an added dimension by the reversal of the minstrel show convention. The floating stage in a sense envelops not only a mythical, bucolic Southern town, but also an exploiting society with such traditions as the minstrel show. We in the audience are very much *in* the play.

*The Visit* is set in another mythical town, the town of Güllen. During the play we witness scenes in the town's railway station, the Golden Apostle Hotel, the grocery store, the Mayor's office, the police chief's office, the church, Petersen's barn and the forest. All these are created suggestively within a setting that stands for Güllen as a whole, a pocket of misery in a land of plenty. Meanwhile, it is a play about collective guilt. The Gülleners, in their desperate need, succumb to the temptation of Mme Zachanasian's bribe, the offer of a fabulous sum of money in exchange for Alfred Ill's death. We are drawn into the play, partly by the engagement of our imagination, and partly by being a crowd ourselves. The opening at the railway station calls for imaginary trains to roar through the auditorium via stereo sound, an effective way to involve the audience. By the high point of the play, when the town turn out in all their finery to conduct an elaborate ritual accepting blood money and strangling Alfred Ill, we are ourselves enclosed in the town meeting with them, after the dismissal of the reporters and the media. Güllen's town limits expand to include us. Would we really do otherwise under such circumstances?

A floating stage might also be used to give a kaleidoscopic picture of an individual life. Milan Stitt's *The Runner Stumbles* portrays the struggle of Father Rivard with his own emotions over several years. He reconstructs his past while conversing and ruminating in his prison cell in the present, so that the floating stage encompasses essentially his memory, his mind and mental anguish. Indeed, the floating stage is most often used to engage either a collective, social conscience, as in *Day of Absence* or *The Visit*, or a personal vision, as in *The Runner Stumbles*.

There are, we need to note, those plays that are deliberate hybrids, usually joining the fixed stage with either the floating or the fluid. Tom Stoppard's *Rosencrantz and Guildenstern Are Dead*, for example, puts Rosencrantz and Guildenstern in a fixed, downstage area from which they must deal with an annoyingly fluid upstage, the world of *Hamlet*. Peter Luke's *Hadrian VII* uses upstage for the fixed, mundane, pitiful room of Frederick Rolfe and downstage for the floating, mad imaginings of his mind. It is also possible to define the same space in two different ways simultaneously, as Peter Weiss does in *Marat/Sade*, wherein the confines of the stage stand both for the asylum *and* for Paris in the time of the Revolution.

These three types of stages and their mixtures may describe how the stage is being used in any particular play more accurately than the ideas of presentationalism versus representationalism or concentrated versus comprehensive action. These types of stages also cut across the distinctions we are used to making between one style and another. True enough, Realism tends to the fixed stage, Epic Theatre to the fluid, Symbolism and Expressionism tend to the floating, and the Theatre of the Absurd tends to the fixed. Nevertheless, there is no direct correspondence. Realism's reliance on the fixed stage characterizes not only the plays of the early masters such as Ibsen and Chekhov, but also many very contemporary plays like David Mamet's *American Buffalo* or Sam Shepard's *True West*. Increasingly, however, there are realistic plays employing floating stages (John Guare's *Landscape of the Body* or Lanford Wilson's *Rymers of Eldridge*, for example). Epic Theatre occasionally abandons the fluid stage in favor of the floating stage, as in *Mother Courage* or *The Visit*. The Theatre of the Absurd turns typically to fixed stages (*Endgame*, 'The Chairs') but will occasionally adopt the floating, as in Ionesco's *Rhinoceros* or Arrabal's *Garden of Delights*.

Moreover, the variety of ways in which stages can be of one type or another, or even mixtures, provides the playwright with a wealth of choices that ultimately makes every play unique. The challenge of that empty space is basic to the composing of any play and should also be basic to analyzing any completed play. The restrictions of space imposed by the stage are one of the sources of inspiration to playwrights. The response we witness in the form of their plays deserves investigation and appreciation.

# Subverting/alienating performance structures*

## JAMES S. MOY

*Life's but a walking shadow, a poor player*
*That struts and frets his hour upon the stage*
*And then is heard no more: it is a tale*
*Told by an idiot, full of sound and fury,*
*Signifying nothing.*

— Shakespeare

*One thinks one is tracing the outline of the thing's nature over and over again, and one is*
*merely tracing round the frame through which we look at it . . . A Picture held us captive.*
*And we could not get outside it, for it lay in our language and our language seemed to repeat it*
*to us inexorably.*

— Wittgenstein

Most investigations into the nature of theatrical locales have centered on the ability of such spaces to focus attention on the performance being offered. Within this panoptic theatrical enterprise, the privileged gaze of the renaissance ideal viewer has dominated until quite recently.[1] During the twentieth century, Artaud, Brecht, Piscator, the Russian Experimentalists of the 1920s, Grotowski, Schechner, and many others sought to break the hold of the picture frame by posing alternatives. Accordingly, their experiments brought about new staging techniques along with radical reconfigurations of the physical relationship between audience and performed event. Despite the experimentation, however, the primary perception of the role of the theatrical space remained the same: to provide both a physical (architectural) and metaphorical (scenic) grounding for a performed event. The performance site, then, still served the substance of representation.

This study, however, will examine the ways in which performance structures (both architectural and scenic) can serve actively at once to alienate an audience from a staged representation and to elevate that audience to what might be called a simulacral plane. As the proscenium theatre remains the dominant architectural mode for performance, the

* A draft of this paper was read at the *Themes in Drama* International Conference held at the University of London, Westfield College in March 1985.

study will begin by treating subversions of the picture-frame theatre and then move on to other formats.

In the conventional proscenium theatre, the alienation of an audience from a performance can easily be achieved through the subversion of its metaphorical grounding, forcing the viewer to read background against the performed text. The space created by this tension disrupts and ultimately displaces the significance of the narrative line. Once alienated, the audience member becomes a free-floating consciousness, intermittently interacting with the performance event depending upon the nature of the sequence developing on stage. Clearly, many of today's cinema and electronically mediated entertainments by their very natures operate under this aliena-tion paradigm.

Accepting the mediated event as a uniquely mass expression, this study will seek precursors in the nineteenth century when theatrical entertain-ments clearly geared to the tastes of the masses first emerged. In addition, as I am primarily involved in American studies, I will focus my attention on American developments although it goes without saying that similar structures emerged in Europe.

Variety entertainments which came to dominate the nineteenth-century popular stage provide unique examples of performances whose internal structures served to distance audiences from the theatrical event. Through their spectacular sequence of episodes, audiences were at once detached and displaced from one lexia to the next, driven by an ever rising horizon of expectations. The proairetic, then, became the driving force in these entertainments with displacement serving as its agent. Unlike the Brech-tian distancing intended to provide space for audience reflection on the didactic content of the performed event, these entertainments displaced viewers through a sequence of lexias, subverting the contents of each episode in the process: '. . . they want spectacle. No effort has been made to convert them to the seriousness of the content, nor even to the seriousness of the code . . . they only want some sign, they idolise the play of signs and stereotypes, they idolise any content so long as it resolves itself into a spectacular sequence.'[2] Alienation in such variety acts was generally accomplished by a radical shift of metaphorical grounding for each episode. This sequential displacement is clearly in evidence on the playbill for the week of 9 May 1898 from Proctor's Pleasure Palace (plate 23). Included in the sequence of fifteen events were several acrobatic acts, 'Australian Ring Experts,' a sketch by Clara Morris, a troupe of performing dogs 'consisting of 15 Snow White Poodles . . . together with a Troupe of Acrobatic Dogs, 5 in number,' 'Miss Edsall's delightful one act Comedietta, "THE TWO RUBIES,"' and a movie depicting views of preparations for war. Other playbills from Proctor's Pleasure Palace included acts like 'THE LUMIERE CINEMATOGRAPH,' jugglers, ethnic comedians, and

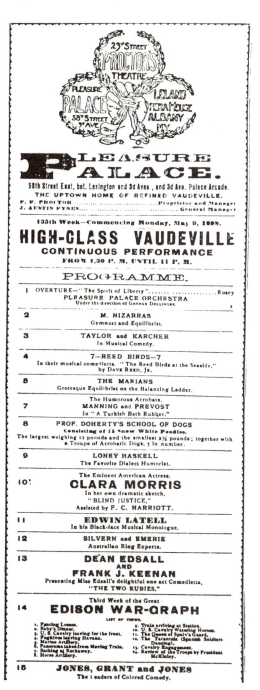

23 Proctor's Pleasure Palace playbill dated 9 May 1898. (Courtesy of the Hoblitzelle Theatre Arts Library, Humanities Research Center, University of Texas, Austin)

'PROF. GEO. LOCKHART'S COMIC ELEPHANTS.'[3] The ultimate attack on the very possibility of a discursive line can be found in the fact that the order of acts varied from day to day depending upon the whim of the theatre manager and the availability of talent.

While the disruptions of the implicit metaphorical spaces in variety entertainments could on occasion be viewed as movement from one neutral space to another, Steele MacKaye in his 1880 renovation of the Madison Square Theatre introduced an architectural mechanism for the displacement of elaborately detailed settings (plate 24). Initially intended to provide for rapid scene changes, it could be argued that the awe with which audience members might have viewed such changes produced a dislocation as well. In MacKaye's elaborate machinery, one can clearly see a precursor to the 'jump-cut' of today's cinema, as the frame of one scene literally displaced its predecessor as it dropped or was elevated into view. Theatre architecture as mediating mechanism at the Madison Square Theatre clearly occupied a position similar to that of the camera and projector in the cinema or television.

Beyond serving dislocations internal to performed events, there existed several other architectural means for alienating an audience from the content of performed texts during the nineteenth century. Significant among these were theatres which provided for the simultaneous performance of several events. Nineteenth-century American theatre spaces designed for such events include the Greenwich Street Theatre (1797), Spalding and Rogers's combined circuses (1850s), Proctor's Pleasure Palace and Garden of Palms (1895), and the Folies Bergere (1911).

The Greenwich Street Theatre opened in 1797 as America's first multi-function theatre.[4] Constructed by John B. Ricketts as a structure to house his entertainments, its flexible interior space allowed for both circus and traditional theatre performances. Indeed, a rendering from the period (plate 25) of an earlier but similar structure by Ricketts shows how the gap between stage and pit could be bridged in performance. A description from a promised entertainment typical of Ricketts's offerings provides insight into how this space might have been used:

New Performances on the Tight Rope. Mr Spinicuta will for this night only dance with large TWIG-BASKETS fastened to his feet. Second a COMIC DANCE, in which he will throw a Half-Summerset, backwards and forwards, and will DANCE UPON HIS SHINS, Instead of his feet. For the first time this season, he will throw himself into the Air, and perform the SINGLE & DOUBLE LEAP OVER THE GARTER, Backwards and forwards, upwards of Ten Feet high; and will likewise PLAY ON THE VIOLIN, and perform several tricks with a CANE ... GROUND AND LOFTY TUMBLING On the Stage By Messrs. SULLY, F. RICKETTS, RENO LANGLEY, Master SULLY, and Clown Mr. Spinacuta; who will jump down from the table and Chair, and throw a summerset, with his FEET AND HANDS TIED. Mr. Sully

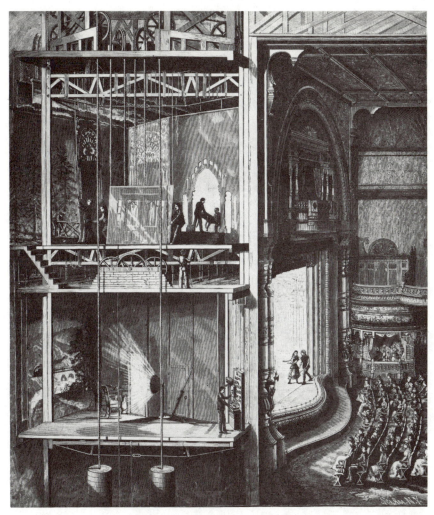

24 Interior of Madison Square Theatre, New York City, 1880. (Courtesy of the University of Wisconsin Libraries)

will throw a summerset tied up in a Bag, and also with an expanded Umbrella in his hand. To which will be added, (for the first time) a NEW PANTOMIME . . .[5]

Clearly, Ricketts's variety entertainments employed the type of displacement discussed earlier. More important here is the fact that two significantly different activities were proceeding simultaneously, a series of tightrope acts in the pit and a sequence of 'GROUND AND LOFTY TUMBLING' followed by a pantomime on the stage. Accordingly,

PONEY RACE WITH REAL PONIES AT THE PANTHEON AND RICKETTS'S AMPHITHEATRE, PHILADELPHIA. Jan.y 14.th 1797.

25 Interior of Ricketts's Circus, Philadelphia, 1797. (Courtesy of The Historical Society of York County, Pennsylvania)

audience members once detached from either sequence would continually shift attention between pit and stage as spectacular moments captured their gaze.

The enterprise of Spalding and Rogers raised the coincidence of performed events to a still higher level.[6] Where Ricketts persisted in the use of the proscenium stage while using the pit for his equestrian entertainments, Spalding and Rogers discarded the proscenium altogether. They owned several travelling circuses and the entertaiments were most impressive when their three circuses converged on one city (plate 26). From the playbill pictured it becomes clear that each member of the audience could expect to register only fragments of the volume of the activity offered, as again clowns, gymnasts, horses, tightrope acts, and pantomimes competed for his attention. Indeed, even when their three companies performed separately as individual units, the entertainments offered were clearly simultaneous events in complex configurations. In both Ricketts's and Spalding and Rogers's circus entertainments one can see a marked tendency away from the picture-frame theatre as the perfect view of the privileged gaze is replaced by the mass audience's privilege to focus on whatever it chooses.

In theatres like the Folies Bergere and Proctor's Pleasure Palace and Garden of Palms can be found the mass audience's appropriation of a variation on the proscenium environment. The Folies Bergere (plates 27, 28) which opened in New York in 1911 appears to be a formalization of the chaotic simultaneity seen in the earlier enterprises of both Ricketts and Spalding and Rogers.

The Folies Bergere advertised a 'Company of 200 Artists including 100 Girls . . . 3 Musical Directors. 33 Musicians,' along with Marthe Lenclud, 'The Prettiest Woman in Paris.'[7] Offering revue entertainments whose reception would not have been unlike that of the less rigidly structured variety form, the Folies Bergere also introduced cabaret entertainments which featured '10 Sensational European Acts' including Marthe Lenclud who performed a 'Venus Apache' dance; LaBelle Titcomb who appeared in a series of poses on horseback; 'Les Marquards,' a team of French eccentric dancers; 'The Amoroso Sisters . . . with their dancing-acrobatic-contortion-aerial turn'; the 'Grizzly Bear' dancers; Olga Petrova who imitated famous celebrities; Simone de Beryl who posed 'gracefully while the cinematograph plays gracefully over her figure'; and Marcel's Living Statues.[8]

While the entertainments were typical of the period, the Folies Bergere introduced some innovations both in content and staging. One of the owners later boasted that 'instead of merely nude murals on the boxes, we had nude murals *in* the boxes. When a bugle sounded in the rear of the theatre . . . lights disclosed Jean Marcel's Living Statues . . . posing in little

26 Spalding and Rogers playbill. (Courtesy of the Hoblitzelle Theatre Arts Library, Humanities Research Center, University of Texas, Austin)

27 Interior of Folies Bergere, New York City, 1911. (Courtesy of the Center for Research Libraries, Chicago)

more than make-up.'[9] To the accompaniment of music from a double concert grand piano on the stage, Marcel displayed his models in 'two miniature stages, high up in the walls of the theatre on either side of the proscenium arch.'[10] Further, in an attempt to foster a more intimate environment during some performances, 'a platform, level with the stage was literally drawn over the orchestra pit, making a sort of extended "apron" that brought the performers very close to the audience. The music at these times was played from the stage itself.'[11]

28 Stage of the Folies Bergere, New York City, 1911. (Courtesy of the Center for Research Libraries, Chicago)

Here again, the alienated audience member would continually shift his attention through the three picture-frame stages. Despite the tacit acceptance of a theatre form which relied on displacement, it is intriguing to note the desire to make the performance more intimate by bringing it closer to the audience. As the tension created between metaphorical space and performed text defined the site for the operation of displacement, so the space created by the tension between the alienation inherent in this displacement form and the desire for intimacy or contact served to create a place for another order of performance, one which transcended mere representation. Within this space of absence there was created a desire which could not be filled by observed performance, but demanded new presences. Into this space the Folies Bergere introduced dinner. Indeed, the Folies Bergere is usually cited as America's first dinner playhouse and nightclub. Audience activity, then, had been added to the fractured events of the simultaneous and alienating staged performances.

Proctor's Pleasure Palace and Garden of Palms which opened in 1895 (plates 29 and 30) not only featured the type of variety/displacing entertainments discussed earlier, but also provided an architectural metaphor for these seemingly chaotic theatricals.[12] For the price of a single admission, one was allowed 'to wander over the entire building and see all the entertainments,' which included the main stage attractions, the beer garden on the roof (plate 31), and variety performances in the cabarets beneath each of the two main auditoria.[13] One of the cabarets was described as a 'theatre-bar-restaurant which . . . included two large bars. Entertainers of all kinds did their specialties and there were tables where meals were served to patrons. The place remained open until three o'clock in the morning.'[14] Most intriguing was the main stage which allowed performances to be '. . . seen by two audiences, one in the theatre and the other seated at tables in the Palm Garden sipping liquid refreshment, or eating hearty dinners.'[15] As depicted in the illustration, several events could be offered simultaneously. Here, then, audience members not interested in any of the main stage performance events could choose to gaze at the audience on the other side of the double stage, concentrate on their drink if they happened to be seated in the Palm Garden, or simply leave for one of the other performance locales in the building.

The picture-frame stage had been transformed from a mechanism for affirming the power behind the privileged gaze of the renaissance elite into an expression of the power of the mass audiences arbitrarily to select new objects of focus, a power which has been characterized as fascistic.[16] The project of the elite theatre had been representation. The masses, however, dreamed of a theatre which could somehow address their unrepresentable existence. 'That the silent majority (or the masses) is an imaginary referent does not mean they don't exist. It means that *their representation is no longer*

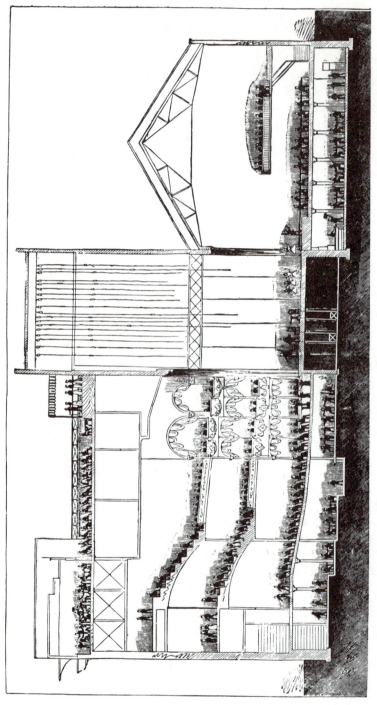

29 Section view showing performance areas of Proctor's Pleasure Palace and Garden of Palms, New York City, 1895 (Courtesy of the University of Wisconsin Libraries)

30  Interior view through mainstage of Proctor's Pleasure Palace and Garden of Palms.
(Courtesy of the University of Wisconsin Libraries)

31  View of a typical turn-of-the-century roof beer garden. (Courtesy of the
University of Wisconsin Libraries)

*possible*. The masses are no longer a referent because they no longer belong
to the order of representation. They don't express themselves, they are
surveyed.'[17] To this end, the theatre of the masses embraced complexity
and displacement over representation. While the elite theatre of the day
focused on the details of difficult family life in an ever more complex society,
the masses chose to avoid the contents and mirror the complexities. In their
involved refractions of these complexities, the new reflections turned back
upon themselves to create a simulacral rehearsal for life, a simulation.[18]

> Representation mingles with what it represents . . . one thinks as if the
> represented were nothing more than the shadow or reflection of the represen-
> ter. A dangerous promiscuity and a nefarious complicity between the reflection

and the reflected which lets itself be seduced narcissistically. In this play of representation, the point of origin becomes ungraspable. There are things like reflecting pools, and images, an infinite reference from one to the other, but no longer a source, a spring. There is no longer a simple origin. For what is reflected is split in itself and not only as an addition to itself of its image. The reflection, the image, the double, splits what it doubles.[19]

As today's advertisements both reflect and inform while creating audience desire, so the architecture of the nineteenth-century popular theatre provided a space wherein simulated utopian-seeking desire could be rehearsed. This utopian project persists to this day in places like Disneyland, while its mediated doubles continue through the cinema and television.[20]

## NOTES

1 For treatments of the affirming renaissance gaze and the proscenium stage, see Stephen Orgel, 'Poetics of Spectacle,' *New Literary History*, 2 (1971), 367–89 and Timothy Murray, 'Theatrical Legitimation: Forms of French Patronage and Portraiture,' *PMLA*, (March 1983), 170–82.
2 Jean Baudrillard, *In the Shadow of the Silent Majorities*, trans. Paul Foss, Paul Patton, and John Johnston (New York: Semiotext(e), 1983), p. 10.
3 Playbills from Proctor's Pleasure Palace dated 9 May 1898, 25 April 1898, and 22 March 1897, all at the Hoblitzelle Theatre Arts Library, Humanities Research Center, University of Texas, Austin.
4 For a detailed treatment of this theatre, see my 'Greenwich Street Theatre 1797–1799,' *Theatre Survey*, 20 (November 1979), 15–26.
5 *Aurora and General Advertiser* (Philadelphia), 12 April 1796, p. 2.
6 For a treatment of this enterprise, see Penelope M. Leavitt and James S. Moy, 'Spalding and Rogers' Floating Palace, 1852–1859,' *Theatre Survey*, 25 (May 1984), 15–27.
7 *New-York Daily Tribune*, 23 April 1911, p. 7.
8 *New York Times*, 23 September 1911, p. 7.
9 Jesse L. Lasky with Don Weldon, *I Blow My Own Horn* (Garden City, NY: Doubleday & Company, 1957), p. 83.
10 *New-York Daily Tribune*, 28 April 1911, p. 7.
11 *New York Times*, 28 April 1911, p. 13.
12 For a detailed study of this theatre, see my 'Proctor's Pleasure Palace and Garden of Palms 1896–1899,' *Nineteenth-Century Theatre Research*, 8 (Spring 1980), 17–27.
13 *New York Times*, 28 July 1895, p. 11.
14 William Moulton Marston and John Henry Feller, *F. F. Proctor Vaudeville Pioneer* (New York: Richard R. Smith, 1943), pp. 163–4.
15 *Brooklyn Daily Eagle*, 15 December 1928, quoted in Marston and Feller, *F. F. Proctor Vaudeville Pioneer*, p. 150.
16 Britta Sjogren, 'Television, The Spectator and Desire,' a paper read at the

Society for Cinema Studies Conference at the University of Wisconsin – Madison, 24 March 1984. In discussing television, she calls the viewer's position 'fascistic' because of the power expressed by the viewer in turning the set on and off.

17 For a detailed discussion of his ideas regarding the simulacrum, see Jean Baudrillard, *Simulations*, trans. Paul Foss, Paul Patton, and Philip Beitchman (New York: Semiotext(e), 1983).

18 Baudrillard, *In the Shadow of the Silent Majorities*, p. 20.

19 Jacques Derrida, *Of Grammatology*, trans. Gayatri Chakravorty Spivak (Baltimore: Johns Hopkins University Press, 1976), p. 36.

20 Louis Marin, 'Disneyland: A Degenerate Utopia,' *Glyph* 1 (Baltimore: Johns Hopkins University Press, 1977), pp. 50–66.

# Rich joy of the sixties: the streets of New York City as theatrical space*

## WILLIAM W. FRENCH

In 1966 Robert Brustein lamented that American theater fell between 'sense and sensuality' and endorsed John Millington Synge's words that:

> On the stage one must have reality and one must have joy; and that is why the intellectual modern drama has failed, and people have grown sick of the false joy of the musical comedy, that has been given them in place of the rich joy found only in what is superb and wild in reality.[1]

At the very time Brustein wrote, the avant-garde, experimental theatre, whose 'whey-faced solemnity' he deplored was being trucked – literally – into the streets and undergoing some astonishing metamorphoses under the conditions of performance in the open space and natural daylight, with noise and confusion and a restless and sometimes hostile audience.

By 1965 the streets of New York City became the last frontier past which the experimental 'serious' theater movement pushed. The streets, playgrounds, parks – especially in the tenement sections of the city – became the ultimate theatrical space because playing in the streets represented the ultimate aesthetic and political dare. Performed in the open air, usually in natural daylight, under conditions primitive by the standards of modern, indoor theater, the street theater of New York between 1965 and 1975 was characteristically highly mobile and fluid in form and style; it varied with the different motives – political, aesthetic, religious – that drove people into the streets. The one powerful and pervasive motive they shared was a desire to break down barriers, especially those they felt had been arbitrarily erected to keep theater indoors serving a frivolous, elite audience. By destroying traditional conceptions of theater as indoor, class-bound, and largely verbal, and by giving birth to what Gerald Berkowitz calls a 'theatrical movement of direct experience rather than a depiction or description of an experience,'[2] the street-theater people hoped to make a theater that brought actors and audiences together in a shared space. Thrust stages, theater-in-the-round, 'total' theater in

---

* A draft of this paper was read at the *Themes in Drama* International Conference held at the University of California, Riverside in February 1985.

which the actors became part of the audience and part of the audience became actors, were all fine; but they stopped short of the ultimate playing space, the streets, a theatrical space with no barriers at all. Naturalism in the European theater had long since treated environment as a dynamic element of human experience.[3] In the United States many people in street theater would move to the idea that the streets themselves are a phenomenon of theater, others to the idea that actors should neither display their histrionic skill nor screen themselves behind an assumed character, but depict themselves as they are naturally. To most, street theater assumed a religious significance. To all, it offered the widest possibility for interchange between audience and performers on the widest of all stages.

By the mid-1960s street performance developed in three modes, each growing out of forms and theories extended from mainstream theater. The first, forms of ethnic or racial or working-class theater, were simply moved outdoors and refashioned to serve in the expanded physical environment and political atmosphere of the sixties. Forms of political theater such as the agit-prop of John Bonn's *Prolet Buehne* never died; certainly the spirit was easily resurrected by people like Marketta Kimbrell when the time was ripe. This kind of street theater did not spring from the counter-culture, with which street theater is often associated, though, like street theater since the nineteenth century, it responded to social conditions and political agendas affecting large numbers of working-class people. Second, altered forms of traditional classical theater were brought outdoors, notably by Joseph Papp with his mobile Shakespeare theater and by Patricia Reynolds. These groups had no counter-culture affiliations nor specifically political motives. Third, the avant-garde, experimental theater extended into the streets. This mode is, indeed, associated with the counter-culture – one thinks of Peter Schumann – though many notable exceptions must be made. In other cases, like that of Maryat Lee, connections with the experimental theater were tenuous.

This street-theater movement reached its apex in 1971 when the New York City Department of Cultural Affairs and the Black Theatre Alliance sponsored a two-day seminar to spread information about street-theater techniques. By 1965 political bodies had strong reasons to encourage urban street theater. The ghetto riots of the mid-sixties shocked many Americans into a political awareness. For some, street theater presented a way to keep people too busy to riot. August Heckscher, Commissioner of New York City Parks and Recreation, said that the street theaters would keep the city 'cool.'[4] City officials favored a commercialized approach: draw together talent, add a few stars, give them a Broadway musical script, and package up a show. A troupe called Broadway in the Streets was thrown together which offered, with considerable condescension, 'quality entertainment' to the 'culturally deprived.'[5] It soon failed; victim of inflated costs and casts and material inappropriate to its audience. Where Joseph Papp succeeded by bringing a theater of classics, and Peter Copani and Maryat Lee succeeded by bringing material out of the audience itself, Broadway in the Streets soon failed, child of funding agencies. Synge's 'false joy' would not migrate to the wild streets.

However, the sense of social urgency loosened foundation and granting agency purse strings, and large amounts of funding became available. Dozens of individuals and groups won sponsorship, and a movement was underway. Among questions discussed at the 1971 seminar was the role of lighting and sound equipment. Some argued that such equipment is more than supportive to outdoor performance: it is vital. East Harlem's Third World Revelationists, for example, used no sound equipment at all, relying on audience participation. Other groups eschewed amplifiers in favor of 'projection' or 'location,' performing in closed-off streets or small parks and places where the architecture would assist vocal projection. Others, like Brother Jonathan Ringkamp, took a philosophic position: use of technical equipment was out of the question because 'theater is an accident that occurs on the street corner.'[6] Another important topic was enlisting community help – especially children – to achieve security, a heavy consideration in street performance. Also, everyone agreed on the necessity of a platform stage: even a minimal height of two or three feet was felt to be helpful. Mobile flat-bed trucks with stages that could fold out and flats that could be erected rapidly were favored.[7] Indeed, 'floats' or pageants became the most commonly-used space, almost a standard.

One who inspired the use of the mobile stages was Joseph Papp, whose Riverside Shakespeare offered free Shakespeare outdoors as early as 1956. Papp set out to bring a form of traditional classical theater outdoors, working through a group based in a Lower East Side church. He outfitted an elaborate trailer truck that moved among parks and streets. He did not hesitate to use amplification, though he cannily sought locations where buildings or trees would help absorb street noise. In the late-fifties Papp expanded the operation to a two-vehicle caravan and later to three flat beds that could be set up as a semihexagon. The arrangement – which could be readied in about two hours – created a wide playing space and allowed performance on different levels, from the ground up to several feet above the truck bed. Some of the audience could sit or stand very close to the outer edge of the wings. Papp's design was an elaboration of the Federal Theater's Portable Theater Caravan, of which he had fond memories; the Caravan first exposed him to culture, and he has always been intent upon providing the same opportunity to others. He has found street audiences astonishingly receptive. Of a production of *A Midsummer Night's Dream* some years ago he says, 'You think tough kids are going to say, "What garbage is this?" But people listen, kids get quiet. They say that music has charms to soothe. Well, Shakespeare does.'[8]

Patricia Reynolds also brought theater classics to the streets. She operated Theater in the Street from 1963 to 1975, playing to audiences in the humblest, poorest streets in the city. Trained at the Royal Academy of Dramatic Art, Reynolds had performed with the Old Vic and taught at the American Theatre Wing and at the American Academy of Dramatic Arts. She was in part motivated toward street theater by her distress with the cultural deprivation of ghetto dwellers; she saw her role as the bringer of culture. She was appalled that people could live their entire lives twenty minutes from Broadway and never see 'legitimate' theater. 'So many people in the United States grow up without theater. It's a great tragedy, like being denied one's birthright.'[9] Reynolds initiated Theater in the Street as a non-profit Equity project after organizing a play for the East Fourth Street Betterment Association's annual street fair in 1962.

Once she had experienced working with street audiences she never wanted to stop. She was thrilled by their enthusiasm. She points out that street audiences were absolutely free to walk away at any time; but they did not. Audiences would grow during the performance. 'When we would get there,' she says, 'no one would be there. But by the time the show started people seemed to come out of the wall.' The audience would pitch

> . . . their whole hearts into a show put on in the middle of their teeming block. . . . Chairs are sometimes donated by parish houses, but the audience is happy enough to sit on crates or front stoops or in balcony seats in their windows. After the show, people push to meet the actors, touch their beards, help cart away chairs. Nobody is truly just a spectator but an excited participant in everything that goes on.[10]

Theater in the Street literally played on the street and sidewalk surfaces. Reynolds was especially thrilled by the propinquity and involvement of the audience: 'The people are so close to you, sometimes you have to step over them or between them to continue performing. And since it's daylight you can see their faces. They cheer when anybody kisses anyone else. They yell, "He's behind you!" or "He's dead!" They shudder when a gun is pointed in their direction.'

In 1965 Reynolds added a flat-bed truck that carried a stage with canvas backdrop and two side flats, elevating the action a foot or so in order that the audiences of 500 to 1,000 could see the action better. Equipment – scenery, costumes, props, sound system – was brought in a van which then served as a dressing room. The 1966 season for Theater in the Street consisted of thirty performances at sites throughout Manhattan and Brooklyn and The Bronx including playgrounds, parks, housing projects, and blocked-off streets. Spectators sat on curbs, boxes, folding chairs, balconies, or looked out of windows. Street noise always accompanied the performances and became part of it: dogs barking, airplanes droning overhead, trains going by, sirens blaring. The hum of traffic and audience never ceased. The repertory, in Spanish and English, included *It Should Happen to a Dog*, an adaptation of a Chekhov story entitled 'The Chameleon,' and *The Bungler*, adapted from Molière's *L'Etourde*, a *commedia dell'arte* piece.

Where Reynolds sought to spread culture through Theater in the Street, Marketta Kimbrell wanted to 'bring good theater to the working people of the United States,' those not in the cultural mainstream. Kimbrell started the New York Street Theatre Ensemble as a multi-ethnic troupe in 1968 with a political commitment, performing throughout the Lower East Side adaptations of Brecht's *The Exception and the Rule* and Lorca's *The Puppet Play of Don Cristobel*.[11] Trained at the Theatre Academy of Prague, Kimbrell rehearsed her company by her own rigorously professional standards. The company, still currently active and called the New York Street Theatre Caravan – a nod to its political roots in the thirties Federal Theater – finances its street-theater operation through tours of major European theaters and festivals and paid performances on college campuses and in union halls. The group is not agit-prop. But Kimbrell borrowed some agit-prop techniques, especially easy portability. Groups in the 1920s and 1930s like John Bonn's *Prolet Buehne* performed flat on the street.[12] Kimbrell used a flat-bed truck convertible to a pageant within twenty minutes. Her adaptations of Brecht and Lorca and her versions of folk tales and historical material such as the Sacco and Vanzetti trial rely on a certain amount of stereotyping and generalizing and dialectics. But Kimbrell remains committed to the artistic standards of her European theater heritage, which accounts for the endurance of the Caravan.

Another group that performed on a pageant and had a strong but unique artistic and social commitment was Maryat Lee's Soul and Latin Theater. Also known as SALT, this group operated in East Harlem between 1968 and 1970.[13] Lee was teaching street theater at the New School for Social Research when she moved into street theater after a hiatus of over twenty years. She wrote four plays for SALT based on improvisations and oral history, *Day to Day* (Samuel French, 1970), *After the Fashionshow*, *The Classroom*, and *Luba*, all with strong social themes. These plays were crafted through an unusual process involving oral history, improvisation, and authorial emendation; they were acted by 'indigenous' actors, dwellers of the East Harlem community whose lives they dramatize. They constitute a kind of Theater of Phenomenology or a Theatre of Physical Fact.[14] Rooted in the historical phenomena of the daily lives of slum dwellers, they convey with immediacy the experiential reality of living in East Harlem during the sixties. They depict family quarrels, drug use, homosexuality, class confrontations in schoolrooms, unrelieved anger, in a language very close to the real. Rather than the sort of historical facts that make newspaper headlines, they embody the force of sensuous life lived beneath the headline events.

During the summer of 1968 the SALT troupe of ten actors and five staff members gave thirty-five performances in the meanest streets of Manhattan, Brooklyn, and The Bronx. Operating out of a settlement house on East 116th Street, the troupe travelled in an old automobile that pulled a rented hay wagon into place. The wagon was outfitted with portable steps, flaps, wings, and loudspeakers, and could be set up as a stage measuring 8' × 14' in about twenty minutes. A public address system with three microphones and two loudspeakers amplified the actors' voices. Lee estimates that SALT played to 15,000 to 20,000 people that summer on $13,500. Audiences threw water bombs and shouted obscenities; many spectators were apathetic; the fringes of the street audiences were alive with movement and chatter; but a core always paid careful attention and rewarded the actors with backtalk, applause, cheers, and jeers, and questions following the performance. SALT was deliberately a primitive theater, embodying Lee's notion in a paraphrase of Lope de Vega, that theater at its best consists of 'three planks, two actors, and a passion.' She strove seriously to bring this primitive theater 'not,' she insists, '*to* the streets but *out* of the streets,' a theater whose medium was the people who constituted both audience and actors.

As different as they were, all these groups had certain features in common. The most important was the propinquity of the audience to the players. Especially for groups like the Pageant Players or the early Theater in the Street that performed flat on the ground, the theatrical space dissolved completely: street event and theater, and street space and theater space became one. Theater can go no further to destroy illusion and to foster the kind of primitivism that had inspired the painters and sculptors of an earlier generation.

Further, street audiences were usually invited to participate in a discussion following each performance. The SALT actors and crew, for example, would sit on the edge of the stage and talk for up to two hours with the audience. These sessions were considered part of the performance; they were a way of tearing through masks, shunning 'false roles,' being honest. Such 'rapping' owes something, perhaps, to the Becks' Living Theatre techniques of 1968–9 of inviting their audiences to participate in presentations such as *Paradise Now*. A 'sense of mission' informed their behavior.[15] But in the ghetto streets behavior such as the Becks foisted upon their intense middle-class audiences would not do.

Only in the streets could a truly radical theater like that proposed by Artaud happen, a theater that abolished stage and auditorium and established 'direct communication between the spectator and the spectacle, between the actor and the spectator.'[16] Artaud had in mind not a city street but a 'hangar or barn' reconstructed to become a holy place. But in the summer heat of the sixties and early seventies the city streets became to many a holy place, a ground on which a sacred event could take place. Peter Brook envisioned a similar theater with his 'rough theater,' a 'theater that's not in a theater, the theater on carts, on wagons . . . audiences standing, drinking.' This 'rough theater' is allied to his idea of a 'holy theater' that makes the sacred invisible visible.[17] Also, this street theater was more like Robert Brustein's traditional Theater of Communion than his modern Theater of Revolt;[18] it was a revolt against the theater of revolt, making a stab at refashioning belief in a coherent universe. Writing in 1968, for example, Maryat Lee set the principal aim of SALT as to 'increase communication between estranged peoples – between parents and children, between individuals, between Puerto Ricans and Blacks.'[19] Lee thought of theater as a way for actors and audiences to participate in acts of self-discovery that would 'help bridge divisions and create a cleansed and loving community.'[20] Lee's idea of theater stressed an intimate relationship among location-drama-actor-audience. Actor and audience should reside together in the same *locus* (for this reason, among others, she has been critical of people like the Becks, who she felt constituted a community totally separate from that of their audience); the drama emerges directly from the audience, being based on oral history and improvisations; the drama is presented in the space where audience and actor reside – in the street where they live.

Peter Schumann was even more forthright about his sense of religious mission and theatrical commitment when he took Bread and Puppet Theater to the street: the loaves of bread that actors and audience break and share manifest Schumann's desire for all to understand that the act of theater is also a religious ritual, a sharing of the staff of life. He has said that Bread and Puppet is 'rooted in a nineteenth-century Romanticism that envisions man as divine, sacred and good.'[21] His immense puppets and masks – ten to fifteen feet tall – stress their archetypal significance. Appearing in open spaces outdoors, they call attention to easily recognizable features – sharp, jagged teeth or a tear on a cheek – in order 'to make the world plain,' Schumann says, 'to speak a simple language that everybody can understand.'[22]

The same sense of religious mission informs street theater to this day. Crystal Field of Theatre for the New City calls acting a 'form of preaching,' an idea she generated in 1967 when she and George Bartenieff produced their first street play on an open-bed truck in Central Park as part of a peace parade. At first skeptical, she was deeply impressed with the work she saw there of Schumann and Robert Nichols. 'Religion was dead,' she says, 'but street theater was a religious thing.' She and Bartenieff have been doing street theater every summer since then, and she still thinks of it as a 'kind of poetry'; it must have, she says, 'a religious element and a poetic element: the plays for the street must reflect back to the community the moral and religious truths in which they believe.'[23]

What the environment of the street as theater meant to a spectator must remain mysterious except for the persistent physical facts: the constant hum and rumble of traffic, of trains below, airplanes overhead, sirens, the rustling and movement of the fringes of the crowd, their chatter, their catcalls. All became part of the performance. Your own street was your theater. You could go indoors and watch a war happening on the evening news as if it were a show brought into your living room; you could walk out your door and watch a show happen on your block in which you witnessed a teenager stealing his family's possessions to buy drugs. You knew it *was* happening all around you. You could yell remarks to the actors and hang around afterwards to argue with them. All the world became a stage. Or, if one prefers, the illusion of a stage.

Working from these phenomena as a reinvention of the theatrical environment, Richard Schechner sought to become spokesman of an avant-garde faction. Schechner was inspired by a mystical event that affected his idea of 'environmental theater.' Describing the experience of being on East Seventh Street one night with people sitting on stoops and enjoying films being shown and children dancing to live music, Schechner found himself 'participating, celebrating.' The event became important to him because 'celebration, casualness, non-professionalism, ritual, necessity, and environment confronted one another ... The multiplicity of images, sounds, and street life made a newly discovered art. An artless art that cannot be "reviewed" or "criticized".'[24] To Schechner, as to many others, the city streets and parks became the theatrical environment, the most proper environment for a 'living theater' or an 'open theater' or a 'poor theater.' In the streets, theater occurred in open spaces free to all; the streets were where the poor lived. Those who performed in them were always limited by narrow budgets but not by the restraints of commercial theater. If they were limited by a political philosophy, that limitation was self-imposed only by some. If free of demands placed upon craft and technical skill, street theater imposes conditions demanding one of two highly contrasting styles of acting. It requires either a broad, stylized mode of acting, the actor competing with the distractions of the environment; or, if the actors are 'indigenous' – street people – it fosters a *vérité* mode in which 'style' or illusion or mimesis is broken down altogether, and the actors do not perform at all in the ordinary sense but behave with conviction as if in 'real life.' The actor is not a character but a person. He is the nextdoor neighbour. In either case the idea of illusion is lost: the actor is either a performer playing a character or someone sharing a part of himself. Any idea of 'realism' is also thrown out. What remains is a pre-illusionistic theater of heroic or comic action, or perhaps a theater akin to Schechner's *wholemask*, a performance of the performer himself.[25] Again, in either case, emphasis falls on the actor, on his words and movements and gestures. The open-air space simply absorbs anything else short of gunfire or loud music. As a result, the audience do not expect to enter passively into an illusion of reality created for them. Rather, a street audience understands that the performance excites their ability to respond to the conditions of their own lives and life about them. They come to expand the possibilities of life in the streets and therefore may be enabled to place a greater value upon the reality of their own lives, for they have been authenticated, as it were, by the presence of the theater in their street.

The streets were – and still are – the ultimate redefinition of theater. They were totally environmental and totally democratic. Any consideration of the theatrical space of the American theater since the 1960s must take into account the urban streets as a space for theater, a space in which masses could be mobilized, culture spread, self- and community-awareness enhanced, the concept of theater itself expanded, barriers broken, a mystical communion achieved. What was carried back indoors of this rich joy remains another question.

## NOTES

1 Robert Brustein, *The Third Theatre* (New York: Knopf, 1969), p. 3.
2 Gerald M. Berkowitz, *New Broadways: Theatre Across America, 1950–1980* (Totowa, NJ: Rowman and Littlefield, 1982), p. 114.
3 John Gassner, *Directions in Modern Theatre and Drama* (New York: Holt, Rinehart and Winston, 1967), p. 23.
4 C. Ray Smith, Editorial, *Theatre Crafts*, 6:2 (1972), 1–19, p. 9.
5 *Ibid.*
6 Smith, *ibid.*, p. 15.
7 Smith, *ibid.*, p. 17.
8 Interview with Joseph Papp, New York City, June 1983.
9 Interview with Patricia Reynolds, New York City, July 1983. Ms Reynolds also kindly permitted me access to her private papers. Unless otherwise noted all material pertaining to Theater in the Street is based upon this interview and articles appearing in the *National Observer*, 20 July 1964; the *Brooklyn World-Telegram*, 6 July 1964; and the *New York Times*, 8 July 1964.
10 'Theatre in the Street', *Life*, 6 September 1963.
11 Interview with Marketta Kimbrell, New York City, July 1983.
12 Stuart Cosgrove, '*Prolet Buehne*: Agit-prop in America,' *Performance and Politics in Popular Drama: Aspects of Popular Entertainment in Theatre, Film, and Television, 1800–1976*, ed. David Bradby *et al.* (New York: Cambridge University Press, 1980), pp. 201–123.

13 Material on Maryat Lee is based on interviews conducted with her between 1981 and 1983 in Hinton, West Virginia. See also my article 'A Double-Threaded Life: Maryat Lee's *Ecotheater*,' *Drama Review*, 27:2 (1983), 26–35. Ms Lee has been kind enough to permit me access to her private papers. She has made many suggestions for this paper, for which I am very grateful.

14 I refer to the so-called Theatre of Fact of the 1950s and 1960s, documentary dramas deriving from the Federal Theatre's *Living Newspaper* and based on historical 'facts,' such as Heinar Kipphardt's *In the Matter of J. Robert Oppenheimer* (1964). My reference to a 'Theatre of Phenomenology' is merely a suggestion to be explored.

15 Brustein, *The Third Theatre*, p. xiii.

16 Antonin Artaud, *The Theatre and Its Double*, trans. Mary Caroline Richards (New York: Grove Press, 1958), p. 96.

17 Peter Brook, *The Empty Space* (New York: Penguin, 1968), p. 73.

18 Robert Brustein, *The Theatre of Revolt: An Approach to the Modern Drama* (Boston: Little, Brown, 1962) pp. 1–16.

19 'Soul and Latin Theater: A Street Theater Project, 1968.' Unpublished pamphlet.

20 Maryat Lee, 'Legitimate Theater Is Illegitimate,' *Toward the Second Decade: The Impact of the Women's Movement on American Institutions* ed. Betty Justice and Renate Pore (Westport, Conn.: Greenwood Press, 1982), pp. 1–14.

21 Margaret Croydon, *Lunatics, Lovers, and Poets: The Contemporary Experimental Theatre* (New York: McGraw-Hill, 1974), p. 20.

22 *Ibid.*

23 Interview with Crystal Field, New York City, July 1983.

24 Croydon, *Lunatics, Lovers, and Poets*, pp. 195–6.

25 Richard Schechner, *The End of Humanism: Writings on Performance* (New York: Performing Arts Journal Publications, 1983).

# Comic space

MICHAEL ISSACHAROFF

As the etymology of the word 'theatre' demonstrates (theatre $<$ θεατϱον, 'a seeing place'), space is as basic to that medium as time is to fiction or to music. I am not just thinking of the theatre as a building, an architectural space whose stage and auditorium design impinge directly on the performance occurring therein. The place of performance needs, I think, to be considered in the broadest sense, from the stage in Theatre X to the city (and country) in which that theatre is located. I am also referring to the manner in which a specific dramatist utilizes imaginary space, the producer the available space. The producer is limited by the facilities at his disposal; the playwright is limited only by the confines of his imagination. Theatrical space could thus be conceived of as a series of concentric circles, the smallest being the use of the stage area in a given theatre, the largest, the country of performance. Needless to say, this pattern of concentric circles frames what is said and what happens in the theatre. And as we shall see, it is by no means a one-way process: stage utterances can shape the way we perceive the context of their occurrence. In its turn, the context lends meaning or may modify meaning considerably. A non-theatrical example will suffice to illustrate the point succinctly. In uttering the words 'I name this ship the Spirit of Burgundy,' if the speaker is out of doors with a champagne bottle in his hand which he is about to smash against the side of the ship, he is doing what J. L. Austin calls a performative, a speech act in which the utterance of the words and the accomplishment of an act are simultaneous.[1] If, on the other hand, the speaker were, shall we say, somewhat tipsy, at dinner in boozy company, about to serve the sixth bottle of wine he has just uncorked, the meaning of the words would be rather different. Though the words are identical in both cases, their context of utterance has a major impact on their meaning. Thus in Beckett's *Endgame*, for example, the ashbins in which the protagonist's parents, Nagg and Nell, are confined throughout the play frame their discourse, lending it automatically a tragicomic flavour, opposing it implicitly to that of the wheelchaired protagonist.

Beckett, especially in later plays, such as *Happy Days* and *Not I*, shows us

how to discard from the drama most of the constituent elements traditionally thought indispensable: movement, decor, gestures, even dialogue (in
*Act Without Words*). Yet the one dimension that must be retained is space. To
be enacted, a play must take place *somewhere*. The same cannot be true of a
novel or a poem, though either, of course, may attempt to represent space,
but only through the verbal channel. If we speak of space in a novel or
poem, what we are talking about is space mediated by words (or rather by
black marks on the page), scanned, then imagined and recreated by a
reader. Fictional or poetic space is never 'there' literally as it can be in the
theatre.

If time – time represented or time of performance – is in some way present
in all art forms, if only minimally in the case of painting (where we are
dealing with the time it takes the eye to scan the canvas), space as thus far
defined, is a characteristic component of theatre, which is the only literary
art form in which it is concretely manifested.

I shall not be examining the technicalities of theatrical space here, but
suffice it to say that it may be either shown or described, or as I have
expressed it elsewhere,[2] *mimetic* or *diegetic*, adapting for my purposes the
Aristotelian distinction between showing and telling. In exploring the kinds
of space peculiar to comic drama and especially to farce, my focus will be
shown space rather than described space evoked by characters on stage.

If, as we have seen, the context of utterance can modify or even determine
the meaning of what is said, my premise is that in comic drama, and in farce
in particular, space can determine the comic mode, lending utterances their
comic flavour, just as, conversely, utterances may at times render the
location ludicrous. My corpus is European and American drama. In order
to verify and generalize my hypotheses, I have purposely ignored national
and chronological boundaries, checking what happens, say, in French farce
against examples from American, British and other (Western) traditions.
No Western theatrical tradition is hermetically sealed in a xenophobic sort
of way; cross-fertilization is the norm rather than the exception.

I

If we turn now to how space works in drama, it rapidly becomes apparent
that one could map out a grammar of possibilities, a spatial paradigm
which would include the following pairs (opposite).

Now in comic as opposed to non-comic or tragic drama, space tends, as
we shall see, to be non-closed (that is, permitting numerous exits and
entrances, as in much nineteenth-century French farce by such authors as
Feydeau, Labiche and Courteline), and multiple (that is, entailing several
changes of set). The action may take place inside or outside; the set is

| closed | non-closed |
|--------|------------|
| fixed | multiple |
| divided | undivided |
| moving | stationary |
| inside | outside |
| stage | auditorium |

sometimes divided into two or three stage areas simultaneously in use as in Feydeau, Ayckbourn and Stoppard; the place of utterance is occasionally represented as moving, as in Thornton Wilder's *Pullman Car Hiawatha*, Beckett's *All That Fall*, Tardieu's *Les Amants du métro* in which we find a train, a car and an underground carriage respectively. Whereas in traditional, pre-Artaudian and non-comic drama the stage/auditorium divide is strictly observed, the convention being that the audience is looking through the fourth wall, in modern comedy, the barrier between stage and auditorium is sometimes lifted as in Cocteau's brilliant *L'Impromptu du Palais-Royal*, in which a bogus spectator interrupts the performance, corrects actors' pronunciation, and so forth.

Comic drama raises another spatial issue: to represent or not to represent, that is the question – which comic playwrights may not always take very seriously. Alfred Jarry sets the tone for the anti-mimetic stance in *Ubu roi* in which, we are told, 'the action takes place in Poland, that is Nowhere.'[3] In the programme of the 1896 production, Jarry recommended that placards be shown on stage to signal changes of location and similarly, any item of decor required for some special reason, such as a door or a window, should simply be brought on stage as needed.[4] The place of action, Poland, thus becomes abstract; and aesthetically the result of Jarry's ludicrously expressed, though seriously intended, diatribe is an anti-realist stance that privileges the verbal sign (the placard) to the detriment of the visual. The effect, of course, is comic. Yet despite the revolutionary theatre aesthetics exemplified by *Ubu roi*, Jarry's standpoint is in fact closely related to the well-established logocentric tradition of French drama from seventeenth-century tragedians such as Racine down to contemporary absurdists like Ionesco. Writing some thirty years later, Jean Giraudoux made the point explicitly: 'The Frenchman,' he said, 'comes to the theatre to listen, gets tired if he is forced to watch. He believes in the word; he does not

believe in decor.'[5] It was precisely this logocentric notion of theatre that
Artaud attacked vigorously in his famous manifesto *Le Théâtre et son double*.[6]

But the anti-realist stance is by no means confined to the French post-
Naturalist theatre. Thornton Wilder, for example, in the stage directions of
*Pullman Car Hiawatha* (1931) has this to say about his railway car set:

> At the rise of the curtain the Stage Manager is making lines with a piece of chalk
> on the floor of the stage by the footlights.
> STAGE MANAGER: This is the plan of a Pullman car. Its name is Hiawatha
> and on December twenty-first it is on its way from New York to Chicago. Here
> at your left are three compartments. Here is the aisle and five lowers. The
> berths are all full, uppers and lowers, but for the purposes of this play we are
> limiting our interest to the people in the lower berths on the further side only.[7]

Like Jarry, Wilder by de-emphasizing the visual is privileging the verbal.
Since his set is supposedly in motion, Wilder chooses an innovative manner
in which to represent movement – characters take the place of locations that
supposedly are flitting past, thus becoming 'speaking places':

> THE FIELD: I represent a field you are passing between Grover's Corners,
> Ohio and Petersburg, Ohio. In this field, there are 51 gophers, 206 field mice, 6
> snakes and millions of bugs, insects, ants and spiders. All in their winter sleep.[8]

If outside space is represented by actors, inside space – the Pullman car –
rather than being represented by decor, is mimed and suggested bodily,
and thus this stage direction:

> The actors enter carrying chairs. Each improvises his berth by placing two
> chairs 'facing one another' in his chalk-marked space. They then sit in one
> chair, profile to the audience, and rest their feet on the other. This must do for
> lying in bed.[9]

Needless to say, the set, ludicrously though creatively represented in an
anti-realist stylized manner, impinges significantly on discourse, often
triggering the comic effect. This is so especially in the incongruous (and
hence comic) juxtaposition of disjointed exchanges coming from the
various berths, thus:

> LOWER ONE (*in a shrill whisper*): Porter! Porter!   PORTER: Yes, mam.
> LOWER ONE: My hot water bag's leaking. I guess you'll have to take it away.
> I'll have to do without it tonight. How awful!
> LOWER FIVE (*sharply to the passenger above her*): Young man, you mind your
> own business, or I'll report you to the conductor.
> STAGE MANAGER (*substituting for* UPPER FIVE): Sorry, mam, I didn't
> mean to upset you. My suspenders fell down and I was trying to catch them.[10]

The total effect of Wilder's play is a sort of comic symphony of sound and
voice reminiscent of brilliant radio drama, such as Dylan Thomas's *Under
Milk Wood* and Beckett's *All That Fall*.

Clearly, then, if a playwright decides to ridicule the mimetic tradition of the Well-Made Play of the late-nineteenth century, he may undermine the convention creatively and comically as Wilder chose to. Yet perhaps the ultimate example of a dramatist undermining theatrical space, thereby rendering it and what is said within it farcical, is Bernard Shaw's hilarious eternal-triad farce of 1905, *Passion, Poison and Petrifaction* in which the dramatist begins by ridiculing the convention of the fourth wall in an exchange between The Lady (Lady Magnesia) and Phyllis, her maid:

> PHYLLIS: Will your ladyship not undress?
> THE LADY: Not tonight Phyllis. (*Glancing through where the fourth wall is missing*) Not under the circumstances.[11]

In what is undoubtedly the most extreme interaction between a theatrical character and stage space, Shaw has one of his characters EAT the decor (supposedly as an antidote for the poison given him by Lady Magnesia's husband). Shaw's tongue-in-cheek stage direction is unforgettable:

> As it is extremely difficult to find an actor capable of eating a real ceiling, it will be found convenient in performance to substitute the tops of old wedding cakes for bits of plaster. There is but little difference in material between the two substances; but the taste of the wedding cake is considered more agreeable by many people.[12]

Shaw's play is a parody of Victorian melodrama; his dialogue at times has an almost Marx Brothers style comic effect. Before Lady Magnesia retires for the night, there is a hint that she may be murdered in her sleep. The melodramatic stage directions reflect an author almost seduced by narrative temptations:

> *Lady Magnesia switches off the electric light* (. . .) *A white radiance plays on her pillow, and lights up her beautiful face. But the thunder growls again; and a lurid red glow concentrates itself on the door, which is presently flung open, revealing a saturnine figure in evening dress, partially concealed by a crimson cloak. As he steals towards the bed the unnatural glare in his eyes and the broad-bladed dagger nervously gripped in his right hand bode ill for the sleeping lady. Providentially she sneezes on the very brink of eternity; and the tension of the murderer's nerves is such that he bolts precipitately under the bed at the sudden and startling Atscha! A dull, heavy, rythmic thumping – the beating of his heart – betrays his whereabouts. Soon he emerges cautiously and raises his head above the bed coverlet level.*
> THE MURDERER   I can no longer cower here listening to the agonized thumpings of my own heart (. . .) I'll do't. (*He again raises the dagger. The angels sing again. He cowers.*) What is this? Has that tune reached Heaven?
> LADY MAGNESIA   My husband! (*All the colors of the rainbow chase one another up his face with ghastly brilliancy.*) Why do you change color? And what on earth are you doing with that dagger?
> FITZ (*affecting concern, but unhinged*) It is a present from mother. Pretty isn't it? (. . .)
> LADY MAGNESIA   But she promised me a fish slice.
> FITZ   This is a combination fish slice and dagger.[13]

The dénouement of this play is even more hilarious. Adolphus, having consumed large quantities of plaster, some of it diluted in water, becomes totally rigid, a living statue. The character after swallowing the decor is thus turned into decor himself! A stiff in more senses than one . . .

II

The plays by Jarry, Shaw and Wilder thus exemplify the frequent overlap between parody, avant-gardist experimentation and the comic. Central to such experimentation is the realist versus anti-realist debate. This brings us back to the closed/non-closed dichotomy mentioned earlier. It becomes apparent that the choice of closed versus open space very frequently signals the dramatic mode of a particular play. Closedness, resulting in stasis, tends to overlap with the tragic or non-comic, and conversely, openness usually corresponds to the comic or non-tragic. Closed space – in plays such as Sartre's *Huis clos*, Arthur Miller's *Incident at Vichy*, Sartre's *Les Séquestrés d'Altona*, Pinter's *The Dumb Waiter* or Genet's *Les Bonnes* and Beckett's *Endgame* – mirrors a closed situation (or what used to be called tragic destiny). As Roland Barthes has observed in another context, 'the Racinian protagonist is imprisoned (locked in); he cannot escape without dying . . .'[14] This is also true of much contemporary tragic or non-comic drama. The protagonist's remark in *Endgame* could likewise quite well be extrapolated to include plays by Sartre, Pinter, Beckett, Genet, Ionesco and many others in which the setting is a closed room: 'Hors d'ici c'est la mort' (Outside of here it's death).[15] If the closed space is sometimes protective, as in, say, Pinter's *The Caretaker*, it is often deceptively so, as in Pinter's *The Dumb Waiter*, Genet's *Haute surveillance* (set in a prison cell) or in *Les Bonnes* (set in a closed room).[16]

Arthur Miller's *Incident at Vichy*[17] represents perhaps the most extreme point of tragic closedness. It is set in a detention room in Vichy, in 1942. The characters detained there by the Nazis and their French collaborators are waiting to be inspected by a Nazi underling who will decide which of them are to be sent to a concentration camp. The detention room itself is enclosed by an imprisoned country – occupied France – the country in its turn enclosed within an imprisoned occupied Europe – the concentric circles of a modern Hell. There is no escape possible.

Against this tragic backcloth, it is not difficult to see how the reverse – open space – often coincides with the comic mode. Confinement is thus consonant with the fixed (that is, single) theatrical set, while, conversely, comic space is necessarily non-closed, allowing numerous comings and goings. As Albert Bermel has observed of farce in France, 'the drawing-rooms of nineteenth-century French farces went so far in providing access to and from the stage, that some of the sets appear to have more of their surface devoted to window and door frames than to walls, floor and ceiling combined.'[18]

Confinement, of course, is freedom denied; self-imposed closure or sequestration, on the other hand, may serve a comic purpose with serious undertones or implications. Aristophanes' *Lysistrata* exemplifies the point. The women, led by Lysistrata, occupy the Acropolis, which contains the Treasury, in an attempt to coerce the men into ending the war in Greece. This open versus closed motif is paralleled by the women using their bodies as the primary space of conflict – they refuse to have sexual relations with their husbands, hoping thereby to force an end to the war. The two central motifs of the play – the occupation of the Acropolis and the women's sex strike – are linked farcically by the theme of doors and closedness. The men, it will be recalled, attempt to storm the Acropolis, carrying unlit torches and firepots, their strategy being to burst into the Acropolis and smoke the women out. The women easily repulse the attack by pouring cold water into the firepots.

This battle of the sexes, won by the women, is given farcical representation. After the failure of their Acropolis-storming strategy, the men, due to the imposed deprivation, appear on stage with painful erections – the convention in Aristophanes' comedies was the use of costumes for male characters with phalluses affixed (!) The two scenes – storming the Acropolis and parading about with fixed phalluses – are no doubt intended to be linked, the one a farcical variation on the other, the penetration of closed space being the objective in both cases . . . Aristophanes' play thus exemplifies the closed/open dichotomy in the farcical mode, linking physical space (the Acropolis) and corporal space (the women's bodies). It is not surprising, therefore, that comedy and especially farce thrive on openness, which is the antithesis of stasis, and thus on movement, which requires multiple changes of location and hence of decor.

The use of a (supposedly) moving set in such plays as Thornton Wilder's *The Happy Journey to Trenton and Camden* (1931), Günter Grass's *Only Ten Minutes to Buffalo* (1957) or Tardieu's *Les Amants du métro* (1950) is not coincidental. The actual representation of the vehicle or of movement may, of course, be either realistic or anti-realistic and stylized. Thus in Wilder's play, four chairs represent the car (just as chairs are used in *Pullman Car Hiawatha* to represent the berths in the train compartment); Günter Grass subscribes to the realist tradition and we find a rusty old locomotive in the centre of the stage, supposedly moving at high speed.

The point, of course, is that sets such as these lend a faster pace to what occurs on stage – the illusion of movement, just like movement itself, is a useful adjunct for farce, whose effect is, after all, usually contingent on rapid pacing. A vehicle, even motionless on stage, sets up a certain horizon of expectation. It is therefore possible to play on this, exploiting it for comic effect. This is precisely what Arrabal does in *Le Cimetière des voitures*. The set is a collection of old, dirty and rusty cars in a car junk yard, a few of which are lived in. The comic effect stems both from the incongruous discrepancy between location and utterance and from the sight gag of a well-dressed waiter rushing from one car window to the next in response to the 'tenants' hooting for service (calling for breakfast, drinks, etc.) as if they were at a first-class hotel.

If the vehicle as set can enhance the comic, the use of multiple sets or of split sets can achieve the same effect. The obvious instance of multiple sets is French farce of the nineteenth century (by such authors as Feydeau and Labiche), and the quintessential example, Labiche's *Un Chapeau de paille d'Italie* (*An Italian Straw Hat*), filmed many times, but most memorably by René Clair in 1927. *An Italian Straw Hat* has no fewer than five changes of set, corresponding to the mad rush of the protagonist, Fadinard, in desperate search of a particular type of straw hat, to replace the one his horse had eaten that belonged to a young lady, Anaïs, married but in gallant company in the Bois de Vincennes at the time Fadinard's horse gobbled her hat, that was perched on the branch of an obliging tree. Fadinard is about to get married, yet cannot do so until he obtains a replacement straw hat for Anaïs, who is determined to conceal her infidelity from her husband. The 'logic' of the action of Labiche's play is as garbled as this synopsis suggests. The farcical impact of *An Italian Straw Hat* is due as much to the comic odyssey of a desperate protagonist, rushing from one place to the next, as to the absurd quest for a ludicrous prop, whose importance is blown out of all proportion, and foregrounded at the expense of most other elements of the play.

The split set is a technique which consists of dividing the stage into two or sometimes three distinct areas simultaneously (sometimes consecutively) in use. It is the device used by such authors as Feydeau in *L'Hôtel du libre échange* (*Hotel Paradiso*), Alan Ayckbourn in *Bedroom Farce*, and Tom Stoppard in *Every Good Boy Deserves Favour*. Ayckbourn, who calls it the cross-cut device, in speaking of his use of a triple stage area (three bedrooms) in *Bedroom Farce* (1975) considers that 'jumping the action from bedroom to bedroom gives the play an added rhythm over and above what the dialogue normally provides.'[19]

The juxtaposition of apparently separate stage areas opens up interesting possibilities for the comic intercalation of disjointed utterances. This is the device used to great comic effect by Flaubert in *Madame Bovary* in the famous Comices agricoles scene, in which the sounds from the separate areas are interspersed – Emma and Rodolphe's dialogue at the window, the Conseiller and Derozerays on the platform, awarding prizes for the best farm animals, and on the ground, the lowing of the cattle and mumbling peasants. Flaubert uses the device so that snatches of Derozerays' speeches can be read as ironical references to the characters in the other two areas, especially Emma and Rodolphe.[20]

In act II of *L'Hôtel du libre échange*, Feydeau uses a similar device, though on the horizontal plane. The stage in act II is divided into three areas – bedroom, landing, bedroom. In bedroom I, Pinglet is about to seduce Mrs Paillardin when the chair they are sitting on collapses at the same time as, by a farcical coincidence, Mr Paillardin is cooling his heels in bedroom II. And so on.[21]

In this use of the cross-cut device, the crux of what is happening on stage is the implicit linking of what is supposedly separate or distinct – in the example cited, two apparently independent strands of dramatic action. The result of the juxtaposition is a comic collision. In other forms of the comic, the collision may occur on the lexical, phonological or situational planes. The meeting of what might be considered incompatible domains, be they spatial or verbal, triggers laughter. Arthur Koestler coined a useful term for this mode of collision, 'bisociation,' a double-minded 'transitory state of unstable equilibrium,' as he put it, that he thought to be at the heart not only of the comic but also of the creative act itself.[22]

One could therefore argue, perhaps, that most forms of comic space, be they non-closed, anti-realist, moving, multiple, and so forth are inscribed in an implicit dichotomy, each element evoking its respective opposite, rejected by the comic dramatist. As Johann Huizinga reminds us in his suggestive analysis of the play element in culture, 'the arena, the card table, the magic circle, the temple, the stage, the screen, the tennis court, the court of justice, etc. are all in form and function play-grounds, that is, forbidden spots, isolated, hedged round, hallowed, within which special rules obtain.' I would maintain, then, that it is through the transgression of implicit or explicit rules and conventions that the comic dramatist achieves his brilliant and most creative effect.

## PLAYS CITED

| | |
|---|---|
| Aristophanes | *Lysistrata* |
| Arrabal | *Le Cimitière des voitures* |
| | *Guernica* |
| Ayckbourn | *Bedroom Farce* |
| Beckett | *Act Without Words* I, II |
| | *All That Fall* |
| | *Endgame (Fin de partie)* |
| | *Happy Days* |
| | *Not I* |
| | *Waiting for Godot* |
| Cocteau | *L'Impromptu du Palais-Royal* |

| | |
|---|---|
| Feydeau | *L'Hôtel du libre échange* |
| Genet | *Les Bonnes* |
| | *Haute surveillance* |
| Grass | *Only Ten Minutes to Buffalo* |
| Jarry | *Ubu roi* |
| Labiche | *Un Chapeau de paille d'Italie* |
| Miller | *Incident at Vichy* |
| Pinter | *The Caretaker* |
| | *The Dumb Waiter* |
| Sartre | *Huis clos* |
| | *Les Séquestrés d'Altona* |
| Shaw | *Passion, Poison and Petrifaction* |
| Stoppard | *Every Good Boy Deserves Favour* |
| | *Night and Day* |
| Tardieu | *Les Amants du métro* |
| Thomas | *Under Milk Wood* |
| Wilder | *The Happy Journey to Trenton and Camden* |
| | *Pullman Car Hiawatha* |

## NOTES

An earlier version of this paper was presented as a public lecture at Trinity University (Texas) in April 1985. I should like to take this opportunity to thank that institution for the courtesy extended to me and for the facilities generously made available at the Elizabeth Maddux Library during a research leave spent in San Antonio in 1984–5.

1 See J. L. Austin, *How To Do Things With Words* (Cambridge, Mass.: Harvard University Press, 1962). Although Austin rejected literary discourse as, supposedly, not being pertinent to the concerns of 'ordinary language,' his categories in their original form as well as in their modified version in J. Searle, *Speech Acts: An Essay in the Philosophy of Language* (Cambridge: Cambridge University Press, 1969) do, in fact, concern the problem of literary, and specifically theatrical, discourse. See, for example, Stanley Fish, *Is There a Text in This Class?* (Cambridge, Mass.: Harvard University Press, 1980), especially pp. 97–111; 197–245; 268–92. See also M. Issacharoff, 'How Playscripts Refer: Some Preliminary Considerations,' in Whiteside & Issacharoff (Eds.), *On Referring in Literature*, (Bloomington: Indiana University Press, 1987).

2 See 'Space and Reference in Drama,' *Poetics Today*, 2:3 (1981), 211–24 as well as a somewhat lengthier discussion of theatrical space in my *Le Spectacle du discours* (Paris: José Corti, 1985).

3 Cf. Jarry's whimsical comment in his 'Discours prononcé à la première représentation d'*Ubu roi*,' at the Théâtre de l'Oeuvre on 10 December 1896: 'Quant à l'action, qui va commencer, elle se passe en Pologne, c'est-à-dire Nulle Part,' *Oeuvres complètes* (Paris: Gallimard, Bibliothèque de la Pléiade, vol. I, 1972), p. 401.

4 'L'écriteau apporté selon les changements de lieu évite le rappel périodique au non-esprit par le changement des décors matériels, que l'on perçoit surtout à l'instant de leur différence.

Dans ces conditions, toute partie de décor dont on aura un besoin spécial, fenêtre qu'on ouvre, porte qu'on enfonce, est un accessoire et peut être apportée comme une table ou un flambeau.' 'De l'inutilité du théâtre au théâtre,' *Mercure de France*, September 1896, reprinted in *Oeuvres complètes*, vol. I, p. 407. For further comments on the theoretical implications of Jarry's aesthetics, see *Le Spectacle du discours*, ch. 11.

A related problem, of as much interest to philosophers of language as to literary theorists, is the ontological status of real (place)names used in literary texts. Comic effect can stem, for example, from the intentional mixing of references to real places (existents) and imaginary places. Tom Stoppard does precisely this in *Night and Day*, set in any imaginary African country, Kambawe, but in which we also find reference to real places such as Brighton. For a discussion of names and naming in fictional discourse, see my 'How Playscripts Refer: Some Preliminary Considerations.'

5 'Le Français vient à la comédie pour écouter, et s'y fatigue si on l'oblige à voir. En fait, il croit à la parole et il ne croit pas au décor. Ou plutôt, il croit que les grands débats du coeur ne se règlent pas à coups de lumière et d'ombre, d'effondrements et de catastrophes, mais par la conversation. Le vrai coup de théâtre n'est pas pour lui la clameur de deux cents figurants, mais la nuance ironique, le subjonctif imparfait ou la litote qu'assume une phrase du héros ou de l'héroïne.' J. Giraudoux, *Littérature* (Paris: Gallimard-'Idées', 1967), pp. 220–1.

6 A. Artaud, *Le Théâtre et son double* (Paris: Gallimard-'Idées', 1968).

7 Thornton Wilder, *Pullman Car Hiawatha*, in Wilder, *The Long Christmas Dinner and Other Plays in One Act* (Harmondsworth: Penguin Books, 1969), p. 45.

8 *Ibid.*, pp. 52–3.

9 *Ibid.*, p. 45. Note that Wilder also represents time through the use of characters appearing on stage: 'The hours are beautiful girls dressed like Elihu Vedder's Pleiades. Each carries a great gold Roman numeral. They pass slowly across the balcony at the back moving from right to left.'

10 *Ibid.*, p. 46.

11 *The Bodley Head Bernard Shaw Collected Plays with Their Prefaces*, vol. III (London, Sydney & Toronto: The Bodley Head, 1971), p. 206.

12 *Ibid.*, p. 203.

13 *Ibid.*, pp. 207–8.

14 '... il est l'enfermé, celui qui ne peut sortir sans mourir: sa limite est son privilège, la captivité, sa distinction,' Roland Barthes, *Sur Racine* (Paris: Seuil, 1964), p. 20.

15 Beckett, *Fin de partie* (Paris: Minuit, 1957), p. 23.

16 In fact, the tragi-comic ambivalence apparent in much twentieth-century drama is paralleled by a corresponding mixture of open and closed space, the latter being exemplified by such plays as Arrabal's *Guernica* (1961), Beckett's *Waiting for Godot* (1953) and *Fin de partie* (1957). In Arrabal's play, Lira, one of the two principal characters, is trapped in the closed space of a W.C. for the duration of the play, thus remaining invisible, whereas her husband, Fanchou, is visible,

on stage, in a room of their bombed house. Needless to say, the bombed house itself is an ambivalent space, at once open and closed. In *Fin de partie*, Nagg and Nell's ashbins are closed spaces that are nevertheless openable (the lids can be lifted off), though Nagg and Nell are confined to this space. The ashbins themselves are located in the closed space of the room whence no exit is possible ('Outside of here, it's death'). A dichotomy is apparent in the case of the ashbin/non-ashbin places of utterance (i.e., Nagg and Nell versus Hamm and Clov), though given the closedness of the room that precludes access or exit, the tragic mode prevails, despite the farcical frame enclosing Nagg and Nell's discourse. In *Waiting for Godot*, the outside space of the set, though apparently open is in fact the equivalent of closed space (no escape for Vladimir and Estragon, entrapped in their waiting predicament, seems possible), akin to the mound in which Winnie is buried in *Happy Days*.

17 Arthur Miller, *Incident at Vichy* (New York: Bantam Books, 1967; 1st printing, 1965).

18 Albert Bermel, *Farce* (New York: Simon and Schuster, 1982), p. 33.

19 Alan Ayckbourn *Three Plays* [*Bedroom Farce, Absurd Person Singular, Absent Friends*] (Harmondsworth: Penguin Books, 1979), p. 9.

20 Flaubert, *Madame Bovary* (Paris: Seuil 'L'Intégrale,' 1972, vol. 1), pp. 618–26.

21 Feydeau, *L'Hôtel du libre échange*, in *Théâtre complet*, vol. IV (Paris: Le Bélier, 1950).

22 Arthur Koestler, *The Act of Creation* (London: Pan Books, 1964), pp. 35–6.

23 Johann Huizinga, *Homo Ludens: An Analysis of the Play Element in Culture* (Boston: Beacon Press, 1950), p. 10.

# Spatial polarities in the plays of Tadeusz Różewicz*

## HALINA FILIPOWICZ

There are few plays in the history of postwar theatre that use theatrical space in more imaginative and effective ways than Tadeusz Różewicz's. Regarded as one of the outstanding modern European poets and playwrights, Różewicz has revolutionized postwar Polish drama by his fluid dramatic forms, more open and loose than forms developed by causal and discursive dramaturgy.[1] His is a non-narrative, antimimetic theatre where spoken language is often untied from meaning, and characterization and storytelling are abandoned in favor of performer and collage. Liberated from the constraints of a conventional plot, plausible psychology, and rational motivation, Różewicz's plays are structured less to make the audience wonder what is going to happen next than to baffle the spectator with dazzling possibilities inherent in the theatrical medium and thus to raise important philosophical questions about the very nature of reality.

Having dismantled the machinery of the theatre of illusion, Różewicz develops dramatic tension through the spatial dimensions of his plays, rather than through conflict between characters or intricacies of plot development. His basic tools are strong, eloquent images rather than words, and his primary artistic medium is deftly orchestrated movement within a special, arbitrarily constructed space. These theatrical effects render the abstract visually concrete, dramatizing an inner psychological state or a philosophical concept. Moreover, they carry forward the plays' inward progressions, often conveying in purely scenic terms the essence of an entire episode or even a whole drama. Różewicz thus creates in his plays a sense of environment which, however, is not to be confused with the Schechnerian notion of environmental theatre where attention is directed to the configuration of the immediate playing area and audience interaction within it with each other, with the performers, and with the ongoing performance.[2] Różewicz's environments are electrifying *coups de théâtre*, playing with the audience's expectations and destroying any single illusion of reality.

* A draft of this paper was read at the *Themes in Drama* International Conference held at the University of California, Riverside in February 1985.

Intrinsically theatrical, Różewicz's plays explore and manipulate tensions between three spatial realms in the theatre: the actual physicality of the stage, the set, and the actors performing; the imagined reality of the characters' lives, represented symbolically or metaphorically by the set; and the auditorium where the spectators, through their experience and imagination, provide a crucial link between the actuality of the stage and the characters' imagined life on the one hand and the off-stage world on the other.[3] In each of Różewicz's plays examined here, the spatial configuration is different. In *The Card Index*, the stage set, the fractured reality of the protagonist's existence, and the world of the audience, whose presence is acknowledged throughout the play, are played off against each other in a polyphonic compositional design that imparts a sense of perpetual disequilibrium. In *The Witnesses, or Our Little Stabilization* (*Świadkowie albo nasza mała stabilizacja*, 1962) and *The Old Woman Broods* (*Stara kobieta wysiaduje*, 1968),[4] sharp contrasts between the contrivances of the stage and the imagined reality produce steadily mounting tension and deliver a powerful final sensation bearing upon the spectators' lives. In *The Interrupted Act* (*Akt przerywany*, 1964), a dramatic study of the cerebral in the process of becoming sensuously tangible, Różewicz creates a self-contained universe which eschews outside reality and operates according to its own laws of time and space.[5]

Dispensing almost entirely with sequential plot, rational causation, and psychological motivation, Różewicz examines in *The Card Index* the collective consciousness of Polish society scarred by its experience of the Nazi occupation and the postwar Stalinist oppression. In a series of dissociated, open-ended episodes with only slight dramatic action, Różewicz embodies in the protagonist, named generically the Hero, the plight of his own generation whose ethical principles and moral aspirations have proved ironically inadequate when confronted with the atrocities of the modern era. Through the character of the Hero, Różewicz expresses a sense of severe moral dislocation experienced by the survivors of the carnage and the Stalinist terror. The Hero killed and compromised for such lofty abstractions as love of humanity, loyalty, and patriotic duty, but in a darkly ironic process of introspection, permeated with self-mocking disenchantment, he questions the verities that have nurtured him and probes his own malleability. Różewicz ends the play not with a dénouement – the tensions that have been engendered are incapable of resolution – but with a sudden moment of excruciatingly intense, mute stillness. He stresses the indeterminacy of the stage world and thus reflects a parallel uncertainty of values, morals, and social norms in the world of the spectator.

The fragmented action of *The Card Index* is internalized within the mind of the Hero, but his identity shifts from one scene to another. Suspended between waking and dreaming, he finds himself in a morass of flickering

32 *The Card Index*, Wrocław, 1977. Directed by Tadeusz Minc. (Photo Stefan Arczyński)

childhood reminiscences intermingled with free-flowing ruminations and discordant visions of his lost decades. As the action unfolds, the Hero painstakingly tries to piece together the card index of his collective biography. A man 'of indeterminate age, occupation, and appearance,' he assumes different identities including those of a cadet in the Polish anti-communist military underground during the war, a writer, and an insignifi-

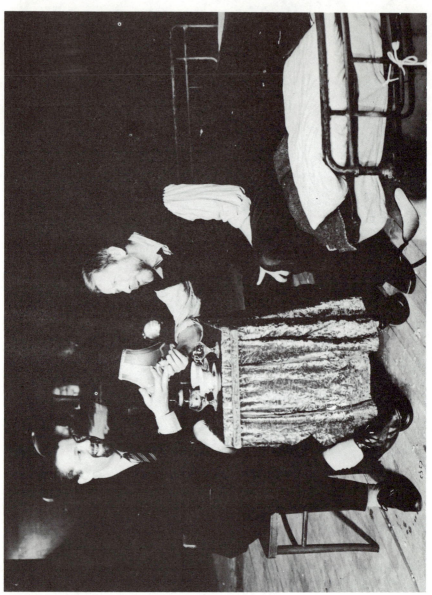

33 *The Card Index*, Warsaw, 1984. Directed by Michał Ratyński. (Photo Renata Pajchel)

cant employee of a ridiculously absurd institution called 'the national operetta.'[6] The Hero, who answers to several names, literally becomes the many personalities that other characters see in him. He exists in the multiplicity of identities, not as a distinct, individualized character of realistic dramaturgy.

This drama of introspection, played out in a private theatre of the mind, occurs in the confined space of the Hero's windowless room. The design of the set, with its maximum of simplicity, carries the spectator's eye to the center of attention, the bed where the Hero remains half-asleep during most of the play. Yet the theatrical metaphor shifts from the actor to the stage as a whole. As so often happens in Różewicz's plays, the setting in *The Card Index* is a direct expression of the protagonist's inner reality. In precise scenic images that supplant words, the setting stresses the absence of any avenue of escape and thereby captures the Hero's sense of entrapment, while the bed, with its connotations of privacy, intimacy, and rest, suggests his quiescence and vulnerability. The room thus has a double identity as a physical space and the Hero's state of mind. It also functions frankly as a stage set, easily accessible to 'various people,' presumably members of the audience (*ST*, 7). They are to wander across the performance area, socializing, questioning the Hero about his life and commitments, and commenting on the characters' lines. This spontaneous interaction between the realm of the characters and the realm of the spectators is designed less to puncture the theatrical illusion than to make the audience feel adrift in the continuum of the Hero's consciousness.

*The Card Index* has no linear progression; the Hero's experience of instability and dislocation has undermined basic notions of time and space. The windowless enclosure of the Hero's bedroom is his parents' home, his office, a coffee shop, and a Hungarian restaurant at the same time. Within this polyvalent space, both naturalistic conventions and dream worlds are invoked, rearranged, and dissolved. The characters – real and imaginary, dead and living – appear and disappear by a process of free association, the result of analogical thinking rather than reasoning. Events in one scene do not seem to depend directly on events in earlier scenes. The past and present are in a process of continuous transformation, and the stage time becomes distorted and rendered excessively slow or fast by the breakdown of causal connections. This dramatic technique of radical disorientation, that never explains or anticipates anything, not only imparts a heightened theatricality to the play, but it also demonstrates the uselessness of insisting on any one level of reality and thus frees *The Card Index* from direct representation. In the play's seemingly unrelated episodes, the totally problematic sense of reality shatters any firm sense of story, and all connecting links must be provided by the audience itself.

In *The Witnesses* and *The Old Woman Broods*[7] the off-stage reality assumes a vibrant, palpable existence on stage, as ominous, mysterious forces threaten the characters' lives. The two plays portray a sickly world that is approximating death and decomposition, while it cherishes the illusion of stability. In each of the plays, the characters evade reality by imposing on their endangered existence illusory, but desperately defended patterns of ownership, power, or clichéd thought. As the action progresses, the audience witnesses a gradual breakdown of all the deceptive patterns that appear to give shape and meaning to the characters' lives. The characters are consequently forced to confront at least briefly, before finding new defenses or patching together the old ones, the fragility of their existence. The plays' movement thus evolves according to a regular pattern of mounting danger, and the atmosphere of growing fear in the face of an unknown menace owes something to Maeterlinck, Witkacy, and Beckett.

*The Witnesses* consists of three autonomous, tightly structured scenes[8] in which the spatial dimensions – the play's 'dramatic geography'[9] – heighten for maximum effect the sense of impending doom and move the action to a jolting climax. In part one, the play's theme is introduced through the distancing technique of a duologue, emotionlessly recited rather than enacted, by two performers standing on the proscenium, in front of a lowered curtain. The duologue imparts the way in which the 'little stabilization' provides a false sense of security by blurring distinctions between ethical polarities and reducing everything to a convenient package of material possessions and prefabricated concepts. In the two parts that follow, the dangers inherent in the stabilization are exemplified through specific situations in which fundamental notions of morality become softened and twisted.

In part two, the deceptive idyll of the stabilization is exposed as a happy and loving couple calmly witness, from the safe enclosure of their apartment, a boy's prolonged torturing of a kitten. The couple's serenity and contentment are reinforced by Rameau's soft, idyllic music and by bright sunlight flooding the apartment. The Man and the Woman have reached this equilibrium by withdrawing from the reality outside into an artificial existence which they have created for themselves. Their apartment is both a shelter and a place of physical separation from others. It is also their most precious possession. The Man and the Woman have reduced reality to patterns of ownership which give them power and security, as do patterns of conventional thought. Formulated into trivial maxims, these habits of thought are a great comfort to them and an important defense against a direct vision of reality. The couple's reliance on verbal clichés is briefly suspended during the Man's disturbing, nightmarish account of the boy's cruelty, which serves as the final test of their placidity. Straightforward and seemingly dispassionate, the Man's monologue derives its mounting urgency from an implied tension between the visible space of the apartment and an invisible space outside, which threatens to subvert the characters' self-centered existence. For the time being, however, the danger is kept at bay. Unaffected by the events outside the apartment and reassured in their complacency, the Man and the Woman resume their daily routine.

Soon after the couple leave the stage, the enigmatic Stranger appears. As he walks across the stage, he rearranges and wipes the furniture, 'as if he wanted to remove traces of the couple's life' (*ST*, 114). His presence takes the scene out of the realm of mimetic realism, framing the action in an obviously theatrical setting. Thus, using the simplest of theatrical means, Różewicz avoids pervasive moralizing yet captures the fragility of the couple's self-satisfied existence.

In part three, in a vivid picture of stasis and spatial isolation, two characters – the Second Man and the Third Man – sit on an empty terrace of a café, one facing the auditorium, the other, upstage. They can neither touch nor see one another, as they hold on to their comfortable chairs, visual symbols of their position in life. Locked away from each other in separate streams of thought, they are nevertheless edgily dependent on each other. Each needs the other as a captive audience for his stories and questions. As the scene goes on, however, their sense of security and well-being slips away from them, for they realize that there is someone in the process of dying just a few feet away. Like the characters in the earlier scene, they ignore signs of approaching danger, symbolized here by the death of the mysterious creature, until, at the scene's closing, their existence suddenly collapses in a moment of apocalyptic silence.

*The Witnesses*, however, never becomes a moralistic tract, manipulating the spectators' emotions. Normal audience sympathies and expectations are undermined by sudden shifts between the actuality of the stage and the world of the characters. It is never clear whether they are *dramatis personae* or actors reciting a poem (in part one) and playing roles (in parts two and three) in a Pirandellian play-within-a-play, with the Stranger, or a stage manager, straightening up the set at the end of part two. Ordinary possibility seems suspended, and the play offers the audience no reality except the one being constructed at each moment on the stage. But the contrived world of the play alludes to a world beyond, which, although invisible, strongly affects the lives of the characters despite their steadfast refusal to face reality. The encasement of the apartment and the café terrace within the stage space extends the boundaries of the play's effects well beyond the walls of the theatre. Confronted by the atmosphere of anxiety and the overwhelming sense of menace, the audience is thus led to the sensation of the very serious dangers to their own existence.

The progressive imminence of the final catastrophe is also central to *The Old Woman Broods*. Różewicz creates here a compelling dramatic universe in which visual opulence carries the play's meaning. There is no plot, only recurrent stage imagery. The focal image is the setting, a steadily growing pile of refuse, suffused with blinding light. As the play unfolds, the setting becomes a metaphor for the violent destiny of modern man and the fatal course of Western civilization. As in *The Witnesses*, the dominant tone is one of ambiguity and menace. Różewicz achieves great intensity through a peculiar form of suspense: beyond a vague feeling of impending doom, no one knows what will happen. Rhythmic acceleration, applied throughout the play, propels the drama forward in a mounting crescendo of insistent sights and sounds, and the frantic action culminates in a frightening vision of the decay and death of a society.

The entire action is performed on a floodlit stage, in an almost clinical brilliance which hides nothing from view and thus heightens the unfolding anomie. Scene one takes place in a large coffee shop at a train station. With its connotations of transience, this locale suggests a temporary suspension of an inevitable passage to destruction and death. The floor is strewn with debris. As the Waiter turns on an electric fan, a stream of air sends the litter flying about. From without, an enormous pile of refuse presses against the walls of the café. When its only window is opened, a steady flow of debris swamps the coffee shop. More trash pours in as the action progresses, while garbage trucks can be heard dumping refuse just outside the train station. In scene two, the garbage dump has already swallowed the coffee shop. The landscape, in the form of a broad, apocalyptically desolate expanse on the edge of time, seethes with motion as the characters crawl through the refuse or unload truckfuls of discarded objects, live people and life-size puppets, and encyclopedias – visual symbols of useless ideologies and obsolete abstractions.

The play opens with a wordless, visually arresting tableau, rich in color, texture, and shape. A striking accent in the bleak interior of the café, the tables and chairs are painted red, black, and white. Made of metal, glass, and plastic, they 'glitter, glisten, and sparkle' (*ST*, 331). There are also other objects which reflect the bright lights against the dull background of the decaying garbage: the Old Woman's sparkling white dentures, numerous rings, and lacquered purse; the Waiter's patent-leather shoes; and the Young Woman's metallic costume. More than mere scenographic embellishments, these objects are symbolic of the deceptive glitter and elegance of the 'little stabilization.'

The Old Woman, wearing several layers of protective coverings, with jewelry and flowers dangling all over her, actually looks like a mound of debris herself. The Waiter scuttles about the cafeteria, pandering to the Old Woman's interminable whims and wishes, while she growls with irritation or coos with delight. Both of them divert themselves with superficial conversation, carried in staccato rhythms, which distracts them from the situation as it really is: a formless chaos, represented by the debris, on which patterns can be fitted only by self-deception. For example, the Waiter meticulously wipes the tables and arranges artificial flowers in a vase, and another waiter, named Cyryl, painstakingly sweeps the garbage with 'a miniature dustpan' and 'a tiny brush' (*ST*, 343).

In scene two, a disaster has apparently struck and reduced the modern civilization to a deathly landscape of graves and battlefield trenches. In slow motion, Cyryl and the Waiter crawl out of the garbage. The Waiter wears an army helmet and holds a knife between his teeth. The two men lock their bodies in a powerful embrace, but it is not clear whether they fight or hug one another. 'They freeze, they move, they freeze again' (*ST*, 348). Later in the scene, the Waiter emerges entangled in dirty bandages, ominously 'spilling out of his body and dragging behind him like intestines' (*ST*, 353).

The world may now be the vast expanse of 'a necropolis,' but life goes on in its normal routine, and the 'little stabilization' prevails (*ST*, 347). Dedicated to a life of illusion, the community continues to structure its existence by imposing artificial patterns on it. For example, the sanitation department preserves an orderly appearance of the dump by sprinkling it with water, sweeping and rearranging the garbage into neat piles, and painting crossings for pedestrians. The coffee shop has collapsed, but it quickly resumes its operation and expands into a beauty salon where the Old Woman, now wearing several layers of summer dresses, gets a permanent and a pedicure. An orchestra rehearses for a concert. Chaises longues have been brought in, and the garbage dump doubles as a beach. Three young women in swimming suits sunbathe on a white beach towel. In the stage directions, they are identified as Clotho, Lachesis, and Atropos, the three Fates of the Greek mythology. But rather than spin the thread of human fates and dispose of lots, they obliviously clip their fingernails, make wreaths out of the trash, and exchange trivialities.

As scene two draws to an end, this fragile, temporary equilibrium is suddenly upset by the arrival of the Old Woman's son. Holding a travel bag, he is dressed simply but colorfully. The colors, however, are 'beauti- fully matched' (*ST*, 363). The most striking features of the Young Man's appearance are his long, curly blond hair, a live flower in his buttonhole, and a snow-white lace jabot at his neckband. A vivid contrast to the emptiness, sterility, and decay of the world in which nothing grows and wreaths are made of debris rather than flowers, the Young Man, radiant and innocent, represents the possibility that life may be renewable. In an ironic travesty of the myth of the Second Coming, however, tremendous aggressions are unleashed against the intruder, which catapult the drama into its final apocalypse. The lights dim, enveloping the stage in 'lifeless' semi-darkness 'as if during a solar eclipse' (*ST*, 365). The Policeman confronts the Young Man, charging him with littering the dump. The

34 *The Old Woman Broods*, Wrocław, 1969. Directed by Jerzy Jarocki. (Photo Grażyna Wyszomirska)

Young Man does not dispute the charges but simply points to their absurdity: '[H]ow can anyone litter . . . a garbage dump?' (*ST*, 366). But, like the other characters in the play, the Policeman refuses to recognize the reality: 'I don't see any garbage here' (*ST*, 366). In a friendly gesture, the Young Man offers the Policeman his flower, but the Policeman, with an uneasy grimace, forces the Young Man to take the flower back. The Young Man's face loses its radiance and freezes in an expression of sadness and sobriety.

Immediately following the confrontation, the lights go on and off several times. In a still more advanced stage in the world's decay, the characters disappear, and all life seems to be drawing to a close. Only the Old Woman, the sole survivor of the sweeping cataclysm, frantically digs through the debris in search of her lost son, until a curtain of heavy metal quickly falls down. This surprising and anticlimactic *coup de théâtre* replaces the final explosion: without warning, the curtain cuts off and encloses the apocalyptic reality evoked on the stage. Thus, in keeping with his dramatic practice, Różewicz shatters any lingering illusion of reality, in which the characters' oblivious existence has possibly been wiped off by an unnamed catastrophe, and he catches the audience unawares with a startling theatrical surprise. The unwary spectator, who has been carried along by the intense interplay of the characters' delusions, is now caught in shocked amazement as the established premises of the play are unexpectedly disavowed. The ironic device of the final curtain leaves the audience disconcerted and perplexed. The playwright has thus manipulated one realm (the contrivances of the stage) to undercut another (the imagined life of the characters) in order to engage the spectators' imagination in a jolting sensation bearing upon their own lives. He has played a trick on them, evoking in the spectators a slightly uneasy feeling of their lack of control over their lives and responses – an effect that parallels the situation of the characters in the play.

*The Interrupted Act*,[10] a deliberately incomplete comedy in four scenes, is Różewicz's most radical denial of what has always been the basis of theatre: a representation of human life in the form of dramatic action. Although it would be possible to unearth several stories buried beneath the surface of the play, seemingly structured around a rift between the Engineer and his daughter, the playwright refuses to develop any of these lines. *The Interrupted Act* starts deceptively as a simple domestic drama but soon shifts to an embodiment of the creative process, which demands a new kind of attention and mental participation from the viewer. The play's title thus refers not only to the Engineer's liaison with the Nurse, but primarily to compositional strategies of the playwright who seeks to divest his work of permanence and boundaries via random spatial and temporary distributions. As in Conceptual, or Idea, Art of the late 1960s and early 1970s,[11] conception takes precedence over form: the idea and its execution are more important than the finished product, which merely documents the idea. In his work-in-progress, Różewicz leads the audience through his creative conscious-ness, combining his objections to dramatic conventions and critical criteria with a clear, radical alternative and a genuinely polemical position which he defines both in the stage directions and the largely wordless scenes.

In print, the stage directions – which are to 'be included in the program notes' (*ST*, 275) – constitute two-thirds of the entire play, but they offer little technical instruction for the actor and the director. Rather, they provide documentation of the playwright's creative process. This extended monologue contains Różewicz's most trenchant comments on the inherent limitations of theatrical illusion. Well aware of conventions and techniques used by dramatists to create a logically believable world on stage, he rips these theatrical forms apart and exposes them as fraud. His method is first to consider possibilities offered by scenic realism, with its preposterously causal explanations, and then to undermine systematically the credibility of such old-fashioned dramaturgy:

> An attractive, nicely built young woman holding a large suitcase walks across the room. She has just said goodbye to her father, a well-known engineer, and is leaving forever to go to America, to stay with the family of her late mother. Her father is not seeing her off because he is lying in his study . . . with his leg in a plaster cast . . . Unfortunately, we cannot prove on the stage – through so-called theatrical means – that the young woman is leaving forever or even that she is leaving for North America. We are helpless. True, we could have used a narrator, a telephone, or the Father's voice from the other room . . . The young woman could have called for information about flights to Hamburg, Lisbon, and New York. But all this has already taken place before the curtain went up . . . [Besides,] these scenes would have taken about forty-five minutes to perform, while the actual 'drama' might have completed its course . . . Unfortunately, we have no time to show in our theatre . . . the reasons which led to the young person's departure. (*ST*, 272–4)

Apart from their function as a carefully controlled attack on scenic realism, the stage directions allow Różewicz to view his creation without the intermediary of the characters. The *didascalies* call for a set representing a large, inconspicuous room in the Engineer's apartment. As the playwright's obsessive stream of thought continues, however, the stage becomes a physical manifestation of his imagination, where he explores different possibilities of developing the play's action. Różewicz thus theatri-calizes the activity of thought, rendering the conceptual in precise visual terms. He consciously distorts and conceals the residual fragments of the creaking plot, and he relieves the characters of conventional narrative functions. Moreover, he delights in maintaining a distanced attitude toward the *dramatis personae* through his prodigious interventions into the realm of their imagined existence. He repeatedly halts the stage action, playing ironically with the illusion, fracturing the reality of the characters' lives, and thus making the contrivances of the stage unabashedly obvious. It is precisely the playwright's ironic distance from his own work that holds together the entire play and gives it its forward motion. Whereas in traditional dramaturgy the action progresses once certain premises have been established, here the longer the action goes on, the more improbable and even impossible it becomes, and transformations within the play are kaleidoscopic and unceasing.

In scene one, the daughter slips a farewell note under a sugar bowl. In the following scene, the Engineer's housekeeper finds the letter and reads it aloud, while mechanically picking up sugar cubes and putting them in her mouth. She then asks, 'What's to be done now?' (*ST*, 284). At this point, the stage erupts in unexpected discontinuities and upsetting jolts, as the playwright brings to life postmodern, surrealist, symbolist, and socialist–realistic variations of the action. With verve and adroitness, he creates spectacularly comic *coups de théâtre*, thwarting the spectators' expectations. The audience is kept in a state of pleasurable suspense, not so much over the details of the scanty narrative but over the way in which Różewicz will resolve the flamboyantly theatrical situations he has contrived. In the symbolist scene three, for example, the Stranger comes in, sits at the table, pours himself a drink, lights a cigarette, and exits not having uttered a word. In such sequences, Różewicz's favorite technique is reminiscent of Witkacy's 'visual emphasis through pointed focus' which 'directs the spectator's eye to a significant detail, character, or area of the stage and then holds his attention there for a prolonged moment, imprinting the scene on his consciousness.'[12] Różewicz's technique is, furthermore, an ironic inversion of a device of the *pièce bien faite* in which the apparently trivial object – the glass of water in Eugène Scribe's *Le Verre d'eau* (*The Glass of Water*, 1840) or a lost love letter in Victorien Sardou's *Les Pattes de mouche* (*A Scrap of Paper*, 1860) – is invested with a deeper significance revealed only later in the play. But the details in Różewicz's close-ups – the daughter's letter, a hole in the Stranger's left sock, a fly sitting on a sugar cube, three white hairs lying on a bookshelf – are intentionally incongruous and meaningless. The result is a sense of spatial displacement which punctures the style of painstakingly intimate realism and confounds rational everyday experiences.

*The Card Index*, *The Witnesses*, *The Old Woman Broods*, and *The Interrupted Act* represent a summation of Różewicz's accomplishments as a playwright. In these visually forceful and evocative works, reality is entirely problematic, existing in a constant state of destruction and reconstruction. Liberated from the clichés of psychology and storytelling, Różewicz's plays derive their unusual power on stage not from the scripted text, but from an ingenious orchestration of spatial polarities. A virtuoso master of dramatic technique and visual effect, Różewicz lifts the plays off the ground of realistic dramaturgy and predictable expectations into the realm of freedom and pure theatricality. The works reveal his brilliant skill in playing with the conventions of the theatre and leading the audience wherever he wishes. Różewicz's manipulation of the shifting planes of reality is his shock tactic to provoke, attack, and arrest the attention of the spectators, thus forcing them to question the stability of their own world – the world outside the theatre.

## NOTES

1 Różewicz's work for the theatre includes fifteen full-length plays, ten one-act plays, and a scenario for an environmental piece entitled *Birth Rate: The Biography of a Play* (*Przyrost naturalny: biografia sztuki teatralnej*, 1960). His first play, *Exposure* (*Ujawnienie*), completed in 1950 when he was twenty-nine, has been barred from production or publication on political grounds. But Różewicz's second play, *The Card Index* (*Kartoteka*, 1960), staged as the arts in Eastern Europe were emerging from a dreary period of enforced socialist realism, signalled the beginning of a stylistically tolerant pluralism and provided an important model for theatre experimentation in Poland.

2 See Richard Schechner, '6 Axioms for Environmental Theatre,' *The Drama Review*, 12 (Spring 1968), 41–64.

3 For discussion of spatial dimensions in the theatre, see especially J. L. Styan, *Drama, Stage, and Audience* (New York: Cambridge University Press, 1975) and *The Elements of Drama* (New York: Cambridge University Press, 1963); Bernard Beckerman, *The Dynamics of Drama* (New York: Alfred A. Knopf, 1970); Stanley Vincent Longman, 'The Spatial Dimension of Theatre,' *Theatre Journal*, 33 (March 1981), 46–59; Kazimierz Braun, *Przestrzeń teatralna* (Warsaw: Państwowe Wydawnictwo Naukowe, 1982); and Arnold Aronson, *The History and Theory of Environmental Scenography* (Ann Arbor: University Microfilms International Research Press, 1981).

4 Since first productions of Różewicz's plays are frequently delayed by the censor – for example, *Dead and Buried* (*Do piachu . . .*), completed in 1972, was not cleared by the censor's office until 1979 – the year given in parentheses refers to the first publication of a play.

5 Różewicz uses theatrical space in a more conventional way – to establish a particular mood and to reflect the characters' cultural milieu or social aspirations – only when he seeks an ironic effect. For example, in one of the astonishing and witty reversals of *Spaghetti and the Sword* (*Spaghetti i miecz*, 1964), act two is ostensibly set for the simplest naturalism and the sentimentalism of the most insidious kind, thus promising a sequential development of events after the slapstick antics of act one. The scene takes place in Italy, in a luxurious seaside villa in Sorrento, where Wanda, a brooding Polish beauty, brings her national culture to the ignorant Italian masses and simmers in self-indulgent, intellectual games. As act one opens, a 'blue expanse of the sky and the sea is visible through

open windows . . . In the parlor, by the fireplace, sits an elegant and beautiful woman, forty years old. Next to her is a platter with grapes, oranges, (green) figs, and olives' (*ST*, 175). From a distance come a soft Neapolitan canzone and the murmuring of the sea, occasionally punctuated by a ship's siren. Różewicz uses this straightforward stage realism to lull the audience into a false sense of security so that the theatrical destruction of that apparent reality will be all the more effective. He subsequently breaks the spell of the opening sequence with broad comedy featuring two ebullient, garrulous Italian women and Wanda's soon-to-be fiancé, Garofano. A caricature of an unctuous Italian lover used to swift conquests, he races feverishly in and out of the performance area on roller skates.

6 Tadeusz Różewicz, *Sztuki teatralne* (Wrocław: Zakład Narodowy imienia Ossolińskich, 1972), pp. 7, 41. Further reference to Różewicz's plays is to this edition, with the abbreviation of the title (*ST*) and page numbers given in the text in parentheses. All translations are mine. For the English translation of *The Card Index*, see Tadeusz Różewicz, *The Card Index and Other Plays*, trans. Adam Czerniawski (New York: Grove Press, 1970). This translation, however, is based on a censored version of the play and does not include a number of scenes which first appeared in Polish in 1971: '*Kartoteka*: fragmenty nie publikowane,' *Odra*, 11 (November 1971), 67–75.

7 For the English translation of the two plays, see Tadeusz Różewicz, *The Witnesses and Other Plays*, trans. Adam Czerniawski (London: Calder and Boyars, 1970).

8 Martin Esslin has compared the structure of *The Witnesses* to 'three movements' of 'a sonata,' which 'together produce the total desired effect of variations on a basic theme.' See his *Theatre of the Absurd* (Garden City, NY: Doubleday, 1969), p. 277.

9 Longman, 'The Spatial Dimension of Theatre,' p. 46.

10 For the English translation, see *The Card Index and Other Plays*.

11 For discussion of Conceptual Art, see especialy Ursula Meyer, *Conceptual Art* (New York: Dutton, 1972); Gregory Battcock (ed.), *Idea Art: A Critical Anthology* (New York: Dutton, 1973); and Nikos Stangos (ed.), *Concepts of Modern Art* (New York: Harper and Row, 1981).

12 Daniel Gerould, *Witkacy: Stanisław Ignacy Witkiewicz as an Imaginative Writer* (Seattle and London: University of Washington Press, 1981), p. 56.

# Samuel Beckett's Doomsday play: the space of infinity*

JAMES E. ROBINSON

Kent:         Is this the promis'd end?
Edgar:  Or image of that horror?

. . . . .

Kent:  Vex not his ghost. O, let him pass!

(*King Lear*)

In so much of Samuel Beckett's fiction and theatre, we seem to be in a Doomsday landscape, in a stripped-down world somewhere at the edge of time, awaiting a 'promis'd end' that never arrives. Beckett's eschatology is uncertain about the after-life or the after-death: 'No, nothing is certain' (*Waiting for Godot*), yet 'Something is taking its course' (*Endgame*).

Seemingly projected into a passage toward eternity, the characters of Beckett yet remain endlessly in passage, infinitely edging on toward the resolution that never occurs. Involved in a process of diminishing time and place that should lead to spiritual reckoning and release according to the paradigms of the theology of the Western world, the characters of Beckett at the edge of Doom remain bound, bound to their dying, bound to each other or to themselves, bound to the consciousness of their unconsummated existence. Summarizing the irony of the Beckett eschatology, one of the narrators of Beckett's fictions playfully provokes himself to do what he cannot possibly do, play the god who should render reckoning and release:

> It is in the tranquility of decomposition that I remember the long confused emotion which was my life, and that I judge it, as it is said that God will judge me, and with no less impertinence.[1]

Although the whole of Beckett's art might be perceived as Doomsday Play in this ironic sense, I limit myself in this essay to selected theatre pieces that allow for especial treatment as Doomsday Theatre. The space of theatre accentuates a bounded world from which the characters struggle for release. The Beckett stage becomes further a space of infinity, endlessly

* A draft of this paper was read at the *Themes in Drama* International Conference held at the University of California, Riverside, in February 1985.

compressing into zones approaching boundlessness, but remaining endlessly a boundary. Two features characterize the Beckett Doomsday stage: (1) a myth of infinity replaces the traditional myth of passage to eternity; (2) the plays, earlier through later, represent an evolving experience in the Doomsday chamber of passage. The progress of Beckett's art as illustrated by the plays selected in this essay is a reflection of the myth of infinity adumbrated by that art. The plays successively diminish in substance and clarity of contour. The more recent plays engage the characters within increasingly narrowing and darkening stage arenas in what becomes an increasingly intense but unresolved flight from the self. The plays endlessly edge on toward an undefined edge: 'Something is taking its course.'

It would be helpful to consider medieval Doomsday plays of the Corpus Christi cycles as a measure of contrast for better perception of the contours of the Beckett Doomsday plays. In England each of the four surviving cycles concludes with a Judgment Day play based on Matthew 25:31–46. Christ summons all to final judgment, separates the sheep from the goats, the good from the bad, welcomes the blessed to heaven and dismisses the cursed to eternal fire. Christ, who displays the wounds of the redeeming Crucifixion, is the key figure in these medieval Judgment plays: judge and savior, He redeems time as He dissolves it. The people summoned to judgment are characters free from the trappings of this-world consciousness and identity, characters like the metaphoric sheep and goats of Matthew 25, identified at the edge of time only as the saved or damned.[2]

A variety of easy and lively theatrical images accentuated the passage to eternity in the medieval Judgment plays. In the Chester play Latin glosses indicate that Jesus will come to Judgment 'as in a cloud' attended by angels carrying the instruments of the Crucifixion (the cross, the crown of thorns, a lance). Records from a fifteenth-century production of the York Doomsday reveal a grand performance featuring a pageant wagon for heaven with an iron superstructure and assorted damasks, artificial angels, red and blue clouds streaming from heaven on sunbeams of gold, an adjacent structure for 'hell mouth,' a variety of sarks, diadems, wigs, and masks. In the final grand passage of this York production, Christ ascended spectacularly into eternity in an iron seat on a pulley.[3] At the end of the Wakefield Cycle, we envision the devil Tutivillus, who has delighted in all the bad souls he has collected at the last reckoning, leading a parade of demons and damned from the *platea* off to the pageant wagon of hell, and we see Christ escorting the good up a staircase of the pageant of heaven, all the good singing, as the text indicates, an ultimate chorus of *Te Deum laudamus*.[4] A Latin inscription concluding the text of the York Judgment summarizes the spectacle that effects the transition from time to eternity: '*Et sic facit finem cum melodia angelorum transiens a loco ad locum*' ('And so crossing over from place to place,

He [God the son] makes end, with an accompaniment of a melody of angels').[5] Simply done, with the song of guildsmen as supporting angels, Christ moves across the spaces of medieval pageantry, and the image of doom becomes a celebration of transcendence, a passage to eternity.

The open theatre management of these medieval Doomsday plays pointed upward for the redeemed and so emphasized ascension and transcendence; Beckett's Doomsday plays collapse in images of theatrical circles or theatrical entropy. The medieval Doomsday play concluded in reckoning and passage to eternity; in Beckett's Doomsday theatre there is no measure for judgment. Although Beckett's characters are in passage, they do not pass. The medieval plays presented a mythology of passage to eternity. Beckett presents a mythology of infinity.[6]

*Waiting for Godot* (English version 1955; *En attendant Godot* 1953) makes direct use, parodic use, of Biblical images of Judgment. Near the beginning of the play Vladimir and Estragon engage in a vaudevillian exchange about the thieves who died with Christ (Luke 23:32–43). 'One of the thieves was saved,' muses Vladimir. 'It's a reasonable percentage' (p. 8).[7] And then in the banter that follows, Didi and Gogo play lightly with the idea of salvation (was the thief saved from hell or death?) and with the mathematics of the testimony (only one of the four evangelists says that one of the thieves was saved). The image of a good and bad thief at the opposite sides of Christ prefigures the sheep and goats to the right and left of Christ at the General Judgment.

Beckett observed this about the image of the thieves: 'Take Augustine's doctrine of grace given and grace withheld: have you pondered the dramatic qualities in this theology? Two thieves are crucified with Christ, one saved and the other damned. How can we make sense of this division?'[8] The inexplicability of arbitrary judgment is one of the major themes of *Godot*. Near the end of the first act the Boy as messenger from Godot meets Didi and Gogo. We learn that this boy minds the goats, and Godot doesn't beat him. His brother minds the sheep; Godot beats the sheepherder, claims the Boy. Godot treats goats and sheep in reverse parody of Christ's judgment in Matthew 25:31–46.

But Godot, of course, is absent, whatever the arrangement of sheep and goats. Godot is absence, the unknowable.[9] All the explainable values of Matthew 25, the corporal works of mercy and the grace afforded by Christ's Passion – all this disappears as explanation of salvation. Didi and Gogo think that when they meet Godot, they will be saved. But salvation is not an explicable matter in the mythology of this play. Didi and Gogo may keep their appointment at Doomsday, but unlike the crucified thieves, or the sheep and goats of Matthew, they wait astride an empty space.

In *Waiting for Godot* the theatrical image of the diminishing edge of existence near Doomsday is a road by a tree and a mound inhabited off and

on by two pairs of mortals and a messenger from Godot. During the course
of the play's two acts two evenings pass and two nights fall (as a stage moon
pops up near the end of each act). The play's action circles round to stasis,
whence it began. The *'four or five leaves'* that appear on the tree in the second
act accentuate compression of time in a myth of infinity.

> Vladimir:  But yesterday evening it was all
>            black and bare. And now it's
>            covered with leaves.
> Estragon:  Leaves?
> Vladimir:  In a single night.
> Estragon:  It must be the Spring.
> Vladimir:  But in a single night!
>
>                                              (p. 42)

In an infinitely circling series, the action and time of *Godot* continuously
shrink; here the division between winter and spring shrinks into a single
night.

Lucky's monologue in act I accentuates Beckett's image of a universe
shrinking. The collapsing Lucky delivers a marvelous theatre piece of
collapsing language which nevertheless makes a kind of sense. Beckett has
explained the sense this way: 'The monologue's theme is: to shrink on an
impossible earth under an indifferent heaven.'[10] The monologue summarizes the process of life diminishing under the aegis of inexplicable
indifference, not proceeding toward end and reckoning.

*Endgame* (1958; *Fin de partie* 1957) is Beckett's most intricate exercise in
presenting figurations of an eschatology of infinity. We are in a room, a
shelter, with a hollow wall, a window right (the earth), a window left (the
sea), a place inbetween that is near being a condition of placelessness.
There are two ashbins containing stumps of the 'accursed progenitors,' Nell
and Nagg: before the play is over, one is perhaps dead; the other is perhaps
alive. At the beginning there is Hamm in an armchair, with castors; he is
blind, unable to stand, his face covered with a bloody handkerchief. There
is Clov, the watcher at the windows, looking out into spaces which we later
understand to be spaces approaching spacelessness, the void. Says Clov at
the beginning: 'Finished, it's finished, nearly finished, it must be nearly
finished.'

During the course of *Endgame* the language of the play brings us more and
more to approach point zero, to experience the edge of life to come or the
edge of oblivion. We learn that outside the shelter 'There's no one else,' and
'There's nowhere else.' 'There's no more nature.' Outside there is 'zero,'
'Nothing on the horizon,' lead waves, no sun, zero. During the course of the
play, we learn there are no more pap, no more sugar plums, no more pain
killer, no more tide, 'no more coffins.' In the very last verbal motion of the
play, we prepare for a final discarding, a final disposal: Clov says, 'This is

what we call making an exit,' and Hamm says, 'Discard.' Hamm throws away some of the few props of the play, the gaff, the toy dog, the whistle. But immediately before these discardings begin, Clov appears with new dressings, and new props, a Panama hat, a tweed coat, raincoat, umbrella, bag. And Clov does not exit. The play does not reach point zero. It returns in substance to the tableau of its beginning, where Clov said '. . . it's finished, nearly finished, it must be nearly finished.' But it is never finished.

What Hamm in his blindness projects as destiny inside the hollow walls of the room of the *Endgame* stage is 'Infinite emptiness.' At one point Hamm tells Clov that one day Clov, like Hamm, will be blind and worn down and will look at the wall and close his eyes and open them to find 'no wall any more.' Rather 'Infinite emptiness will be all around you, all the resurrected dead of all the ages wouldn't fill it, and there you'll be like a little bit of grit in the middle of the steppe' (p. 36).[11] So we look upon the Beckett stage as a space of infinity, a space of 'infinite emptiness,' and we see the players and perhaps ourselves as infinitesimal figures of inexplicable and grimly comic pathos. Like 'little bit[s] of grit' spilling into 'the middle of the steppe,' Beckett characters become part of a process approaching but failing to reach the impossible consummation.[12]

The more severe images of infinite erosion in *Endgame* are relieved by a playfully serene game about endlessness. Beckett constructs a game inside the endgame for the last part of the play. Midway in the play Clov sets up this formula for the possible end of the game: he says to Hamm, 'You whistle me. I don't come. The alarm rings. I'm gone. It doesn't ring. I'm dead' (p. 47). To show Hamm that the alarm is working, that the clock has the power to ring, Clov brings in the clock and sets it ringing, exclaiming to Hamm: 'Fit to wake the dead! Did you hear it?' (p. 48). Later on then as we approach the end of the game, Hamm says 'Ah let's get it over!' (p. 70) and whistles for Clov, thus setting off the terms of the clock formula earlier defined by Clov. So Clov enters with the alarm clock, hangs it on the wall (p. 72), and then puts it on top of Nagg's bin (p. 79). There we watch this theatre mechanism tick off infinite time. We do not hear the clock ring. For the clock not to ring is, according to Clov's formulation, signification that Clov is dead, not gone, but dead. But then, we ask as the play freezes into tableau, how long do we wait for the alarm clock to ring or not to ring to be sure that it has not rung and thus that Clov is dead, not gone, but dead? (At the end he is neither dead nor gone.) When can we say for sure that the condition 'It doesn't ring' is a past fact? We cannot, according to the wit of the game, ever know whether Clov is dead so long as he is not gone, and so long as the alarm is silent. The puzzle of the clock is analogue of the perplexity of the limited human mind trying to conceive of Doomsday and a life to come. We cannot experience the ring of the clock at the end of time so long as we live. We cannot experience the consciousness of death or eternity so long as we live. For Beckett such a paradoxical impasse is a trap of rational consciousness that results in a myth of infinity. This silent alarm clock at the end of *Endgame*, this alarm 'Fit to wake the dead' yet infinitely not ringing, may be a parody of the 'great sound of a trumpet' that Christ's angels are supposed to deliver to announce the decisive moment of Doomsday (Matthew 24:31).

Beckett scholars often refer to the *'large blood-stained handkerchief'* (as the stage directions describe it) that covers Hamm's face at the beginning and end of *Endgame* as a Veronica mask or veil. Such an allusion to Christ's suffering face augments the Christian suggestions of Clov's opening words, 'Finished, it's finished . . .' These words echo Christ's last words on the cross, 'It is finished' (John 19:30). The allusion is parody, since neither Hamm nor Clov bring anything to finish. One might also say that the bloody handkerchief suggests the napkin from Christ's entombed head, the piece of linen left behind in the tomb at the scene of Christ's resurrection (John 20:7).[13] Again, the reference is parody: when he refers to the handkerchief at the end of the play (calling it 'Old stancher' in the English version and *'Vieux linge'* in the French version), Hamm says to the linen, 'You . . . remain.' And Hamm remains with the linen, in the tomb as it were; there is no resurrection.

*Waiting for Godot* and *Endgame* develop a myth of infinity in part by parody of Christian images of eschatology. The characters, tied to each other in pairs, are not so tormented by being tied to their own self-consciousness. Now in the Doomsday plays that follow in Beckett's career the parody of Christian myth disappears as Beckett concentrates on developing his own images of suffering humanity caught in a self-tormenting solipsistic vision of unending, unresolved existence. Characters become more engaged in monologue, or in dialogue with different dimensions of the self. And characters become more and more involved in the attempt to realize negation or erasure of what might be called Cartesian self-consciousness.[14] As they seek erasure of such consciousness the characters of Beckett struggle for passage into an unrealizable zone of some kind of transcendent being, or other being, or non-being.[15]

The Doomsday landscape of *Happy Days* (1961) is a space of scorched earth where the heroine Winnie, buried up to her waist in the first act and up to her neck in the second, delivers soliloquies of empty talk in the face of the enveloping burial. Winnie's man Willie, barely able to crawl, speaking hardly at all, seems threatened with passing out of existence, that is passing out of the existence held tenuously in place by the view and patter of Winnie. Winnie feels that gravity is failing, that she would be 'sucked up' and 'simply float into the blue' except for the mound that binds her (p. 33).[16] Winnie wonders if 'the earth has lost its atmosphere' (p. 51) in this time of 'the great heat' (p. 28). Winnie speaks and thinks in a rattle of trivial talk which she refers to as 'the old style.' Now, in the time beyond 'the old style,' time may be dissolving. 'May one still speak of time?' wonders Winnie (p. 50).

Winnie claims that she lives 'between the bell for waking and the bell for sleep' (p. 21), but in fact when the bell rings in the play it always announces the waking, the day. In the second act Winnie yearns for and waits for the bell for sleep, but several times, including at the play's ending, Winnie closes her eyes, and then the bell rings, each time calling her to the light of day. The play is an infinity of 'holy light' and 'hellish light' (p. 11).

Here we might recall section six of Beckett's novel *Murphy* (1938), where the narrator analyzes Murphy's mind. There are three zones in Murphy's mind, 'light, half light, dark, each with its specialty.' The zone of light is the zone of ordinary consciousness, where the mind is in touch with the phenomena of physical reality. In the half-light, there 'is the pleasure of contemplation.' 'The third, the dark' is 'a flux of forms, a perpetual coming together and falling asunder of forms': this is the zone of 'will-lessness,' which Murphy longs for, where one exists as 'a mote in . . . absolute freedom.'[17] Says J. E. Dearlove about Murphy's quest: 'he seeks himself in a realm where the self does not exist.'[18] So do the characters of Beckett's Doomsday plays come more and more to seek release from the light, to enter a realm where the self does not exist. Winnie in *Happy Days* is still very much caught up in the blazing light of her self-consciousness. But the space of the Beckett stage will become more and more a space of gathering dark.

In *Play* (1963) a spotlight holds three characters in a kind of post-mortem consciousness which keeps death from effecting any kind of passage into transcendent eternity. As in many of the stories of Beckett's prose fiction, consciousness oddly proceeds in an infinite continuum even beyond death. M, W1, and W2 represent respectively a man, one woman to whom the man owed some loyalty of love, and another woman for whom the man betrayed the first. This infinite triangle recalls Sartre's *Huis clos* (1944). However, in the Sartre play the three characters have lived separate lives in the ordinary world and in a post-mortem world are then brought together in a kind of hell to torture each other ('. . . *l'enfer, c'est les Autres*,' says one of the characters near the end of *Huis clos*). The Beckett people of *Play*, on the other hand, have lived in miserable company with one another in the mortal world, and now in the post-mortem world have separate existences. Beckett's characters exist as heads protruding from funeral jars, speaking in response to the play of the moving light, recalling their affair, occasionally speaking in accidental chorus, usually speaking in seeming dialogue, but each actually speaking in monologue isolated from the others' hearing, presence, and consciousness, not knowing the whereabouts (or when-abouts) of the others. The spotlight is a 'Hellish half-light' (as W1 calls it) which brings self-consciousness to each character as it plays on them. Here hell is not others (as in *Huis clos*), but the self.[19] The light keeps the self in hell by keeping the mind working: 'How the mind works still!' says W1. The characters yearn for the dark. Says M, hopefully, 'Down, all going down, into the dark, peace is coming . . .'[20] But the spotlight of *Play* persists. The text of the play at play's ending calls for a repetition, '*Repeat play.*' Possibly *ad infinitum*.

In Beckett's later career there are miniscule plays wherein the unending edging toward the end continues on increasingly darkening stages in strange, haunting, and ever-narrowing rhythms of ebbing and nearly ceasing. In these plays Beckett employs a variety of evocative techniques of language and theatre in continuously fascinating attempts to express erasure of consciousness.

*Not I* (1972) presents upstage right a Mouth, '*faintly lit,*' and downstage left a Death-like figure '*in loose black djellaba, with hood, fully faintly lit . . .*' Otherwise the stage is darkness. In a relentless flow of lyrical fragments Mouth expresses fragmented memories of her fragmented life, referring to herself in the third person. Five times Mouth pauses, strongly holding on to the pronoun 'she'; each time after the pause Mouth 'recovers from vehement refusal to relinquish third person,' says Beckett in a note to the text. Four times in conjunction with the pauses the Auditor in djellaba presents with a raising and falling of arms 'a gesture of helpless compassion.'

In this astonishing play some of the shreds of Mouth's language suggest that she came to full sentience and speech only late on in old age, and thus her experience of being born into consciousness intertwines with her experience of dying. The tale of this fragmented and forlorn woman becomes a compressed tale of the infinite continuum of the life–death process. The space of theatre becomes a microspace wherein this macrostory of the human condition is figured as an intensely narrow focus of bounded light in the midst of a vast and seemingly unbounded darkness. Mouth wants it all to cease: 'all the time something begging . . . something in her begging . . . begging it all to stop . . . unanswered . . . prayer unanswered . . .' It goes on – the words, the fragmented thoughts . . . the fragmented mind . . . consciousness . . . 'the buzzing.' At the end the curtain is drawn. '*House dark. Voice continues behind curtain, unintelligible, 10 seconds, ceases as house lights up.*' The sound of the Mouth briefly ebbs beyond its own scene. As the scene ceases, the light brings the life of the theatre back to its own consciousness, after the darkness, after the play. One of the continuously repeated images in the language of Mouth in the play is 'the buzzing.' The audience should hear the buzzing inside the head, even after the play, even if the self tries to reject the pronoun of the self, 'not I.'

*Footfalls* (1976) is the most delicately complex of Beckett's later-day

Doomsday plays. A woman, May, *'dishevelled grey hair, worn grey wrap hiding feet,'* moves in decisively patterned steps, right to left, left to right, nine steps each way and then a dance-like turn: 'Seven eight nine wheel.' The dim lighting on May accentuates especially the walking. May communes with the Voice of her mother. The Voice metaphorically turns the revolving of the footfalls into an infinite revolving of the mind: 'Will you never have done . . . revolving it all?' . . . 'It all. [*Pause.*] In your poor mind.' The Voice of the mother in monologue recalls when someone, possibly her daughter, engaged in footfalls in an earlier time. In monologue May recalls another time when someone 'quite forgotten' (possibly her mother after death) slipped out 'at nightfall and into the little church,' where she began to 'walk, up and down, up and down . . . At nightfall . . . during Vespers.' In the last part of her monologue, which concludes the play, May tells the story of one Mrs Winter and her daughter Amy who discuss whether Mrs Winter observed a 'strange thing' 'at Evensong.' At the end of the play, says Mrs Winter to Amy or Amy to Mrs Winter inside the monologue of May communing with her mother: 'Will you never have done . . . revolving it all? [*Pause.*] It? [*Pause.*] It all. [*Pause.*] In your poor mind. [*Pause.*] It all. [*Pause.*] It all.'

We have been watching ghosts,[21] hearing *Footfalls* of ghosts, in passage, revolving infinitely in the chambers of the mind. The ghosts want 'it all' to come to conclusion.

In *Rockaby* (1981) Beckett presents a lyrical poem simply arranged for theatre. A grey-haired 'Prematurely old' woman with 'Huge eyes in white expressionless face' under a 'subdued spot' on a darkened stage rocks away, in a rocking chair, while a Voice intones an end-of-time lullaby:

> till in the end
> the day came
> in the end came
> close of a long day
> when she said
> to herself
> whom else
> time she stopped
> *time she stopped*
> going to and fro
>
> . . .

The rocker does not stop time. The Woman says 'More' (with deep anguish, I suggest) four different times in punctuation of the continuing lilt of the Voice and the roll of the rocker. At play's end, the separated Voice whimsically puns on the Woman's presumably increasing desire to get off her rocker:

saying to the rocker
rock her off
stop her eyes
fuck life
stop her eyes
rock her off
rock her off

An echoing chorus of Woman and Voice together intoning 'rock her off' continues as the rocker comes to rest and the spotlight fades.

In such theatre pieces of diminishing cadence and diminishing light in these recent years Beckett has pushed his characters about as far along in the passage toward erasure of self-consciousness as his vision allows. In his series of Doomsday plays from *Godot* to recent years, Beckett has presented shapes of universal destiny, not the meanings of individual death. Like the art of the medieval Doomsday plays, Beckett's art is concerned with universal kind and the figurations of universal destiny. 'All mankind is us,' says Vladimir. But unlike the medieval Doomsday characters, Beckett's figures seem untranslatable into representatives of a human passage to eternity. However much Beckett's theatre disjoints the voices and selves of the characters and attempts to absorb them in a releasing space of dark, the characters remain in passages of ebbing consciousness.

Beckett once said, 'I'm no intellectual. All I am is feeling. "Molloy" and the others came to me the day I became aware of my own folly. Only then did I begin to write the things I feel.'[22] In Beckett's series of Doomsday plays through the years, the characters seek release and transcendence in increasingly intense tempos of feeling. However much Beckett's characters are universally representative, they are not abstract. They are characters of feeling. In the recent Beckett Doomsday plays, the voices, the rhythms of aging, disintegrating, and ghostly sensibilities suggest increasingly desperate characters of feeling. They are in elegiac passage, infinitely pushing back the barriers that hold them from whatever realization, reckoning, or release that they (or we) can possibly imagine as a justification or conclusion for the suffering of being.

We would like to grant Beckett's Doomsday figures what Kent would grant for Lear: 'Vex not his ghost. O, let him pass! He hates him / That would upon the rack of this tough world / Stretch him out longer' (v, iii, 318–20). In the feeling of Beckett's ironic Doomsday Play there is this feeling of passage, this need for passing. There may be no absolutes in Beckett's theatre. But in that space of infinity where the Beckett characters endure, there is a continuing and persistent tension between Beckett's own kind of everlasting no and everlasting yea. 'No, nothing is certain.' Still, 'Something is taking its course.'

## NOTES

1 *Molloy*, in *Three Novels by Samuel Beckett* (New York: Grove Press, 1965), p. 25.

2 The Chester Doomsday includes characters named by occupation as well as by the state of their souls: e.g., *Papa Salvatus* and *Papa Damnatus*, *Regina Salvatus* and *Regina Damnatus*, *Mercator Damnatus*. These characters are nevertheless as without distinctive selves as are the saved and damned of the other cycle plays of the Last Judgment. Matthew, Mark, Luke, and John appear as witnesses at the end of the Chester Judgment, and do manage to maintain their identities as scholars. For my references to the Chester Judgment, I use the text in *The Chester Mystery Cycle*, ed. R. M. Lumiansky and David Mills, The Early English Text Society (London: Oxford University Press, 1974).

3 These various details of a York production of Doomsday are reported in Alexandra F. Johnston and Margaret Dorrell, 'The Doomsday Pageant of the York Mercers, 1433,' *Leeds Studies in English*, n.s. 5 (1971), 29–34, and Johnson and Dorrell,'The York Mercers and Their Pageant of Doomsday,' *Leeds Studies in English*, n.s. 6 (1972), 11–35.

4 Martial Rose discusses the staging of the Wakefield plays generally and the Judgment play specifically in his edition of *The Wakefield Mystery Plays* (London: Evans Brothers, 1961), pp. 17–48, 463–4.

5 Quotations from the York Judgment are according to the text in *York Mystery Plays*, ed. Toulmin Smith (New York: Russell and Russell, 1885, rpt 1963).

6 Hugh Kenner compares Beckett's zone or domain to pi and to the $\sqrt{2}$ and generally to the world of irrational numbers. See Kenner's *Samuel Beckett: A Critical Study*, new edn (Berkeley and Los Angeles: University of California Press, 1968), pp. 104–15. Says Kenner at another point (p. 87), 'The Beckett tension is between the person and the mathematical zero . . .' Richard N. Coe, specifically discussing *Godot*, compares the Self to $\sqrt{2}$, and says that 'Godot is there, at the end of the decimal,' and that 'Didi and Gogo are *almost* there,' having travelled 'hundreds of figures after the decimal point . . .' However, such travel beyond the decimal point is infinite. Says Coe,'. . . just as each successive figure after the decimal is less significant than its predecessor, progressing closer and closer to zero by infinitesimal degrees, yet never getting there, so each day takes them nearer to Godot, yet each day is progressively more insignificant, and at nightfall the "end" still eludes their grasp just as stubbornly as at daybreak.' See Coe, *Beckett* (Edinburgh and London: Oliver and Boyd, 1964), pp. 88–9.

7 Quotations and page references are from *Waiting for Godot* (New York: Grove Press, 1954).

8 From an interview with Tom Driver in *Columbia University Forum* (Summer 1961): see Lawrence Graver and Raymond Federman (eds.), *Samuel Beckett: The Critical Heritage* (London, Healey and Boston: Routledge & Kegan Paul, 1979), p. 220. Beckett also said this about the thieves: 'I am interested in the shape of ideas even if I do not believe them. There is a wonderful sentence in Augustine. I wish I could remember the Latin. It is even finer in Latin than in English. "Do not despair; one of the thieves was saved. Do not presume; one of the thieves was damned." That sentence has a wonderful shape. It is the shape that matters.' As

reported in Harold Hobson, 'Samuel Beckett: Dramatist of the Year,' *International Theatre Annual*, 1 (1956), 153.

9  Alan Schneider reported that when he asked Beckett 'who or what Godot was,' Beckett said 'that if he had known, he would have said so in the play.' Godot is an absent figuration of what the artist doesn't know, what he cannot know, cannot express. See Schneider, '"Any Way You Like, Alan": Working with Beckett,' *Theatre Quarterly*, 5 (Sept.–Nov. 1975), 31.

10  Beckett explained the parts of the monologue in this way: 'The first part is about the indifference of heaven . . . The second part . . . is about man, who is shrinking – about man who is dwindling. Not only the dwindling is important here, but the shrinking, too . . . The theme of the third part is "the earth abode of stones" . . .' About the end of the monologue then, where these motifs gather in conclusion like a musical cadence, Beckett said, 'The threads and themes are being gathered together. The monologue's theme is: to shrink on an impossible earth under an indifferent heaven.' As reported in a 1974–5 rehearsal diary by Walter D. Asmus, assistant director for the German production *Warten auf Godot*, which Beckett directed. See Asmus, 'Beckett Directs Godot,' trans. Ria Julian, *Theatre Quarterly*, 5 (Sept.–Nov. 1975), 22.

11  Quotations and page references are from *Endgame* (New York: Grove Press, 1958).

12  Beckett uses the image of grain spilling into infinity in two places in *Endgame*. At the beginning of the play Clov refers the idea of 'Finished . . . nearly finished' to the image of 'Grain upon grain,' building to 'a little heap, the impossible heap.' Later Hamm uses the image of grain 'pattering down' into infinity: 'Moment upon moment, pattering down, like the millet grains of . . . that old Greek, and all life long you wait for that to mount up to a life' (p. 70).

13  In the French version of the play there is an allusion to the 'lifted stone' at the scene of Christ's tomb after His resurrection. Says Clov in describing the boy he claims to see through his telescope: '*Il a l'air assis par terre, adossé à quelque chose.*' And Hamm responds, '*La pierre levée.*' *Fin de partie* (Paris: Les Editions de Minuit, 1957), p. 104.

14  Beckett's works are dotted with various signs of interest in Descartes and his followers. Beckett's early poem 'Whoroscope' (1930) was a grotesque mockery of Descartes. It is not always clear whether we should say that Descartes influenced Beckett or that Beckett especially delights in parodies of Cartesian philosophy. Generally I think that for Beckett Descartes is a convenient touchstone for the problems of self-consciousness and being in Western culture, and that the kind of reality of being summarized by Cartesian rationalism is a curse. But God knows where and when the pressure of self-consciousness began in civilization. For helpful discussions of Beckett and Cartesianism, see Kenner, *Samuel Beckett: A Critical Study*, pp. 83–91, 117–32; Coe, *Beckett*, pp. 16, 27–34; Lawrence Harvey, *Samuel Beckett, Poet and Critic* (Princeton, NJ: Princeton University Press, 1970), pp. 3–66; John Pilling, *Samuel Beckett* (London, Healey and Boston: Routledge & Kegan Paul, 1976), pp. 112–16.

15  Often in Beckett studies, one finds critics caught in the ambivalent tensions in Beckett's works between the themes of the search for the self and flight from self. For example, Martin Esslin in *The Theatre of the Absurd* (rev. edn, Garden City,

NY: Doubleday Anchor, 1969) subtitles his chapter on Beckett 'The search for the self,' and yet within the chapter says, '. . . dramatically and structurally, the flight from self-perception in an attempt to reach the positive nothingness of non-being, *is* an important theme of all of Beckett's work' (p. 58). In *Beckett*, Coe suggests that 'The central theme of Beckett's philosophy' is 'the impenetrable tangle between the essential Self and the apparent Self . . .' (p. 102). Coe also refers to the distinction between an 'ultimate Self' and 'pseudo-Selves' in Beckett's fiction (p. 71). Such distinctions are helpful in suggesting the difference between the self for which a character might search, and the self from which a character takes flight. Still, I want to push the distinction further and call the tension in Beckett a tension between the oppression of the self and the yearning for self-less-ness. David Read puts the issue of Beckett's art in terms of a struggle between being and non-being: note, for example, this phrasing by Read: '. . . Beckett alternates between the desire to secure being and with it the means of expression, and the longing for the non-being that would enable him to abandon his impossible task,' 'Artistic Theory in the Work of Samuel Beckett,' *Journal of Beckett Studies*, 8 (Autumn 1982), 17.

16 Quotations and page references are from *Happy Days* (New York: Grove Press, 1961).
17 *Murphy* (New York: Grove Press, 1957), pp. 111–13.
18 *Accommodating the Chaos: Samuel Beckett's Nonrelational Art* (Durham, NC: Duke University Press, 1982), p. 28.
19 Katharine Worth calls the spotlight of *Play* 'the light of consciousness,' in *Beckett the Shape Changer* (London and Boston: Routledge & Kegan Paul, 1975), p. 205. The contrast between Sartre's hell as others and Beckett's hell as the self is made in James Knowlson and John Pilling, *Frescoes of the Skull: The Later Prose and Drama of Samuel Beckett* (New York: Grove Press, 1980), p. 70.
20 Quotations from *Play*, *Not I*, *Footfalls*, and *Rockaby* are all from *The Collected Shorter Plays of Samuel Beckett* (New York: Grove Press, 1984). The brevity of these plays renders page citations unnecessary.
21 Cf. this comment by Knowlson and Pilling: 'We realize perhaps only *after* the play has ended, that we may have been watching a ghost telling a tale of a ghost (herself), who fails to be observed by someone else (her fictional *alter ego*) because she in turn was not really there,' *Frescoes of the Skull*, p. 227.
22 From an interview with Gabriel D'Aubarède in *Nouvelles Litteraires* (16 February 1961), trans. Christopher Waters in Graver and Federman, *Samuel Beckett: The Critical Heritage*, p. 217.

# The prison as theatre and the theatre as prison:
# Athol Fugard's *The Island**

## ALBERT WERTHEIM

Athol Fugard works with spare materials in his powerful play *The Island*: an audience, two black actors, the barest of stage properties and an empty playing space. From these he transforms both theatre and playing space into the interior of South Africa's infamous Robben Island Prison, a brutal and brutalizing place just off the coast of Cape Town where many political prisoners have been held in dehumanizing captivity and without known term to their incarceration. *The Island* is a play not so much written by Fugard as devised jointly by Fugard and the two original actors of the piece, John Kani and Winston Ntshona. And these two actors use the stage powerfully to enact the existence, routine and human relationships on Robben Island.

It is singularly important that the two characters of the play, John and Winston are acted respectively by John Kani and Winston Ntshona, for this enables Fugard to use his performance technique in order to transform his playhouse into a large playing space. Kani and Ntshona are not two actors portraying two black fictive characters. They are instead playing themselves incarcerated. The stage does not *represent* the prison, it *is* their prison and their particular prison cell. Similarly, the audience is not a disengaged body watching a representation of a prison; it is, instead, transformed through the dramaturgy into John and Winston's fellow prisoners and guards. In short, the playing space of Athol Fugard's *The Island* is not the actual stage area of the theatre where John and Winston's prison cell is located. Rather the playing space is the playhouse as a whole which becomes Robben Island.

Carefully orchestrating the opening segment of *The Island*, Athol Fugard sees to it that theatre quickly becomes a prison. Even as the audience file into the theatre, revealed to them on stage is a Robben Island prison cell with the two black prisoners asleep on the floor (p. 47).[1] There are no beds on Robben Island. Only a single blanket and a tin drinking cup for each prisoner plus a shared bucket of water make up the stage props. And from

* A draft of this paper was read at the *Themes in Drama* International Conference held at the University of California, Riverside in February 1985.

these the two men in the course of the play will fashion an existence and a political statement.

The action of the play begins with a siren, stage lights coming on and the two men, heads shaven and dressed in shorts, in an extended, seemingly endless mime lasting perhaps ten painful minutes during which the two prisoners engage in a Sisyphusian labor of pointlessly digging sand, filling a wheelbarrow with it, pushing the wheelbarrow to another side of the stage and emptying the sand. The stage directions make a point of saying, '*Their labour is interminable*' (p. 47).

That exhausting, pointless mime serves as a warm-up exercise for the play, at once conditioning the actors and the audience to the dehumanizing spirit of a South African prison. Ten minutes is a long time in the theatre, and ten minutes of repeated, wordless action is an eternity particularly when the audience does not know what the point of the monotonous action is supposed to be. But that of course is the point! The restiveness and the failure to understand why actions are taking place or punishments being inflicted is at the core of the existence created in the South African prisoners. The theatre consequently becomes for the audience a microcosm of a South African prison, for they do not know when the playwright will end his play and release them, they do not see the point of the scenario the playwright has created, and they undoubtedly ask themselves what they have done to deserve the treatment they are receiving from the play.

The seemingly interminable mime with which *The Island* commences transforms the theatre into Robben Island and provides an excruciatingly moving dumb show from which the drama that follows can be built. With the blowing of a prison whistle, a second mime immediately ensues: John and Winston are handcuffed, joined at the ankles and forced to run in tandem. Brilliantly, Fugard portrays the subhuman race with the stage directions, '*They start to run . . . John mumbling a prayer, Winston muttering a rhythm for their three-legged run*' (p. 47). With dramatic concision, Fugard indicates the way the tedium, animal degradation and torture work upon the prisoners, serving to evoke the very things that raise men above bestiality: a reliance upon the spirit, manifested in John's prayer, and a reliance upon reason, manifested in Winston's creating a rhythm so that the two men may with dignity run in unison. At the same time, the audience are made voyeurs either suffering along with the two actors or sadistically enjoying their labors. And it is important here that the mime is not merely punishing, hard physical labor for the characters of John and Winston but is so as well for the actors, John Kani and Winston Ntshona. The sweat and pain shown by the actors is earned on stage. In their short traffic on the stage, the actors are meant to undergo as well as enact what hundreds of men undergo every day of their lives in South African prisons.

What Fugard's opening mimes poignantly show is the way the South

African authorities have created a system that is meant to reduce men to beasts, to annihilate the last shreds of their humanity. Their humanity, however, remains intact, even flowers amid a situation that is meant to be death in life or living death.[2] And it does so because the two men continue to act as humans by using dramatic acting as the means for sustaining their humanity. Improvisation – that tool through which an actor learns to understand and practice a role – becomes the means through which John and Winston understand, practice and enact their humanity. Acting, moreover, becomes both shield and sword to the two prisoners: a means for self-protection, for protection of the self, and a means for taking action or acting against their captors, against the State. Fugard thus asserts that acting is no idle art, no end in itself, but the very essence of life and of being human.

Finally, after the men are beaten and returned wounded to their cell, dumb show yields first to sounds and then to words of rage and pain. Nevertheless, the situation in all its intense physicality creates moving words and pictures enunciating spiritual strength. Winston's pain causes John to act: to urinate and wash Winston's wounded eye. And with the consciously chosen terminology of the theatre, Fugard's stage directions indicate, '*In a* reversal of earlier roles *Winston now gets John down on the floor so as to examine the injured ear*' (p. 48, emphasis mine). As the two men thus act to assuage each other's bodily injuries, Winston exclaims, '*Nyana we Sizwe,*' 'brother of the land,' affirming the power of brotherhood and the indomitability of the two men's human spirit.

In his recent plays, *A Lesson from Aloes* and *Master Harold*, Athol Fugard has explored the ways in which the South African apartheid system is equally and perhaps, finally, far more damaging to the psyche of Whites than it is to Coloureds and Blacks. *The Island*, likewise, and with great intensity, shows the backfiring of a system that wishes to rob John and Winston of their humanity and reduce them to beasts. To show this, Fugard has John and Winston appear on stage constantly affirming their brotherhood. Their white guard, by contrast, is unseen. Only his irritating noises and the sting of his blows are heard. The guard is named *Hodoshe*, an Afrikaans word meaning 'the green carrion fly' (p. 47); and like Ben Jonson's Mosca, whose name also means 'flesh fly', it is the white Hodoshe who is reduced by Fugard to a character in a mean-spirited beast fable. John and Winston remain triumphantly human.

Hodoshe exemplifies the prison guards whose humanity devolves into animal behavior whereas the prisoners create their humanity out of the very bestiality that has been forced on them. John and Winston receive beatings and wounds from their guards. They were transported to Robben Island in vans, crammed and shackled to one another like animals, urinating on one another as they traveled. And yet it is their care for one another's wounds that brings forth and italicizes John and Winston's humanity, and no more painfully so than when Fugard's stage directions read, '*John urinates into one hand and tries to clean the other man's [wounded] eye with it.*' The mimed stage action brilliantly portrays the transilience of inhumanity and animal function into human caring, of Sisyphus' punishment transformed into Antigone's triumph. Such humanity rising from the depths of degradation is reminiscent of the spirit that survived in Nazi concentration camps. And the similarity, as Fugard's recently published notebooks make clear, is not accidental.[3]

Having turned his theatre into Robben Island Prison, Fugard writes a play in which the main action is concerned with John and Winston's turning the prison into a theatre. For the 'entertainment' of their fellow prisoners and their guards, John and Winston plan to present their dramatized version of an ancient drama: the confrontation between Antigone and Creon.[4] Like the devisers of *The Island* – Fugard, Kani and Ntshona – the prisoners are not merely actors but playwrights. They forge drama, an art that is an affirmation of their humanity. And they fashion it from the basic artifacts of their prison life and from the basic resources of their imagination. Using a few rusty nails and some string, John devises Antigone's necklace; with a piece of chalk he has treasured away, he lays out on the cell floor the plot of the *Antigone* skit he has created. Similarly, the two prisoners have in the past produced recreations, have re-*created* their spirits by taking each other to the bioscope, creating cinema without film or screen but through the combination of imagination, narration and physical gesture. And in the course of the first scene, they reach out from the isolation of their island prison in Cape Town to friends and family in Port Elizabeth using an empty prison tin cup transformed into a telephone receiver and using the power of fictive imagination, rhetoric and gesture to create the two-sided conversation. Through acting, in short, comes their survival. And clearly for Fugard, acting in the sense of making theatre and acting in the sense of making a commitment are not two separate meanings for a single word but essential identities.

When Winston and John begin to rehearse their *Antigone*, Fugard reveals his master's touch as a dramatist. Winston appears dressed in false wig, false breasts and necklace all wrought from the scraps the two prisoners have been able to store away or find in their restricted, repressive, bare essentials environment. He is ludicrous not only for John but also for the audience, both of whom laugh freely at the grotesque sight Winston presents. But Fugard and John both know that once the audience has had its laugh at the comic figure Winston cuts, the joke will be over and they can go beyond their laughter to perceive Antigone, not a 'drag' Winston, and to take the meaning of Antigone and *Antigone* seriously:

This is preparation for stage fright! I know those bastards out there. When you get in front of them, sure they'll laugh. But just remember this brother, nobody laughs forever! There'll come a time when they'll stop laughing, and that will be the time when our Antigone hits them with her words . . . You think those bastards out there won't know it's you? Yes, they'll laugh. But who cares about that as long as they laugh at the beginning and listen at the end. That's all we want them to do . . . listen at the end!                              (pp. 61, 62)

What Winston does not at this point in the play realize is that the story of Antigone and his own story are congruent. He exclaims, '. . . this Antigone is a bloody . . . what do you call it . . . legend! A Greek one at that. Bloody thing never happened. Not even history . . . Me? . . . I live my life here! I know why I'm here, and it's history, not legends' (p. 62). The audience, however, begins to realize that John and Athol Fugard have chosen the Antigone story because it is a legend that embodies the history of protest; and Winston's life is thus history and legend in one. And as he ruminates about his imprisonment at Robben Island for having burned his passbook, the obvious parallelism of his defiance of the state and Antigone's is hidden for him but understood by the audience.

*The Island* forces its characters and its audiences to grow. It is only at first a simple play merely about incarceration and about time 'Experienced,' as Fugard says in his *Notebooks*, 'as a loss of Life, as a Living Death. You are no more.' But, to evoke the absurdity of life on Robben Island, Fugard swings his play around, moving it from a depiction of imprisonment to a consideration of the meaning of freedom: measuring freedom against the absurdity of incarceration. When John suddenly learns that his case has been reviewed and that he will be freed in a matter of months, clock time – counting the months and weeks and days – returns to him, separating him from Winston who has only the time without end of open-ended imprisonment.

For Winston, John's forthcoming release serves to underline the pointlessness, the absurdity of his own lot; and with that, his spontaneous joy for his friend is transformed into temporary jealousy and hatred. A jealousy and hatred that he releases through playwriting; and it is a playwriting that is meant at once as a self-defense and as a pointed attack on John. Whereas John and Winston's earlier creative efforts had been written for mutual entertainment or, as in the case of their imaginary telephone call to Port Elizabeth, had permitted joint creativity, Winston now implies his divorce from John by writing a monologue, using the same subject matter as their telephone call, taunting John with very graphic descriptions of relationships and events that will soon be, but are still not, within his reach.

But writing and acting out a dramatic monologue about John's freedom creates heuristic experiences on several levels for Winston. He is able to give vent to his envy and purge it. He is able to punish John for his good fortune.

He is able to recognize his own absurdity. And, at last, he comes to terms with that absurdity, sensing for the first time its power. Here Fugard adeptly brings Camus' *The Myth of Sisyphus* directly to bear on *The Island* and does so without a heavy hand. After concluding his dramatic monologue, Winston sees himself projected in old Harry, a seventy-year-old prisoner serving a life sentence and working in the quarries:

> When you go to the quarry tomorrow, take a good look at old Harry. Look into his eyes, John. Look at his hands. They've changed him. They've turned him into stone. Watch him work with that chisel and hammer. Twenty perfect blocks of stone every day. Nobody else can do it like him. He's forgotten himself. He's forgotten . . . why he's here, where he comes from. That's happening to me John. I've forgotten why I'm here.                    (p. 71)

The picture of old Harry, like the opening stage picture of Winston and John with the sand and wheelbarrow, is a version of Camus' picture of Sisyphus. Camus writes: '. . . Sisyphus is the absurd hero. He *is* as much through his passions as through his torture. His scorn of the gods, his hatred of death, and his passion for life won him that unspeakable penalty in which the whole being is exerted toward accomplishing nothing.'[5]

Yet Camus argues that Sisyphus, each time he descends from the heights to find his stone and his eternal torment, gains a special consciousness:

> At each of those moments when he leaves the heights and gradually sinks toward the lairs of the gods, he is superior to his fate. He is stronger than his rock . . . [he] knows the whole extent of his wretched condition: it is what he thinks of during his descent. The lucidity that was to constitute his torture at the same time crowns his victory.                    (p. 121)

Camus concludes his description of Sisyphus saying, 'The struggle itself toward the heights is enough to fill a man's heart. One must imagine Sisyphus happy' (p. 123).[6] Elsewhere in his essay, Camus addresses the question of freedom and absurdity. And what he says there is precisely what Fugard shows as Winston's situation:

> The only conception of freedom I can have is that of the prisoner or the individual in the midst of the State. The only one I know is freedom of thought and action. Now if the absurd cancels all my chances of eternal freedom, it restores and magnifies, on the other hand, my freedom of action. That privation of hope and future means an increase in man's availability.
>                                                            (pp. 56–7)

In short, Winston looks with fright at old Harry who, like Camus' Sisyphus, 'loves stone'; but after his drama is over, Winston, as Fugard's stage direction makes clear, reflects upon his fate and for the first time understands it: '*Winston almost seems to bend under the weight of the life stretching ahead of him on the Island. For a few seconds he lives in silence with his reality, then slowly straightens up. He turns and looks at John. When he speaks again, it is the voice of a man who has come to terms with his fate, massively compassionate* (p. 72). The result is the repeated exultation of brotherhood and renewed commitment, '*Nyana we Sizwe!*', brother of the land.

In the final scene of *The Island*, John and Winston present their *Antigone* play, but it is a presentation that is informed simultaneously by John's understanding and Winston's new understanding of the Antigone legend on the one hand and by their understanding of the Sisyphus legend in much the way that Camus understood it on the other. And in his last scene, Fugard pulls out all his stops to create a *coup de théâtre* that is not an end in itself but a means to enlightenment and political engagement.

As John and Winston take the stage to provide the closing act for the prison entertainment with their *Antigone* play, the role of the audience, of the prisoners and guards, is played by the members of the actual theatre audience, who are addressed as though they were guards and prisoners. And thus the connection between the Antigone story and the story of apartheid in South Africa, between the stage and life, is made immediately, stunningly clear. John's address to the audience in his role of Presenter or Prologue is one filled with the irony of Fugard's dramatic situation:

> Captain Prinsloo, Hodoshe, Warders, . . . and Gentlemen! Two brothers of the House of Labdacus found themselves on opposite sides in battle, the one defending the State, the other attacking it. They both died on the battlefield . . . But Antigone, their sister, defied the law and buried the body of her brother Polynices. She was caught and arrested. That is why tonight the Hodoshe Span, Cell Forty-two, presents for your entertainment: 'The Trial and Punishment of Antigone'.                                                    (p. 73)

The pause indicated in the text of the first sentence – 'Captain Prinsloo, Hodoshe, Warders, . . . and Gentlemen!' – pointedly endows the prisoners with gentility while separating them from the officials of State power. Furthermore, using the word *arrested* to describe Antigone's situation raises the spectre of the modern polity, and in particular the South African state. It is a word that succinctly captures the bond between the ancient Antigone legend and the events of contemporary history. It fixes the Antigone story as a symbol for John and Winston's plight as well as for all who protest and resist in South Africa. This is nicely and pointedly italicized when after his exposition of Antigone's actions and subsequent arrest, John states that '*that is why*' they are presenting their play.

The conflation of ancient and contemporary, of Greek legend and the apartheid state, continues as Creon becomes the symbol for the State as well as for compliant blacks: 'Creon's crown is as simple, and I hope as clean, as the apron Nanny wears. And even as Nanny smiles and is your happy servant . . . so too does Creon – your obedient servant! – stand here and smile' (p. 73). Creon, moreover, as he does in Sophocles' play, upholds the letter of the law of the State. Antigone upholds a higher law, but relates the issue at once to the dilemma in Sophocles as well as to that in South

Africa by declaiming, 'What lay on the battlefield waiting for Hodoshe to turn rotten, belonged to God. You are only a man, Creon. Even as there are laws made by men, so too there are others that come from God' (p. 75). Antigone's defiance of the laws of the Greek state justifies the defiance of the passbook and apartheid laws of the South African state. Antigone, like Sisyphus and like the Robben Island prisoners, knows the consequences of her deeds, knows that her defiance will cause her to be immured; but she thereby comes to know an existential, happy transcendence over tragedy. Winston playing Antigone can say to Creon, 'Your threat is nothing to me' (p. 76).

John and Winston take the Antigone story only as far as her trial. But with the words, 'You will not sleep peacefully, Creon' (p. 76), Winston as Antigone hints at the remainder of Creon's story for Fugard's audience. As a result of his unjust treatment of Antigone, Creon's own son, Haemon, and his wife, Eurydice, die; and at the close of Sophocles' drama, it is Creon who loses power and is reduced to nothingness:

> This is my guilt, all mine. I killed you, I say it clear.
> Servants, take me away, out of the sight of men.
> I who am nothing more than nothing now.[7]

The tragic nothingness awaiting the inflexible upholders of the State's laws in South Africa is obviously foreshadowed.

As John and Winston's Antigone leaves to be immured, she goes not to the tomb of the ancient story but to an all too familiar South African fate. John as Creon exclaims, 'Take her from where she stands, straight to the Island! There wall her up in a cell for life, with just enough food to acquit ourselves of the taint of her blood' (p. 77). And Antigone acknowledges that on the Island she will, like the other prisoners there, 'be lost between life and death.' Having said this, however, Winston goes beyond Antigone's tragedy, stepping out of his costume movingly to assert his own renewed defiance and to reaffirm his absurdity as he returns, like Antigone, to his cell and to the pointless existence he must bear for having had the courage to honor a law of mankind higher than South African civil law.

In forging the connections between ancient myths and modern history, Fugard relates the plights of Sisyphus and Antigone to those of prisoners on Robben Island. As John and Winston play Creon and Antigone, they feel the immediacy of the Greek legend. But *The Island* has another dimension, a dimension that is there at the beginning in John and Winston's names and is there at the end as Fugard forces the theatre audience consciously to recognize that it is also the prison audience.

Fugard's actors and co-dramatists, John Kani and Winston Ntshona, themselves black South Africans, have kept their own names. The play in which they act is a metaphor, as is *Antigone*, the play in which the two prisoners act. The Island is not merely Robben Island but South Africa itself, an absurd prison with absurd rules enforced by absurd officials. South Africa's citizens, be they non-white or white, are as much immured and imprisoned as the heroine in Sophocles' play or the prisoners in Fugard's. If Fugard's play has been effective, the audience will come to recognize that they have been part of the cast and that their seats have been part of the playing space of *The Island*. The enactment of the imprisonment of Antigone is a microcosm of John and Winston's situation which is in turn a microcosm of the theatre as prison, which is in turn a microcosm of South Africa. In the course of *The Island*, we come to realize that John will soon be released from prison and we wonder whether, when he returns to normal life, he will repress his Robben Island experience or whether, as seems likely, he will be energized to work with zeal for an end to the inhumanity he knows his friend and brother Winston as well as other South African prisoners continue to face. Similarly, by extending the playing space from stage to theatre, Fugard suggests that the audience, like John, is released from prison back into normal life when *The Island* concludes. Will we, Fugard implicitly asks then, repress our theatre experience or will we use it to know that we must work to end a polity that transforms society into a prison?

## NOTES

1 Athol Fugard, *The Island*, in *Statements* (Oxford: Oxford University Press, 1974), p. 45. Parentheses following quotations from the play refer to this edition.
2 See Athol Fugard, *Notebooks* (Johannesburg: Ad. Donker, 1983), p. 212.
3 *Notebooks*, p. 209.
4 An extended comparison of Sophocles' *Antigone* and Fugard's has been done by Deborah D. Foster, '*The Blood Knot* and *The Island* as Anti-Tragedy,' in *Athol Fugard*, ed. Stephen Gray (Johannesburg: McGraw Hill, 1982), pp. 202–17. An earlier version of this essay under the same title appeared as Occasional Paper no. 8 of the African Studies Program, University of Wisconsin (Madison, 1977).
5 Albert Camus, *The Myth of Sisyphus and Other Essays*, trans. Justin O'Brien (New York: Alfred A. Knopf, 1969), p. 120. Parentheses following quotations from Camus refer to this edition.
6 See Germaine Bree, *Camus* (New Brunswick: Rutgers University Press, 1959), p. 202.
7 Sophocles, *Antigone* (trans. Elizabeth Wykoff) in The Complete Greek Tragedies, vol. II, ed. David Grene and Richmond Lattimore (Chicago: University of Chicago Press, 1959), lines 1319–21.

# Space invasions: voice-over in works by Samuel Beckett and Marguerite Duras

MARY KAY MARTIN

Our theatrical space, hallowed over the centuries by association with the risings and fallings of great kings, queens, and civilizations, with the rites of passage of many noble endeavours, with the very ritual rhythms of our species, this theatrical space is now being invaded by an alien force. As yet the infiltration of our atmosphere is minimal, but this foreign influence has had and will continue to have long-range effects on the public. I am speaking of the theatre's own bastard child, the cinema, which severed its relations with the theatre, following instead in the footsteps of its photographic ancestry, but which has nevertheless returned repeatedly to raid our populations and undercut our relations with the people. The cinema's latest thrust into our territory is its most potent to date: invisible, it fills our spaces and lulls our senses; omnipresent, it plays upon our imaginations. It is our own voice, the human voice, except it is recorded. It is the time-worn third dimension of the movies, the voice-over. It has infiltrated the theatrical corps in such plays as Beckett's *Rockaby* and Marguerite Duras' *Eden Cinema*, and there it has taken hold and thrives. From these key positions, the voice-over is likely to exert greater influence, not only on the conventions of twentieth-century plays, but on the assumptions, predispositions, and perceptions of twentieth-century audiences.

Theatrical criticism, and even theory, hesitates to say anything definitive about the role or the experience of the theatrical spectator. How can conclusions be drawn about something so dependent on a given production of a play, on its interpretation, its execution, its space? A play is written once and interpreted for production many times, in an infinite variety of spaces, from a 60,000-seat open-air amphitheatre to a 200-seat darkened studio. It is much easier to speculate and even draw conclusions about the cinematic spectator, who invariably settles into a dark theatre, and for whom the surrounding space ceases to exist. The cinematic spectator watches a film which was interpreted for production once, to be played back in the same exact state to whatever audience as long as the celluloid lasts.

How can we even compare the cinematic and theatrical experiences? The theatre is a live event, fluid in its interplay between performer and spectator, and its space conducts currents of emotional feedback between the two. The actors themselves respond to the spatial relationships, as do the spectators. In the movie theatre, on the other hand, the spectator is in relation with a two-dimensional image of movement, a flat surface of light like a giant retina, which displays the illusion of a time and space preserved but unmistakably absent. Beyond pointing out these and numerous other differences, what can be said about correspondences between theatrical and cinematic space, the latter only having occurred as a technological baby of recent history?

We must remember that film at its inception was virtually dependent on live entertainment, in form as well as in content. The 'dramatic' content of silent movies relied either on nineteenth-century melodrama or music-hall farce, both of which exhibited the formal tradition of noncoincidence – or counterpoint between sound and image – in the theatre. The silent movies, having at first no technical capacity to produce synchronous sound, originated in a kind of counterpoint: image track with no corresponding sound track. Yet soon enough the producers of silent film discovered that cinematic two-dimensionality could be disconcerting in its dreamlike unreality and its easy manipulation of time and perspective. Hence music was amended to the silent moving image, a juxtaposition which nevertheless maintained a counterpoint or noncoincidence between sound and image. Music, as composer Kurt London has said, seemed to add a needed 'third dimension' to the silent image,[1] and to lend temporal rhythm and continuity to the discontinuous, disembodied screen picture. Like the dramatic content in the early silent films, this addition of music – live, at first – was derived from the theatre. In an unpublished 1982 dissertation entitled 'Music as Narrative Structure in Hollywood Film,' Kathryn Kalinak of the University of Illinois pointed to numerous theatrical periods, notably the Greek, Elizabethan, and more directly the opera and nineteenth-century melodrama, as antecedents for the original musical accompaniment in the movie houses.[2] The structural principle of 'emotional underscoring,' as well as the Wagneresque leitmotif, has dominated Hollywood and other film scores ever since.

Originally employed, then, to help the diverse visual images cohere, cinematic sound came into being as a medium separate from the visual images. Only much later, when it became possible to synchronize image and sound recording, did the two correspond. By the time of the advent of recorded movie sound, the tradition of counterpoint was solidly entrenched in film-making, possibly because of the efforts of the proponents of visual montage, notably the Russians Pudovkin, Eisenstein, and Alexandrov. In a passage from their 1928 manifesto 'Sound and Image,' quoted by David Cook in his *History of the Narrative Film*, the Russians proclaim their approach to sound:

Only the use of sound as counterpoint to visual montage offers new possibilities of perfecting montage. The first experiments with sound must be directed towards its noncoincidence with visual image. Only this method will lead to creation of a new orchestral counterpoint of image-vision and image-sound.[3]

As a natural extension of the counterpoint tradition, as well as of film's capacity to move freely through time and space, the voice-over convention became established in the cinema in such films as Wilder's *Sunset Boulevard* and Lang's *Dr Mabuse*. Voice-over is to be distinguished from voice-on, the synchronous voice of a visible character, and voice-off, a voice which corresponds to a character who is not visible but is understood to be just 'off camera'; i.e., within the diegesis, or time–space reality of the play, to borrow a term from film criticism. Voice-over, or disembodied voice, became an extreme manifestation of the Russians' 'noncoincidence.' It was also natural that the camera's Peeping Tom perspective should be supplemented by a narrative voice not unlike that of the novel, which moves as easily as film through space and time. Like the third-person narrative in the novel, the voice-over can enable the spectator to know the characters' thoughts, which is exactly what it does when adapted to theatrical space. How fitting that disjunctive sound, originally borrowed from the theatre to fill the cinematic space, should return as a high-tech filmic convention to restructure theatrical space.

One may be inclined to ask, at this point, how the introduction of such a technological intruder as the voice-over can be accepted by the audience as a convention in the live theatrical context. The truth is that the audience has no trouble adjusting to the innovation, as long as the 'unrealistic' format is clearly established, as it is in Duras' plays by the direct address and the constant accompaniment of recorded music, and in Beckett's by the scene. Christian Metz explains about recorded sound:

> . . . auditory aspects, unlike visual events, undergo no appreciable loss in relation to the corresponding sound in the real world . . . the sounds . . . spread into space as do sounds in life, or almost.[4]

Recorded sound is altered relatively little from live sound, unlike recorded image from live image. Both live and recorded sound carry into three-dimensional space.

As noted by Chion in his work *La Voix au cinéma*,[5] voice-over critics have either relegated the recorded voice to its mere semantic, representative function, as if it were news commentary, or described it in Freudian terms as a fetish, like an unconscious memory of the fetal-stage sound of the mother's voice. René Major, in an article in a psychoanalytic journal entitled 'The Voice Behind the Mirror,' analyzes the 'acousophilic instinct,'[6] or the 'wish to hear,' through a discussion of Ovid's Narcissus, who sees only his own reflection and hears only the echo of his own voice.

Major asserts[7] that '. . . the formation of unconscious fantasy hinges on the
. . . auditory zone especially.' This thought might imply the evocative
power of sound without visual reference: a phenomenon familiar to us via
radio and the telephone. My intent here, however, is not to psychoanalyze
the voice-over, but to assess its theatricality.

In 1977 Marguerite Duras wrote a rich and compelling play entitled *Eden
Cinema*,[8] which was based on her 1953 novel *Dam Against the Pacific*,[9] and
which has not yet been officially translated into English. Fascinating on its
own account, the play is equally intriguing for being close, I do not yet know
how close, to the story of Duras' own life, which is also approximated in the
novel for which she won the Prix Goncourt, *L'Amant*.[10] The play is set in
Southeast Asia, what is now Cambodia but was then the colony of French
Indochina. It tells the story of a family breaking up: the son and daughter
come of age and are separately initiated into the harsh realities of political,
social, and personal life, and the mother dies. The story is told from the
daughter's perspective, both directly in the time of the play, and through a
recorded voice, the daughter as an older woman looking back at the events
of long ago. In this way it is a memory play.

The play begins with a long and curious introductory narrative delivered
directly to the audience by the son and daughter alternately. They tell of
their father's death and the subsequent financial ruin of the mother at the
hands of corrupt colony officials, who had sold her a huge lease of land
which was flooded yearly during the rainy season. The mother had tried to
cultivate the salt-soaked soil by leading the wretched local peasants in an
effort to build a dam to hold back the Pacific. During this introduction,
while they tell their history, the children are fondling and stroking the inert,
catatonic body of their mother, who exhibits the insane stupor to which she
will return near the end of the play, just before her death.

After the introductory narrative, the play moves into the 'present' of its
fictional action, the events leading to the mother's death. However, the
narrative memory continues as the play's action shifts: from live played
scenes to direct-address narration by the live daughter, who is played at
different ages; and to narration by the daughter as an older woman looking
back, via the lyric voice-over recording.

The cinematic presence in *Eden Cinema* is thematic as well as structural.
After the father's death, the mother had augmented her meager life savings
by playing the piano at a silent movie theatre in Saigon called the Eden
Cinema. She had played there for ten years, until the end of the silent
movies. A waltz theme from the Eden Cinema and fantasy memories from
sleeping on pillows around the piano haunt the children as young adults in
the play.

Structurally, like the daughter's live and recorded voice, the music is
both inside and outside of the play, inside on an old Victrola they play over

and over, and outside interwoven with the recorded voice. The music scores the live dialogue and action, just as the voice looking back scores the silent and mimed action. As composer Hanns Eisler said[11] of the 'talkies,' music in Duras '. . . takes on the task of closing the gap between voice and body.' Like her music specifications, Duras' descriptions of the silent mimed action sequences are as precise and as vivid as the dialogue. Accompanied either by music or voice-over or both, the mimed sequences are visual scenarios. They are as integral to the text as the music, and as the live and recorded dialogue.

In 1981, four years after the publication of *Eden Cinema*, Samuel Beckett wrote *Rockaby*,[12] which employs a single live character and her recorded voice-over. Beckett had already tried using recorded sound for the majority of the duologue in *Krapp's Last Tape*,[13] but in that play the recorded voice is different. Krapp's recorded voice is specifically within the diegesis – or time–space reality – of the play. In *Krapp's Last Tape* the recorded voice comes directly out of the old man's reel-to-reel machine, and therefore does not overtly alter or shift the time and space of the story.

The voice in *Rockaby*, like Krapp's voice, is the recorded voice of the single character; however, it is outside the time–space reality of the fiction. The old woman signals the sound of her recorded voice, which tells her story, by her live 'More.' The story the voice tells is presumably that of the simple events which have led to the live moment the audience sees; the tape catches up, as it were, with the present time and space of the fiction. She replays her story as she sits in her best black at the bottom of the steep stair, just as her mother did before her, and it is her story that rocks her to sleep the sleep of death. The voice could be her thoughts, a part of or a perspective on herself; it suggests many things. However, the *Rockaby* voice-over, unlike Krapp's tape, cannot be objectively located within the time–space reality of the play. That is, it cannot unless the audience is prepared to imagine, for example, that the old lady has in her basement a pre-programmed, computerized recording system controlled by remote voice; but this the audience does not need to believe. The audience naturally assumes that the recorded voice is a voice-over, like in the movies, where the audience can hear the character's thoughts or is privy to another perspective of the character, a perspective from a time and space other than the time and space of the fiction.

In each of these two plays, then, *Eden Cinema* and *Rockaby*, we find a true voice-over. While watching and hearing the live play, the audience hears a voice. It is recorded, and because it is recorded it is intimate; that is, the voice has what's called a strong presence, or close proximity to the microphone. Therefore it seems intimate; it seems very close to the audience; the softest whisper, as at the end of *Rockaby*, can fill the entire theatre. The audience learns that the voice is the voice of one of the characters in the play, but the voice is somehow removed from the play's story. The physical source of the sound is invisible: it may seem to surround the audience, or come from behind. Neither is the fictional reference of the voice immediately clear, and it remains indefinite. Chion[14] talks about the voice-over as 'en errance à la surface de l'écran': wandering over the surface of the screen. Likewise, we could say that the voice-over in live theatre floats through the air, through the space of the event, like a ghost of the character, its disembodied spirit, its thoughts. The voice-over is neither completely inside the fiction nor outside of it; it is both; it hovers between them. In both *Eden Cinema* and *Rockaby* the voice is the main character's, but in both it seems to watch the play from the outside, as the audience is doing. As Mary Anne Doane says of voice-over in film:

> As a form of direct address, it speaks without mediation to the audience, by-passing the 'characters' and establishing a complicity between itself and the spectator – together they understand and thus *place* the image. It is precisely because the voice is not localizable, because it cannot be yoked to a body, that it is capable of interpreting the image, producing its truth.[15]

Likewise in the theatre, the voice-over blurs the demarcation between spectator and spectacle. The audience internalizes the voice-over as a commentary, an inner monologue, a process which is as familiar as thought itself.

In other words, the audience accepts the convention of voice-over as a narrator, not omniscient or even impartial, yet still removed from its own story. In this it is like narration in the novel which, whether it is third or first person, draws the reader into sharing its thoughts, and moves its audience through time and space and in and out of fictional characters' thoughts. The narrator is subjective, and the audience is drawn into that subjectivity. Like the reader of a novel, the audience listening to the voice-over experiences the play in part through the mind of a character-voice. Like the reader of a novel, the audience listening to the voice-over identifies with the narrator, with the weaver of the tale, with the daughter in *Eden Cinema* or the old woman in *Rockaby*.

This process works in part because of the conventions of the novel and the cinema; the convention carries over from the novel and film into live theatre. The audience has read characters' narrations in books and heard them at the movies, so it adapts to them in the theatre. Beckett and Duras use the assumptions of novel-reading and especially movie-going audiences to advantage. Beckett and Duras are both novelists and film-makers: both have written many novels; Beckett did the film *Film* and the video *Eh Joe*, and Duras has made at least sixteen films.

In summary, because this filmic convention is neither inside nor outside the diegesis of the play; because it is recorded; because neither its referential nor physical sources are apparent; because it is disembodied: this extra-terrestrial voice-over restructures the theatrical space. It fills the commonly shared space with its hovering perspective and, like the convention of silence, links the audience and the actors in a commonly shared experience. Furthermore, since theatre is a live event, where spectators and actors interact, the voice-over affects that interaction, which is the core of any theatrical event. Spectators and actors alike listen and react to the voice. In this voice-over functions like music, which has '. . . a tendency to stimulate the listener's receptiveness in general,' as Siegfried Kracauer suggests.[16] Like an invisible Greek chorus, the voice-over is an intermediary between audience and play, part spectator, part character, and like the Greek chorus its sound or musicality is as important as its meaning. In an article on 'The Disembodied Voice,'[17] Marie-Claire Ropars-Wuilleumier describes the voice-over in Duras' film *India Song*[18] as 'oscillating between meaning and music.' In both *Eden Cinema* and *Rockaby*, the voice-over is rhythmic and lyric.

I have been speaking here of *Eden Cinema* and *Rockaby* as if they were initial forays into new theatrical territory, or as if they were groundbreakers in the alliance between filmic and theatrical conventions. In truth, the filmic disjunction of recorded sound from image had already been carried to its inevitable conclusion in the theatre, in Duras' *India Song*. In that play/novel/film, published in 1973, Duras specifies that all the dialogue is to be recorded. *India Song* is narrated by characters who never appear as live characters, but whose story is bound to the story of the characters portrayed live. Even the central character in the live play is in a sense disembodied; she is understood to have already died. In *India Song*, disembodied recorded voice is the structuring principle of the whole play.

## NOTES

1  Kurt London, *Film Music* (1936; New York: Arno Press, reprint, 1970), p. 35, quoted in Kathryn Kalinak, 'Music as Narrative Structure in Hollywood Film' (Dissertation: University of Illinois at Urbana-Champaign, 1982), p. 40.

2  Kalinak, *ibid.*, p. 35.

3  Eisenstein, Pudovkin, and Alexandrov, 'Sound and Image,' Manifesto 08–05–28, quoted in David Cook, *A History of the Narrative Film* (Toronto: W. & W. Norton, 1981), p. 252.

4  Christian Metz, 'Aural Objects,' trans. Georgia Gurrieri, *Yale French Studies*, 60 (1981), 24–32, p. 29n.

5  Michel Chion, *La Voix au cinéma* (Paris: Editions de l'Etoile, 1982), p. 12.

6  René Major,'The Voice Behind the Mirror,' *International Review of Psycho-Analysis*, 7, 459 (1980), 459–68, p. 460.

7  Major, *ibid.*, p. 460.

8  Marguerite Duras, *L'Eden cinéma* (Paris: Mercure de France, 1977).

9  Marguerite Duras, *Un Barrage contre le Pacifique* (Paris: Gallimard, 1950).

10 Marguerite Duras, *L'Amant* (Paris: Editions de Minuit, 1984).

11 Hanns Eisler, *Composing for the Film* (New York: Oxford University Press, 1947), pp. 75–7, quoted in Mary Ann Doane, 'The Voice in the Cinema: The Articulation of Body and Space,' Yale French Studies, 60 (1981), 33–50, p. 46.

12 Samuel Beckett, *Rockaby and Other Short Pieces* (New York: Grove Press, 1981).

13 Samuel Beckett, *Krapp's Last Tape* (New York: Grove Press, 1957).

14 Chion, *La Voix au cinéma*, p. 15.

15 Doane, 'The Voice in the Cinema,' p. 42.

16 Siegfried Kracauer, *Theory of Film: The Redemption of Physical Reality* (New York: Oxford University Press, 1965), quoted in Kalinak, 'Music as Narrative Structure in Hollywood Film,' p. 37.

17 Marie-Claire Ropars-Wuilleumier, 'The Disembodied Voice,' trans. Kimberley Smith, Yale French Studies, 60 (1981), 241–68, p. 268.

18 Marguerite Duras, *India Song* (Paris: Gallimard, 1973).

# Multiple and virtual: theatrical space in *The Elephant Man**

## VERA JIJI

Theatrical convention has granted stage space the remarkable ability to represent any location (including itself) in or out of this world. Further, the stage can be split into various zones or areas representing different locations seen serially or simultaneously. Through this division, the live theatre provides a physical analog to the splitting of the one authorial voice into the various voices of the characters in the play. The live theatre can provide, therefore, a very subtle and highly satisfying multiple vision through the interplay of these two kinds of shifting perspectives –visual and aural. Moreover, both the various physical zones in the theatrical space and the multiple voices can be manipulated to represent different kinds or levels of reality. Thus the theatre can seem to present both reality and illusion, dealing with that duality which has troubled our culture at least since Plato stated the problem in his allegory of the caves.

This remarkable quality of theatrical space has not received much critical attention, in part because it seems, at first, so self-evident. On one hand, the audience *does* have reality before it; living people move about on the stage, use common artifacts, sit on real chairs, and perform ordinary human actions. However, even when there is only one locale on stage, the audience knows it is in the presence of a dual reality. These people are actors; the clothes costumes, the items of furniture props, the seemingly spontaneous actions an imitation of an action. Rather than life, it is the illusion of life which is before the audience. To use Susanne Langer's term, theatre provides a 'virtual' experience, as does any other art form.

Every artistic form, Langer explains, 'is immediately given to perception, and yet it reaches beyond itself; it is semblance, but seems to be charged with reality.'[1] We cannot do justice to Langer's discussion here, but it is suggestive of her point when Langer tries to explain her concept by using such other terms as 'transparency' (p. 52) and 'pure essence' (p. 54). After defining art in this way, Langer concludes that the audience's desire to take

* A draft of this paper was read at the *Themes in Drama* International Conference held at the University of California, Riverside in February 1985.

what it sees on the stage as a representation of reality is merely a vulgar mistake.

Brechtian aesthetics, on the other hand, involve an insistence on the stage action as presentational: that is, like a circus act, it belongs to the same reality, the same ambience, as that occupied by the audience. In fact, Brecht insists on using a number of techniques designed to prevent the audience at a play from falling into an empathic, illusionist reverie, an acceptance of 'semblance.'

Between the extremes of Langer's virtual state and Brecht's reality-testing, the psychoanalyst D. W. Winnicott would like to stake out another theoretical realm, this one described as the 'transitional space' occupied by the artistic work in which the reality of the work is placed outside the realm of discourse: it is avoided, and the issue never comes to question.[2]

But none of these theorists has been able to control the reactions of actual audiences. Despite Langer's scorn and Winnicott's 'transitional space,' people do bring their real-life interests into the theatre, enjoying Burton and Taylor more in *Private Lives* because of some presumed resemblance between the on-stage action and the real lives of the stars. Despite Brecht's strictures on Mother Courage's greed and her collusion with war as a source for profit, audiences do empathize with the character's suffering at the loss of her children.

In practice, then, there is a range of audience response which might be charted on a continuum. At times the stage may duplicate an intractable, limited and unpleasant 'reality.' At other times, it may lift the audience out of the ordinary, enabling it to approach the world of pure essence, thus fulfilling one of our most delicate and exquisite desires. Most often, the theatrical audience hovers, veering between a willing suspension of disbelief and a retreat into a self-conscious, critical checking with reality.

To a major extent, this hovering mental state depends on the psychology of the individual viewer. However, it can also depend on the skill with which the playwright and director have manipulated the audience. This paper shows how this manipulation can result from the effective utilization of theatrical space by a play, using as an example that extraordinarily inventive drama, Bernard Pomerance's *The Elephant Man*.

The power of *The Elephant Man* derives, in part, from the audience's necessarily active involvement in the imaginative creation of the virtual state and partly from the audience's retention of its sense of reality. For the audience is forced by the play itself to remember that John Merrick, the play's subject, was an actual human being. Indeed, if we didn't know that he had existed, the play would be dismissed as unbelievable, and would be of very little interest to anyone.

The audience's first glimpse of the actor playing Merrick occurs as the physician, Treves, who has examined him after finding him in a freak show, delivers a medical lecture about him while 'projected slides of the real Merrick' are shown. The vivid, horrifying details are highlighted: 'From the brow there projected a huge bony mass, like a loaf. . . From the upper jaw there projected another mass of bone . . . like a pink stump, turning the upper lip inside out, and making the mouth a wide, slobbering aperture. . .'[3] and so on. Meanwhile, the handsome young man who plays Merrick, clad only in a loincloth and bathed in a spotlight, gradually twists himself into a grotesquely tortured posture on stage to provide a physical metaphor for the described disfigurement. It is essential to the creation of the virtual state that the actor's body should not resemble or simulate Treves' description. On the contrary, the actuality of the actor's body, his handsomeness, forces the audience to continue working actively in order to sustain the analogy, to imagine the virtual or illusory character demanded by the play.[4]

Several theatrical critics mentioned the effectiveness of this moment, Walter Kerr of the *New York Times*, for example, referring to 'the theatre's silken slipperiness.'[5] But this use of a physical metaphor is more than a clever maneuver to avoid an awkward problem of theatrical representation. It is a creative utilization of the theatre's power to transform 'real' into 'virtual semblance.' Here, the physical transformation is analogous to the play's larger theme: the recurring transformations and confusions between what is seen as reality and what illusion.

During the lecture scene (scene III), this theme is successfully presented on stage through the careful creation of three separate physical staging areas which may be seen as analogous to three theatrical states of experience: presentational, representational (which might roughly correspond to Winnicott's 'transitional space') and virtual. On one side of the stage, the Treves lecture which shows the slides of the real John Merrick converts the audience into observers at the Medical College. Thus that portion of the stage must be in Brechtian, presentational 'reality.' Treves, the lecturer, dominates that space and presents that kind of 'realistic' thinking. In fact, throughout the entire play, Treves' discomfort at treating Merrick as anything more than a scientific object will plague their relationship and his own conscience. The stage space Treves occupies throughout the play will be skeptical, scientific and presentational in tone.

Meanwhile, the actor's transformation into Merrick, the monster, on another part of the stage, forces the audience to participate through their imagination, to assent to the analogy created by the actor's distortions of his voice and body. They agree to let his squeaky voice and twisted arm and posture stand for the freakish aberrations described above. Thus they assist in the movement of the actor's reality toward 'semblance,' contributing the 'as if' required for a willing suspension of disbelief.

In the third area, upstage, sits a 'cellist, formally dressed, who plays music between scenes. Nor is the music here just background. Rather, it creates a third, most 'transparent' zone of feeling and beauty to contrast with the play's presentation of horrors. Since music is the most abstract of the arts, corresponding to no tangible object (the 'cellist in his tie and tails is too dissimilar to the sounds of the Bach suites for us to confuse him with the reality of the sound) we now have the 'ineffable' world of music, the representational illusory state of theatre and the presentational 'realistic' world of the lecture hall present simultaneously.

The impossibility of separating 'reality' from 'illusion' becomes the subject of the play on a number of levels analogous to the division into the various zones of physical stage space. The subject of the first half of the play is the surmounting of the disgust which Merrick inspires by those who get to know him. We are led to consider his appearance the illusion, while the unseen, inner man provides the reality. In fact, this position is explicitly asserted by the physician, Treves, when he chooses an actress as a social companion who is to visit Merrick at the hospital. Treves explains to the actress, Mrs Kendal, that she's been selected because she 'won't give in, you are trained to hide your true feelings and assume others' (p. 29). The truth here is explicitly defined as her *inner* reality. The same point is reinforced when Merrick, upon meeting Mrs Kendal, remarks that, as she is an actress, she 'must display yourself for your living then. Like I did.' But she corrects him. 'That is not myself,' she replies. 'That's an illusion. *This* is myself' (italics added, p. 32). But it too is hardly a spontaneous self without illusion. The audience has watched the actress create the self with which she greets Merrick as, before her first meeting with him, she rehearses four different ways of saying 'I am very pleased to have made your acquaintance, Mr. Merrick' (p. 29). Much later, she again explains that her reality is her artifact when Treves wonders about the role of the many toilet articles given to Merrick as gifts. 'Props,' explains Mrs Kendal, 'To make himself. As I make me' (p. 39).

Akin to the visual dichotomy presented between the handsome actor and Merrick the monster are thematic dichotomies such as: Mrs Kendal as sincere friend versus Mrs Kendal as actress on a mission of mercy; Merrick as natural man versus Merrick as society's pet; Merrick as beneficiary of Treves' and London society's generosity versus Merrick as a prisoner of Victorian morality and prurience; Merrick's model of St Phillip's Cathedral as a work of art versus the model as a mockery of his spiritual aspirations; Treves' life as benevolent physician versus Treves' life as complacent jailer. All these views are presented within the play where they are held in suspension, simultaneously.

I was disappointed to find a number of critical comments which refused to allow the play these ambiguities, resolving them into one truism or another by ignoring half of what was going on. Thus we could read that (and this is typical) the play is 'a haunting parable about natural man trading his frail beauty and innocence for the protection and prison of society . . .'[6] And again, Treves begins to realize that 'the free and boundless spirit of his patient has been gradually crushed. The Elephant Man gradually loses the questioning vitality he has at the start. His energy is channeled as he sickens, into completing a model of a church. Art, for Mr. Pomerance, is a substitute for the natural grace that we lose in living.'[7] While these implications are undeniably there, so are the opposing views.

Unprotected by Treves and London society, Merrick would have died much more quickly and miserably. 'The free and boundless spirit' referred to above is a sentimental creation of the critic's, who has forgotten the humiliation of the scene (scene IV) in which Merrick, too offensive even for a Belgian freak show, is discarded as a bad investment, cheated, and abandoned by his trainer. And, as we shall see, the model of the church also takes on contradictory meanings which are carefully developed during the second half of the play.

It is true that we never lose our sense of Merrick's imprisonment within the stage space given to the hospital, though Treves teaches him to call it 'home.' We see Merrick literally penned in his bath, while Treves teaches him to say that 'rules are for our own good' (p. 7). On one of Mrs Kendal's visits, she brings a picnic basket and rug so they can pretend to go outdoors. But the rug is spread on the wooden floor. The 'pretense' is deliberately flaunted to reinforce the Brechtian alienation. Other Brechtian techniques are also employed, such as the breaking-up of the play into many short titled scenes, the use of actors in multiple roles, the insistent return to the factual. Equally distancing is the repetition of the lecture scene in the dream sequence in which the characters are reversed, with Treves anatomized rather than Merrick. Thus we are again set to questioning the values the play seemed to set up, and our sense of 'reality' and 'illusion' is deranged once more.[8] One of the tenderest love scenes ever staged is that between Merrick and Mrs Kendal, because of the complex interweaving of levels set up in the play. The audience by now is thoroughly disciplined into creating the imagined monster. However, it has been captivated by the charm of a real actress 'playing' a real actress, and has accepted Carol Shelley almost completely on the presentational level as Mrs Kendal. But at this moment, when she starts very slowly to undress, she appears to stop 'playing a role' with the self-control, distancing and irony which the character has previously shown. As she drops her clothes, she seems to drop her defences. Her face now acquires a new softness. She then turns her back to the audience, forcing them (again) to imagine her loveliness. At that moment, the audience's image of her shifts from the presented to the imagined, and she takes on Merrick's transcendence. When the clumsy and unimaginative Treves interrupts the moment, destroying it, the transparency of the world of the ideal itself seems to shatter. This remarkably effective moment of theatre works so well, in part, because the association of the three characters with different levels of theatrical experience has been so carefully built.

Sitting on the edge of these ambiguities places us precisely where the differing zones of the theatrical space, almost alone, can put us. We are invited to see our world as gross, failed – a mockery of our aspirations. Simultaneously, as we in the audience imaginatively enter into the world of the play, we accept that illusory 'paradise' which between them, Merrick and Mrs Kendal momentarily create.

The theme of the ambiguous relationship of reality to illusion is played out again in the church model which appears in the play's second half. Like Merrick's first appearance in a spotlight when the actor is transforming himself into the character, this model exists in a space palpably different in quality from its surroundings. It occupies the center of the forestage, bathed in its own light. It is almost as if the model is trying to exemplify Langer's views on the nature of the artistic work, insisting on itself as more than the physical object given to perception, reaching beyond itself into transparency and pure essence. At the same time, its absurd inadequacy as an expression of what Merrick wants it to signify is equally apparent.

During the play's second half, Merrick slowly and patiently builds the model of St Phillip's Cathedral on stage. In an introductory note to the play, Pomerance writes, 'I believe the building of the church model constitutes some kind of central metaphor, and the groping towards conditions where it can be built and the building of it are the action of the play' (p. v). Indeed, Pomerance underscores the model's significance in the following dialogue:

> Mrs. Kendal: Look Freddie, look. The model of St. Phillip's.
> Treves: It is remarkable, I know.
> Merrick: And I do it with just one hand, they all say.
> Mrs. Kendal: You are an artist, John Merrick, an artist.
> Merrick: I did not begin to build at first. Not till I saw what St. Phillip's really was. It's not stone and steel and glass; it's an imitation of grace flying up and up from the mud. So I make my imitation of an imitation. But even in that is heaven to me, Mrs. Kendal. (p. 38)

If the audience can accept the model of the cathedral as 'an imitation of grace' rather than a plaything whose construction helps Merrick pass the time, then Merrick can be seen for his 'virtual' or 'transparent' qualities as an artist rather than as a monster. Yet my quotation has been deliberately incomplete. The next line belongs to Treves, who says:

> Treves: That thought's got a good line, John. Plato believed this was all a world of illusion and that artists made illusions of illusions of heaven.
> Merrick: You mean we are all just copies? Of originals?

Treves: That's it.
Merrick: Who made the copies?
Treves: God. The Demi-urge.

Going back to his work, Merrick says 'He should have used both hands, shouldn't he?' This remark has legitimately wide reverberations. It is likely that here Merrick is mocking not only the injustice of his own grotesque malady, but also other injustices of God's world to which he has previously shown some sensitivity – for example, in his protests over the firing of an orderly at the hospital for staring at him. So in Merrick's mockery of God's and his own creations as 'one-handed,' we can also see the model as being, as one critic fairly put it,'a mock building made by a mock man.'[9]

The construction of the model of the cathedral on stage, beautiful and yet absurdly inadequate as a symbol of Merrick's longings, encapsulates the play's reverberating ambiguities. A few of the better theatrical critics, notably Walter Kerr and Gerald Weales, did try to deal with some of the play's utilization of the stage's given dualities, Kerr remarking that 'The theatre is asserting itself here, insisting upon its power of suggestion,' and that 'life and the theatre – the "real" look of things and the deeper look *into* them [italics his] are examined, entangled and questioned.' However, most of the reviews either overlooked this issue or reported on the play's 'conventional dramaturgy.'[10]

Yet I submit that much of the play's power comes from the playwright's and director's almost uncannily skillful use of the multiple possibilities inherent in theatrical space. Not only have the possibilities of the stage been beautifully exploited, but the relationship between the stage, audience and theatrical environments are made to yield remarkable results.

If we now broaden our view to take in the entire theatrical environment, we find ourselves discussing, as before, the obvious whose implications have not been sufficiently detailed. To recapitulate, the stage space is there so that the audience can gaze at it – unabashed – while it holds 'the mirror up to nature.' Among the satisfactions available to the audience may be mentioned their vicarious enjoyment of the events on stage. In addition, they often get reinforcement and entertainment while remaining superior (in control, sitting comfortably in semi-darkness while the actors expose themselves to view and criticism).

That this gazing at a show corresponds to a fundamental human need has always been evident. It has been made more so by Freud's analysis of scoptophilia (the desire to look, the obverse of exhibitionism), and by Lacan's discussion of the 'stade du miroir,' the stage of development setting the infant's self image through the mirroring he receives from his image in the glass as well as the psychical mirroring which he receives from his mother. So that we might even say, in a kind of shorthand, that the theatrical stage provides a kind of mothering for its audiences, giving them back an image which might or might not be to their liking, but is intended to increase their pleasure in or understanding of themselves and this world.[11]

That the image of the mirror is central in this play about a man who looked like a monster is not surprising. During Merrick's first meeting with Mrs Kendal, it is when he speaks of Romeo's use of the mirror that he begins to endear himself to Mrs Kendal. Merrick claims that Romeo doesn't love Juliet, because he uses a mirror to see whether she is dead.

> Merrick: Does he take her pulse? Does he get a doctor? Does he make sure? No. He kills himself. The illusion fools him because he does not care for her. He only cares about himself. If I had been Romeo, we would have got away.
> Mrs. Kendal: But then there would be no play, Mr. Merrick.
> Merrick: If he did not love her, why should there be a play? Looking in a mirror and seeing nothing. That is not love. It was all an illusion. When the illusion ended he had to kill himself.

To the Elephant Man, looking into a mirror will always give back 'nothing,' because the mirror gives back only the external self, not the beloved or 'other.' The play expands this image further in scene xii, which is a series of recitatives by Merrick's visitors, speaking in turn about why each of them identifies himself with the Elephant Man, finding him, in one respect or another, like themselves. In other words, he is seen as nothing other than a mirror image of those aspects of his visitors which they would like to have reinforced by this Christ-like scapegoat figure of patience and faith.

As Ross, his cynical keeper puts it,

> Dukes. Ladies coming to see you. Ask myself why? Figure it's the same as always was. Makes 'em feel good about themselves by comparison. Them things don't change. There but for the grace of.

Of course, this cynical view has some truth to it, and can be applied to the audience which has come to the theatre, as well as to the fashionable visitors on stage. Audiences who ignore the applicability of Ross' speech to themselves, or who find themselves 'uplifted' by Merrick's saintliness without feeling uncomfortable at their own complacency, or satisfied to see the model of St Phillip's as simply an imitation of grace, are choosing to ignore half of the play. It should be noted that Merrick's embracing of religion is set against both Treves' and Dr Gomm's scepticism, allowing each viewpoint to place the other in question.

That the model must fail to express Merrick's longings is also necessary to the play, for it can be inferred that Pomerance does not want the audience to evade such implications. In a *New York Times* interview, he explains his purposes: 'If you point out an error and then appeal for the reason, then that is a step in the right direction.' The theatre 'brings back points that are too volatile, too dangerous to be lived every day – the skeletons in the closet, the guilt.'[12] Where would the guilt lie if not in the audience's collusion with those who patronize Merrick?

It is significant that Pomerance seeks to create 'a unity, a community' in the audience akin to a congregation. As Janet Larson puts it, 'The broader community that comes into being in the theater audience is the "church" built through the whole action of *The Elephant Man* as a dramatic parable.'[13] Thus the model of the church on stage mirrors the larger church whose congregation is the audience. Interestingly, the first New York production of this play took place in an actual church, St Peter's, a small but very beautiful auditorium with a powerful spiritual and aesthetic ambience of its own. Larson reports that 'the Broadway cast have also said that performing *The Elephant Man* resembles the conducting of a religious service, requiring for certain scenes reverent silence in the theater.'[14] But the message of *this* church remains unclear. The last line of the play is an echo of Christ's 'It is done.' But just what is it which is done? Are we to take toward Merrick the reverent attitude we feel toward Christ's self-sacrifice in the service of mankind? The line is said by the hospital administrator, Dr Gomm, about the letter he is sending to the newspapers explaining Merrick's death and the disposition of the funds which were charitably contributed by the public to the hospital for Merrick's maintainance. Deliberately ignored and omitted are the references to Merrick's human qualities suggested by Treves. Thus we see the Elephant Man here primarily as an exploited artifact of Public Relations. The line also repeats the earlier 'It is done,' said by Merrick as he completes the model of St Phillip's. At the moment Merrick says the line, however, on stage in the adjoining area, Treves is breaking down at his inability to solve the problems of 'an England which informs me daily by the way it lives that it wants to die' (p. 65). Addressing the Bishop as Merrick is completing his model, just before Merrick utters the line, Treves has a long speech about the poverty of the lower classes, and the greed and dissipation of the middle and upper classes. 'What you like, sir,' says Treves to the Bishop, 'is that he [Merrick] is so grateful for patrons, so greedy to be patronized, and no demands, no rights, no hopes; past perverted, present false, future nil' (p. 66). Surely, if we are meant to see Merrick as a consoling example of the power of faith, he is also a sacrifice on the altar of tokenism, and Treves' criticism of English society counterpoints Merrick's straightforward 'I believe in heaven' (p. 54).

In the New York production, the play did not end on the line 'It is done' as enunciated by Dr Gomm. A last silent tableau was added. As the actors finished their bows, the 'orderlies' carried the model of St Phillip's downstage center, where it remained in a pool of light (even as the model remains at the original hospital site in London to this day). As the audience filed out of the church, their reactions to this final image apparently ranged from reverence to resentment, Jerome Max in the *Village Voice* saying, 'Hadn't we had enough significance?'[15] It seems to me that Jerome Max's resentment, which he no doubt believed to originate within himself and to be strictly his own, would not have been unwelcome to Pomerance. The use of presentational techniques (reminding the audience to critique what it sees instead of merely accepting it) is fundamental to this play with its careful use of various zones of the stage space undercutting each other.

Whatever the viewer chooses to think about *The Elephant Man*, there is no question that the play's intensely sensitive use of the theatrical environment adds in no small measure to its effectiveness. Thus Pomerance, like many other contemporary playwrights whose work I might have used to illustrate this point, places the audience into a complex world in which the clear boundaries between reality and illusion are con-fused (that is, both confounded and fused together), crossed and recrossed. As a result, we can give credence to and then re-evaluate magical stories of the human spirit's triumph over horror and meaningless suffering on multiple physical and psychological levels.

## NOTES

1 Susanne Langer, *Feeling and Form* (New York, 1953), p. 52. Subsequent references will be acknowledged in the text.
2 See *Playing and Reality* (New York: Basic Books, 1971) for a discussion of this interesting concept. But since Winnicott is concerned with the inner life of the auditor, not with the characteristics of the artwork which influence the way in which the artwork is perceived, his concept cannot be directly compared with those previously cited.
3 Bernard Pomerance, *The Elephant Man* (New York, 1979), p. 5. All further quotations from the play will be acknowledged in the text.
4 Michael Issacharoff, speaking in 'Space and Reference in Drama,' *Poetics Today*, 2:3 (Spring 1981) talks of 'the rivalry between the realm of the visible which is pitted against the realm of the invisible, the latter finally being overcome by the former.' But in *The Elephant Man*, the invisible is not overcome. Rather, the two remain forever in suspension, like those ridged pictures which change from one view to another – Christ with eyes open or shut – as we tilt our own heads.
5 'A Riveting New Serious Play,' 28 January 1979, section 2, p. 1.
6 Gerald Weales, 'An Elephant for All Seasons,' *Commonweal*, 30 March 1979, p. 181.
7 Richard Eder, 'Theater: "Elephant Man" Opens,' *New York Times*, section C, p. 5, 25 April 1979.
8 Pomerance clearly is influenced by Brecht. Oddly, perhaps, he adapted *The Elephant Calf* by Brecht for the Hampstead Theatre in 1975.
9 Weales, 'An Elephant for All Seasons.'
10 Tish Dace, 'Freak Shows,' *Soho Weekly News*, 18 January 1979, p. 54.

11 For an interesting psychoanalytic discussion of theatrical architecture, see Donald M. Kaplan, 'The Primal Cavity,' *The Drama Review*, 12:3 (Spring 1968), pp. 105–16. For the implications of the mirror and the other in childhood development, see Jacques Lacan, 'The Mirror Stage as Formative of the Function of the I,' *Ecrits* (New York, 1977), pp. 1–7.

12 See Michael Owen, 'The Enigmatic Author of *The Elephant Man*,' *New York Times*, 4 February 1979, section 2, p. 4.

13 Janet L. Larson, '*The Elephant Man* as Dramatic Parable,' *Modern Drama*, 26:3 (September 1983), p. 353.

14 Larson, *ibid.*, p. 354.

15 'Treading Too Heavy,' 29 January 1979, p. 77.

# Multiple spaces, simultaneous action and illusion*

## STEPHANIE K. ARNOLD

Changing the nature of the actor–audience relationship has been a primary concern of experimental or avant-garde theatre throughout the twentieth century. Fundamental to that reform has been change in the spatial arrangements of the theatre. Brecht and Meyerhold dismantled the proscenium arch to eliminate the illusion of traditional, fourth-wall realism, frankly exposing the mechanics of theatre production. Later, the division between audience space and performance space was modified further as theatres were no longer conceived as fixed architectural structures. Grotowski developed a unique, metaphorical shape for each production of the Polish Laboratory Theatre. In *Dr. Faustus*, the audience were the guests at Faustus' last supper and sat at long tables around which the action took place. The actors of the Living Theatre moved into the audience, the San Francisco Mime Troupe into the parks, the Bread and Puppet Theatre into the streets. The Performance Group transformed its Garage into multi-leveled, flexible environments which allowed freedom of audience movement for such productions as *Dionysus in 69* and *The Tooth of Crime*. Using found, alternative spaces, Snake Theatre performed *Somewhere in the Pacific* on the beach and *Auto* in a gas station.

A term used by Richard Schechner to describe theatre works which use 'whole space' is 'environmental theatre.'[1] Focusing on the actor–audience relationship from the point of view of acting style, Timothy J. Wiles identifies such productions as performance theatre. 'Instead of speaking from within a character, as in Stanislavskian acting, or stepping outside of it, as in Brecht's theatre, their actors stand in place of traditional characters, and address the audience directly.'[2]

From the 1950s to the 1970s, spatially innovative theatre works appear to have several interrelated common intentions: (1) to increase audience involvement in the theatre event, involvement which may be physical, intellectual and/or emotional/psychological, (2) to create a theatre experience in which the spectators are not observers of a separate, illusory world

* A draft of this paper was read at the *Themes in Drama* International Conference held at the University of California, Riverside in February 1985.

but participants in an immediate theatre experience which occurs primarily in real time and space rather than in the fictive time and space of a story, (3) to restore vitality to the theatre.

Fixed architectural structures which separate actor and audience provide protected physical spaces for both actor and audience just as the traditionally performed play creates a private world which the audience may view but not enter. Inspired by Artaud's vision of the 'elimination of the stage'[3] ('It is in order to attack the spectator's sensibility on all sides that we advocate a revolving spectacle which, instead of making the stage and the auditorium two closed worlds, without possible communication, spreads its visual and sonorous outbursts over the entire mass of the spectators'),[4] experimental-theatre practitioners have sought to destroy the protective nature of the traditional theatre in order to shock or urge the audience into a more active participation in the event. Grotowski writes of psychic confrontation in which the actor and audience join in a process of self-examination. The more formalist approach, encouraged by John Cage, calls on the audience member to integrate the visual and aural signs of the performance. Actual physical participation ranges from the audience member as actor in Allan Kaprow's *Happenings* to the sharing of puppet-making and bread of the Bread and Puppet Theatre.

While the nature of audience participation varies, theatre artists generally have shared an assumption that illusionistic staging precludes participation. Writing from a historical perspective, Brooks McNamara points out the early naturalistic environmental experiments of Nikolai Okhlopkov and Blanding Sloane in the 1930s but concludes, 'although naturalism has informed some environmental work, anti-naturalism has been a far more potent force.'[5] In his definition of environmental theatre, designer Jerry Rojo emphasizes the anti-illusionistic nature of the shift from two separate spaces to one integrated space. 'All aesthetic problems are solved in terms of actual time, space, and materials with little consideration given to solutions that suggest illusion, pretense, or imitation.'[6]

Two recent plays continue the spatial experimentation of the environmental-theatre movement but do not use the actor who directly addresses the audience in his or her own person. While pursuing increased audience involvement, these plays return to the idea of a theatre which presents an illusory world inhabited by fully impersonated characters. The illusory world is now created in more actual depth than in plays written for the proscenium stage because of the use of multiple playing spaces that have four actual walls rather than three fictitious ones.

*Fefu and Her Friends* (first performed 1977) by Maria Irene Fornes and *Your Place Is No Longer With Us* (first performed 1982) by Ellen Sebastian both use women's homes as their performance spaces. *Your Place Is No Longer With Us* is written to take place in an actual home. *Fefu and Her Friends* requires a central stage space and several additional rooms adjacent to the main stage space. In both plays, as the scene changes, the audience moves to different spaces. And in both plays, action occurs in more than one space at the same time.

Although both plays explore the strength which comes from women's relationships with women, *Your Place Is No Longer With Us* and *Fefu and Her Friends* differ substantially in structure and in technique. Ellen Sebastian uses the highly technical, sleight-of-hand visual imagery associated with other California performance-theatre artists such as Alan Finneran, Laura Farabough and George Coates. Maria Irene Fornes creates a naturalism so complete as to be called 'flat' by supporters and detractors alike.[7] However, the two plays are linked not only through the use of multiple spaces and simultaneous action to create rather than deny illusion but also by the way in which the nature of the action and character relationships govern the actor–audience relationship.

*Your Place Is No Longer With Us* by Ellen Sebastian follows a black child's journey through the house she shares with her grandmother in her search for self and reconciliation to her grandmother's values. The journey is an inner one expressed through fantasies played out in the different rooms of the house. The fantasies combine adolescent rites of passage and flirtations with an artistic life which exists beyond the grandmother's kitchen. The child's dreams of opera singers and actresses lock her away from the practical realities of trips to the market for cabbage and fishing expeditions with her grandmother's elderly friends. While the audience accompanies the child, the presence of the grandmother is always felt although the character does not actually appear until the end of the play. The child's struggle is in the foreground but the ongoing background of the grand-mother's chiding voice and the sounds and smells of cooking emanating from the kitchen constantly anchor the child's actions.

*Fefu and Her Friends* is unified by the underlying quest of the central character to transcend her fear of living on her own terms. This larger movement is shared by a group of women characters who come to Fefu's house to plan an educational program about self-realization. The struggle with fear emerges in a series of seemingly fragmented encounters between pairs of characters and in one monologue. Playful interaction which bonds the women leads to revelations of visions and nightmares.

Fefu speaks of the lack of a 'spiritual lubricant,' the absence of which makes her life terrifying. She claims that she is visited by a fearful black cat, mangled, missing an eye, with diseased skin, shitting foul diarrhea all over her kitchen.[8] The theme of fear is concentrated and enlarged in the character of Julia, who was 'once afraid of nothing,'[9] but is now confined to a wheelchair because of psychosomatic paralysis. A hunter shot a deer and although Julia was not physically injured by the shot, she has been crippled

ever since. Julia hallucinates that she is being attacked by men whom she
has threatened by her independence. Only if she repents and accepts
women as biologically defined will she be allowed to live. In her hallucina-
tion she repeats a prayer about the nature of women's sexuality to an
invisible panel of judges.

> Julia.   Women's spirit is sexual . . . Their sexual feelings remain with them till
> they die. And they take those feelings with them to the afterlife where they
> corrupt the heavens, and they are sent to hell where through suffering they shed
> those feelings and return to earth as man.

> . . .

> Julia.   They say when I believe the prayer I will forget the judges. And when I
> forget the judges I will believe the prayer. They say both happen at once. And
> all women have done it. Why can't I?[10]

In the climactic scene of the play, Fefu and Julia struggle with each
other's understanding of necessity: Fefu to fight, Julia to retreat.

> Julia.   May no harm come to your head.
> Fefu.   Fight!
> Julia.   May no harm come to your will.
> Fefu.   Fight, Julia!
> Julia.   I have no life left.[11]

Fefu shoots a rabbit with a gun. Julia dies. Julia becomes a ritual figure who
dies through Fefu's force of purpose on behalf of all the women in the play so
that they may defy her vision.

*Fefu and Her Friends* has a more formal structure than *Your Place Is No
Longer With Us*. In part I, the audience gathers as a whole just as all the
characters assemble in Fefu's house. The audience is then split into four
groups as the characters separate and move into different parts of the house.
Guides lead the smaller audience units to four different rooms where scenes
between two or three characters are repeated until they have been witnessed by all four groups. Each audience group sees the four scenes in a
different order. The scenes are intricately arranged so that characters move
from location to location in the same time-frame. Fefu who begins playing
croquet on the lawn with Emma exits part way through the scene, enters the
study and invites Christina and Cindy to join the game, exits from the study
and enters the kitchen where she gets lemonade and returns to the lawn, all
during the same repetition. In part III, the audience and the characters
return to the original playing space, the characters to plan the public
presentation and more significantly to resolve the various conflicts between
them.

In part I, the characters enter for a genteel gathering of lunch and tea.
Most are old friends. They banter. They introduce new members. They fill
in the gaps about Fefu's eccentricity and Julia's loss of courage. As they are

introduced to each other or renew old ties, they are introduced to the whole audience who as a group are like a new member of the circle, although the actors do not acknowledge the audience's presence. The audience remains at a distance like the more tentative characters. In part II, as the characters reveal more of themselves, the audience is drawn deeper into the house and closer to the performers. In the intimacy of small spaces and reduced numbers, delicate secrets are shared. Paula and Cecilia hesitantly touch on their old love affair while drinking tea in the kitchen. Cindy describes a painful dream to Christina as they read together in the study. Alone in a guest room, Julia hallucinates. On the lawn, Fefu confides her fears to Emma. Time is drawn out. The moment is experienced over and over from differing perspectives. Because some characters pass from one space to another, the audience is reminded of what it has already seen. In the original production, the audience in one space could hear snatches of dialogue from other spaces. Joan Larkin writes, 'We have a sense of the texture of time that the theater has never given us before.'[12]

When the audience reassembles in the larger space for the last part of the play, they bring with them a feeling for the characters deepened by the act of entering private spaces and having shared with the characters a suspended moment of time. In evaluating the splitting of that moment of time into four simultaneous scenes, Joan Larkin writes, 'And we have seen each character at a different stage of recognition of Julia's truth of women's condition.'[13] Bringing both groups, the full audience and all the characters, back to the public space of the living room, allows all to share in the moment of Julia's death which is a signal for the future. The movement through the house underlines the progression of the various characters on the journey to awareness.

Similar to *Fefu and Her Friends*, the audience progression in *Your Place Is No Longer With Us* parallels the progression of the action of the play. The event begins when the audience members arrive at the house and are directed by the guide to the living room where it is dark except for a fire in the fireplace. Sounds of cooking, pots and pans, refrigerator and oven doors opening and closing, and Gospel music are heard from the kitchen. When Dee, the child, replaces the Gospel music with a tape of *Richard II*, an argument begins in the kitchen between Dee and her grandmother. The audience only over-hears the opening scene. They remain at a distance.

Mama.    What's this mess you listenin' to on my tape player?
Dee.     Mama, that's Shakespeare's play . . .
Mama.    Well, shake it off my tape deck, cuz I don't like it. Put my church music back on.
Dee.     Mama! It's King Richard. You never heard Shakespeare? He's . . .
Mama.    Naw, and I don't want to hear him now . . . You gone have to go someplace else with that madness. Girl, please get out of my way. Can't you see I'm tryin' to cook? . . . Go on now, baby.[14]

Dee leaves her grandmother's space, the kitchen, the family center, exiled to wander and explore the free, but more dangerous, space of the rest of the house. In this free space, she can experiment with images of growing up. The audience's initial visual contact with the characters occurs when Dee enters the living room and the first character of her fantasies appears, a boy in horn-rimmed glasses and Spiderman pajamas. They play a game, acting out people of different nationalities, punctuated by the grand-mother's admonitions called out from the kitchen. 'Dee, you better stop goin' into coniption fits in there. You gone end up in Medical Lake State Hospital, you just watch.'[15]

The boy leads Dee and the audience upstairs away from the public space of the house, the living room, to the private spaces of bathroom, closet and bedrooms, where Dee's fantasies become increasingly personal, related to the physical and psychological changes of puberty. *Your Place Is No Longer With Us* demands more active audience participation than *Fefu and Her Friends* which allows the audience to maintain a polite distance, essentially in the same scale as the characters' psychological distance to each other. *Your Place Is No Longer With Us* overtly physicalizes Dee's state of mind and the audience is asked to take a more direct part in order to fully perceive that physicalization. However, as in *Fefu and Her Friends*, the actors do not acknowledge the audience.

Dee, followed by the audience, passes through a maze of women's lingerie. The stage directions describe a multi-sense experience.

> The maze corridors begin with white underthings – bras, slips, panties, girdles, etc. – modulating to pink and flesh colors. As the maze becomes more complicated, the colors darken to black and there are dangling stockings that must be pushed aside to continue forth. The final corridor is of colored and printed underwear. When the audience enters the maze, projections of dark red, green, and yellow drops are scattered through the room and lingerie. The projections crossfade through a series of images – musical scores, webs, circles, grids, branches. There is also a sound tape playing the voices and songs of the child's realities and fantasies – her grandmother's sayings, Gospel music and preaching, opera, and Shakespeare. Throughout, there is the undercurrent of a heartbeat which increases in volume until it drowns out all other sounds.[16]

Other fantasy images which the audience observes in a more traditional manner, although not in traditional spaces, include the Opera Singer dressed in a lavender evening gown covered with soap suds seated in a bathtub singing the notes of a musical score projected on the soap suds and the actress, seated inside a closet, the walls of which are covered with cracked mirror, talking to a black doll dressed like Dee on her lap.

Through the fantasies, the problems of growing up, developing a womanly body, defining feminine identity, falling in love, are considered with curiosity, longing, and fear. The question recurs, asked by Dee and the fantasy characters, 'Have you ever been lonely?'[17] Unifying the piece is the painful alienation of adolescence, what it means to be a child in an adult world.

The end of the fantasy section of the play erupts in wild behavior, violent music and movement, the living room furniture overturned. Frightened by the intensity of her own rebellion, Dee seeks refuge in the security of her grandmother's company. The fantasy characters disappear as Dee and the audience enter the kitchen together. Dee can now place the previously more seductive world of intellectual culture in a balance with her grandmother's spiritual values. The play ends with the planning of a celebration meal of home cooking which, after the performance formally ends, the audience is invited to join.

In *Your Place Is No Longer With Us* and *Fefu and Her Friends*, the houses are not used metaphorically as they are in the plays of more traditional realists such as Ibsen or Miller: the doll house which reflects the doll existence of Nora and Torvald, Willy's house overpowered by the looming skyscrapers surrounding it just as Willy is overwhelmed by the circumstances of his life. The images of the houses are not as significant as they are for other realistic or illusionistic playwrights because we don't see the houses at a distance. They don't affect us in their entirety.[18] Environmental theatre designer Jerry Rojo writes,

> It is interesting to note that environmental designs are not readily translated into pictorial renderings that depict mood or idea. This is because these productions exist in concepts which rely on transactions among audience, performer, text, time, and space; and are, therefore, only perceived internally during production.[19]

We comprehend the houses in pieces because we are inside with the characters. The metaphorical significance is focused on the spatial progression through the house.

In *Your Place Is No Longer With Us*, when Dee has experienced her independent exploration of the private spaces of the house, symbolic of herself, she can re-enter her grandmother's kitchen, where older woman and adolescent girl may come to an understanding. This kind of symbolic progression is not unlike that of Chekhov's three sisters whose movement from drawing room to bedroom to garden suggests their dispossession by Natasha and her middle-class values. In the environmental piece, however, the actors and audience also approach. The warm smells of cooking which give the house much of its atmosphere are in fact for the audience who are invited to dine with the actors. The caring of the characters for each other is extended to the audience.

The significance of the spatial progression in *Fefu and Her Friends* is much more elusive than in *Your Place Is No Longer With Us*, partly because of the random sequencing of the four inner scenes. Writing in *The New Republic*,

Stanley Kauffmann expresses the skeptic's view that the movement of the actors and audience is unnecessary.

> Since the small content in these scenes would in no way be damaged by traditional serial construction, since this insistence on reminding us that people actually have related/unrelated conversations simultaneously in different rooms of the same house is banal, we are left with the feeling of gimmick, intended or not – the feeling that mechanical aggrandizement has been impasted on a play . . .[20]

Bonnie Marranca answers this criticism with her observation that, 'Experiencing the play, moving from room to room, becomes more important than following a story.'[21] The nature of that experience, moving into the rooms, for both characters and audience is heightened intimacy and that is what the play is about. For women to overcome their self-loathing which generates fear, they must recognize the worth of other women. Early in the play, Fefu says, 'and if they shall recognize each other, the world will be blown apart.'[22] The spatial progression in *Fefu and Her Friends* is part of that process of recognition.

If the houses themselves do not convey a specific metaphoric image, in both plays they serve as refuges for the characters where their innermost secrets may be revealed. Although society has long considered the home as a woman's sphere, many other American women playwrights have seen the home as a trap.[23] *Your Place Is No Longer With Us* and *Fefu and Her Friends* share a basic assumption that in a woman's home a woman may be herself, that the home is a natural arena for exploring the nature of these women's relationships. The image of the house as refuge is partially defined by the absence of men. In *Your Place Is No Longer With Us*, the only male character exists in Dee's fantasies. The absence of men is dictated by the familial situation of the play, two women living alone. In *Fefu and Her Friends*, men are discussed and appear to be staying at the house, but they remain outside throughout the play. The absence of men is necessary to the characters' ability to reveal themselves. The image of the home as refuge is crucial to the development of intimacy which gives the plays their significance, in Ellen Sebastian's words, 'full of fire and love and fantasy and criticism.'[24]

Creating an illusionistic theatre work which is environmental implies the need for an acting style different from either that used in most illusionistic productions where actors and audience are separated or in most environmental productions where actors do not attempt to create a fiction. Both Maria Irene Fornes and Ellen Sebastian describe the acting in the original productions of their plays as 'film acting,' the kind of naturalism that would be compatible with a close-up camera.[25] This cinematic style extends the traditional understanding of Stanislavskian or method acting, eliminating the need to expand gesture or voice in order to project character. Both playwrights also refer to the audience members as witnesses because of the way they share apparently real space with the characters and because of their proximity to the actors. Fornes says, 'I expected that the audience would feel as if they are visiting people in their house.'[26]

In order to maintain the heightened illusion created by multiple playing spaces and simultaneous action, in the original production of *Fefu and Her Friends*, the audience members were always seated on two sides of the playing space so that they would not look across the action at other audience members. In contrast, a basic goal of staging *Your Place Is No Longer With Us* was to encourage a relationship not only between the actors and the audience that would go beyond the performance itself in the sharing of the dinner but between audience members during the production. Because the audience space was fluid, that is, there was no defined audience space and the size of the space kept changing, co-operation was required for everyone to see comfortably. Ellen Sebastian observed a generosity of spirit in her audiences which grew at least in part out of a planned gentleness in the way the actors moved around the audience and through the availability of a guide to answer questions and put audience members at ease.[27]

While *Fefu and Her Friends* creates a more introspective experience and *Your Place Is No Longer With Us* is more concerned with the development of community, both plays are based on an attitude of receptivity rather than attack. Timothy Wiles writes of the 'aggressivity' of performance theatre 'which demands a reaction from – that is, participation by – its audience.'[28] But 'aggressivity,' which could be defined as any participation, also suggests the atmosphere of much environmental theatre rooted in confrontation. The illusionistic environmental theatre of Fornes and Sebastian moves away from confrontation. While the audience members do not have the comfort of remaining in one protected spot, the nature of their participation is controlled by the lack of direct address. Although they are drawn further and further into the created world, there is still a line between actor and audience if not one between performance space and audience space. Rather than falsely being insisted upon or taken for granted because actors address the audience directly or audience members take roles, intimacy grows through the unfolding of images related to the spatial progression of the actors and audience through the houses.

## NOTES

1  Richard Schechner, *Environmental Theater* (New York: Hawthorn Books, Inc., 1973), p. 25.
2  Timothy J. Wiles, *The Theatre Event* (Chicago: The University of Chicago Press, 1980), p. 111.

3 Antonin Artaud, *The Theatre and Its Double* (New York: Grove Press, 1958), p. 125.

4 Artaud, *ibid.*, p. 86.

5 Brooks McNamara, 'The Environmental Tradition,' in Rojo, McNamara and Schechner, *Theatres, Spaces, Environments: Eighteen Projects* (New York: Drama Book Specialists, 1975), p. 8.

6 Jerry Rojo, 'Some Principles and Concepts of Environmental Design,' in Rojo, McNamara, and Schechner, *Theatres, Spaces, Environments: Eighteen Projects* (New York: Drama Book Specialists, 1975), p. 14.

7 'Like the script, it is naturalistic with discontinuities, certain details left out and an eerie, disturbing flatness imposed at times as if a photo-realist painting was being performed live,' Michael Feingold, *The Village Voice*, 23 January 1978, p. 75.

'The style of the production seems to be a kind of untheatrical naturalism – a certain flatness that appears stylized, very casual,' Bonnie Marranca, 'Interview: Maria Irene Fornes,' *Performing Arts Journal*, 2:3 (Winter 1978), p. 110.

'She has been so anxious to have her people "unactorish" that they are figuratively invisible . . .,' Stanley Kauffmann, *The New Republic*, 25 February 1978, p. 38.

8 Maria Irene Fornes, *Fefu and Her Friends* in *Word Plays* (New York: Performing Arts Journal Publications, 1980), p. 20.

9 Fornes, *Fefu and Her Friends*, p. 15.

10 Fornes, *Fefu and Her Friends*, p. 25.

11 Fornes, *Fefu and Her Friends*, p. 40.

12 Joan Larkin, 'On the Arts,' *Ms.* (June 1978), p. 28.

13 Larkin, *ibid.*, p. 28.

14 Ellen V. Sebastian, *Your Place Is No Longer With Us* in *West Coast Plays 13/14* (Los Angeles: California Theatre Council, 1982), p. 203.

15 Sebastian, *Your Place Is No Longer With Us*, p. 205.

16 Sebastian, *Your Place Is No Longer With Us*, p. 208.

17 Sebastian, *Your Place Is No Longer With Us*, pp. 204, 207, 211.

18 In the original productions of the plays, an additional factor contributing to the lack of a metaphorical image for the whole house was the available space. *Your Place Is No Longer With Us* was performed in borrowed houses full of the actual owner's furnishings rather than in a designed house, although modifications were made for the fantasy sequences. In *Fefu and Her Friends*, the functional spaces of the Relativity Medi Lab, green room, dressing room, office, were converted to playing spaces.

19 Rojo, 'Some Principles and Concepts of Environmental Design,' p. 19.

20 Kauffmann, *The New Republic*, 25 February 1978, p. 38.

21 Marranca, 'Interview: Maria Irene Fornes,' p. 108.

22 Fornes, *Fefu and Her Friends*, p. 13.

23 In *Trifles* by Susan Glaspell, Minnie Foster's home is like the cage of her strangled bird. Lulu Bett's only hope for a rewarding life is to escape the drudgery of her sister's home in *Miss Lulu Bett* by Zona Gale. In *Machinal* by

Sophie Treadwell, the home is one more representation of the oppression that drives the Young Woman to murder her husband.

24 Author's interview with Ellen Sebastian, 11 August 1984.
25 Marranca, 'Interview: Maria Irene Fornes,' p. 110.
26 Marranca, *ibid.*, p. 108.
27 Author's interview with Ellen Sebastian, 11 August 1984.
28 Wiles, *The Theatre Event*, p. 117.

# Index